"*Teaching Translation: Contexts, Modes and Technologies* stands out as an essential addition to the realm of translation and interpreting education. Its compelling content, which seamlessly intertwines theoretical foundations with practical applications, features a diverse range of perspectives, pedagogical strategies, and ethical considerations. This comprehensive volume not only engages readers but also offers profound insights into the evolving educational landscape, providing invaluable guidance for the translators and interpreters of tomorrow."

Lucía Pintado Gutiérrez, *President of APTIS,*
Dublin City University, Ireland

"The editors successfully gathered high-quality contributions by well-established scholars and by young voices in a cutting-edge volume on translation pedagogy, which successfully combines topics emerging from widespread geographical contexts, diversified teaching modes, and pioneering technologies, and which will certainly serve as reference material to students, lecturers, professionals, and scholars alike."

Daniel Dejica, *Politehnica University Timişoara, Romania*

CW00823092

TEACHING TRANSLATION

The field of translation and interpreting (T&I) training has been undergoing rapid and far-reaching transformation in recent years, as a result of technological advances and sweeping shifts in the international environment within which T&I seeks to mediate.

Teaching Translation: Contexts, Modes and Technologies provides a cross-section of multi-national perspectives on teaching various dimensions of translation both within dedicated programmes and as part of individual modules on translation-adjacent programmes. This volume offers essential up-to-date perspectives to ensure that T&I training remains robust and resilient far into the 21st century.

Examining key topics of concern across academia, professional translation practice, and collaborative pedagogies, as well as offering crucial insights from the voices of the trainees themselves, this is an essential text for professionals, scholars, and teachers of translation studies and interpreting studies.

Martin Ward is an Associate Professor of Chinese and Japanese Translation at the University of Leeds. He chaired the organising committee of the APTIS 2022 conference, and his research has been published in *The Translator* (2023, DOI: 10.1080/13556509.2023.2239388).

Carlo Eugeni is an Associate Professor of Audiovisual Translation at the University of Leeds. He chairs the Intersteno scientific committee, and is member of the ITU experts group on accessibility in the metaverse, onAIR, and the Italian Academy of Multimedia Writing "Aliprandi-Rodriguez". He is editor of *Tiro*, *CoMe*, and *SPECIALinguaggi*.

Callum Walker is an Associate Professor of Translation Technology at the University of Leeds, where he is currently the Director of the Centre for Translation and Interpreting Studies. His research focuses on translation industry studies and economics, culminating in the Routledge textbook entitled *Translation Project Management*.

TEACHING TRANSLATION

Contexts, Modes, and Technologies

Edited by Martin Ward, Carlo Eugeni, and Callum Walker

Routledge
Taylor & Francis Group

LONDON AND NEW YORK

Designed cover image: Ildo Frazao

First published 2025
by Routledge
4 Park Square, Milton Park, Abingdon, Oxon, OX14 4RN

and by Routledge
605 Third Avenue, New York, NY 10158

Routledge is an imprint of the Taylor & Francis Group, an informa business

British Library Cataloguing-in-Publication Data
A catalogue record for this book is available from the British Library

ISBN: 9781032577838 (hbk)
ISBN: 9781032571850 (pbk)
ISBN: 9781003440970 (ebk)

DOI: 10.4324/9781003440970

Typeset in Sabon
by Newgen Publishing UK

CONTENTS

CONTRIBUTORS

José Ramón Calvo-Ferrer holds a PhD in Translation and Interpreting from the University of Alicante, Spain, where he has taught different modules on Translation, English, and teacher training since 2008. His research interests lie in ICT in general and video games in particular for second language learning and translator training. He has published various books and papers on video games, translation and second language learning, and is a Visiting Lecturer at the Department of Language of Linguistics of the University of Essex, UK, where he delivers lectures and workshops on video games and translation.

Xijinyan Chen is an assistant teaching professor in the Graduate Program of Interpreting and Translation Studies at Wake Forest University, USA. Dr. Chen received her PhD in Translation Studies from the State University of New York, Binghamton University, USA, and her master's degree in Translation and Interpreting from Beijing Foreign Studies University, China. She has worked as a freelance translator and interpreter since 2010. Her research interests include translation pedagogy, multimedia translation, and literary translation.

Luz Belenguer Cortés holds a degree in Translation and Interpreting and a Master's in Translation and Interpreting Research from Universitat Jaume I (UJI), Castellón, Spain. She also has a Master's in Conference Interpreting (UEV) and is a PhD candidate in the Applied Languages, Literature and Translation Doctoral Programme, in which her thesis won the 2nd UJI Social Commitment Research Projects Banco Santander 2022 award. She is member of the TRAMA (Translation for the Media and Accessibility) and WIKITRAD (Wikipedia and Translation Educational Research Group) research groups. Since 2018, she has worked as a live and SDH subtitler in À Punt Mèdia, where she also does audio description. Since 2020, she has combined this professional activity with that of associate lecturer at UJI, where she has taught French, French culture, French to Spanish translation, Audiovisual translation, and Accessibility. Her research interests are focused on Audiovisual Translation and Accessibility.

Peter J. Freeth is Senior Lecturer in Translation at London Metropolitan University, UK. His research primarily focuses on understanding the sociological position and role of translators in relation to their visibility, particularly as manifested in digital paratextual spaces. His PhD thesis on the subject is available open access and he has published more broadly on topics including adapting paratext theory for use in digital contexts, the digitization of translation archives and sources, and the international reception and translation of Timur Vermes' novel *Er ist wieder da* (*Look Who's Back*). Freeth was awarded the 2023 Martha Cheung Award for the latter. He has also co-edited the volume *Beyond the Translator's Invisibility* (2024) and the special issue *Literary Translatorship in Digital Contexts* and joined the editorial board of *Translation in Society* as an assistant editor in spring 2024.

Yves Gambier is a professor emeritus of the University of Turku, Finland, where he taught translation and interpreting, and was visiting professor at the Immanuel Kant Baltic Federal University in Kaliningrad, Russia, and fellow researcher at the Kaunas Technological University, Lithuania. Author, editor, or co-editor of more than 40 volumes, he is the author of over 200 publications on sociolinguistics, specialised discourse, translation studies, discourse analysis, bilingualism, audiovisual translation, and translators and interpreters training. Involved in Nordic and EU research projects, he has served as General Editor of the Benjamins Translation Library, co-editor of the Handbook of Translation Studies, and member of the editorial board of journals like Babel, Hermeneus, MonTI, Target, Terminology, Sendebar, Hermeneus, Synergies, and TTR. Among his numerous academic achievements, he was chairman of the group of experts of the European Master's in Translation, member of the EMT Board, vice-president and president of the European Society for Translation Studies, and CETRA professor.

Barbara Guidarelli is a Fellow of the Higher Education Academy, UK, and she teaches Italian language and culture at undergraduate level at Newcastle University, UK. She is a DPSI interpreter and she has 18 years' experience in teaching Italian. Her research interests include CLIL and innovative teaching methods.

Yu Hao is a lecturer in Translation Studies at the University of Melbourne, Australia. She does research on translation and translator education. Research interests include translation curriculum development, teaching translation technology, and the role of language translation in crisis communication.

Qifei Kao is a lecturer in Chinese at Binghamton University, State University of New York, USA. Prior to becoming a full-time lecturer, she taught Chinese and translation workshops as an adjunct lecturer at the same university. Her language pedagogy speciality is the design and teaching of online Chinese courses. She is currently working on her PhD in translation studies and writing her dissertation on the translation of contemporary Chinese literature.

Joseph Lambert is a lecturer in Translation Studies and Director of the MA Translation Studies at Cardiff University, UK. In the past, he has also lectured at Durham University, UK, the University of Birmingham, UK, and the University of Hull, UK. He teaches a broad range of modules across the BA and MA programmes in Translation and his primary area of research interest is the ethics of translation. Like his teaching, this work sits at the interface between translation theory and practice. He has recently published a textbook with Routledge entitled *Translation Ethics* and has authored and co-authored several articles and book chapters relating to the translation profession, questions of pay, status, and regulation in the UK, and translation codes of ethics. His current research includes a range of projects exploring the related themes of working conditions, self-care, and wellbeing among translators.

Lulu Lun is currently a lecturer at Tianjin University of Finance and Economics, China, teaching interpreting and translation classes to both undergraduate and postgraduate students. Her research interests focus on interpreting and translation teaching and practices.

D. Carole Moore is an associate lecturer at Newcastle University, UK, and currently teaches Italian and French to English translation. With over 50 years teaching and translation experience, she has written several Italian language textbooks and spent 13 years as Managing Director of her own translation agency. Her research interests include Flexible Learning methods and post-war education in Italy.

Maria Teresa Musacchio is Chair of English Translation at the Modern Languages for Interpreters and Translators branch of IUSLIT, University of Trieste, Italy. Her research focuses, in a functional, pragmatic, and cultural perspective, on descriptive and applied translation studies issues in specialised translation and the relating fields of special languages, terminology and translation pedagogy with a focus on corpus-based and corpus-driven studies of scientific, business, economics, finance and technical communication. From 2014 to 2017 she was head of the University of Padua unit of the EU FP7 Project Slándáil – Security System for Language and Image Analysis – focusing on the use of language and translation to empower emergency response using social media. She currently studies economics language and translation in a diachronic interdisciplinary perspective within the PRIN research project LexEcon.

Cristina Peligra is an associate lecturer at Newcastle University, UK, and is responsible for English to Italian translation practicals. She was awarded her PhD in Translation Studies from Newcastle University, UK, in 2019, with a thesis comparing English and Italian translations of selected works by Dutch author Hella S. Haasse. Her research interests include issues of culture and multilingualism in literary translation, postcolonial translation, paratexts, innovation in language teaching.

JC Penet is a reader in Translation Studies, Newcastle University, UK, and a Certified Personal and Executive Coach. At Newcastle University, he teaches on a wide range of courses in Translation Studies, including on translation theory; the language service industry; translation project management; institutional translation; AI literacy for translators, and interpersonal relations, emotions, and wellbeing in the translation profession. Nationally, he founded the Association of Programmes in Translation and Interpreting Studies (UK and Ireland) and served as its first President until 2021. His research explores how recent developments in the language industry may call into question the perceived sustainability of the translation profession(s). His research also looks at the impact these changes may have on the way we understand and deliver translator training. Recent publications have explored the way(s) in which Trait Emotional Intelligence theory can be applied to translator training to help students develop the adaptive expertise they will need to thrive in the language industry.

Carla Quinci is a tenure-track researcher in English Language and Translation at the University of Padua, Italy. She holds a PhD in Interpreting and Translation Studies from the University of Trieste, Italy. Her PhD dissertation was awarded the CIUTI Prize in 2016 and formed the basis for her recent Routledge monograph titled *Translation Competence: Theory, Research and Practice* (2023). Her research and publications primarily focus on specialised translation, particularly in the areas of translator training, revision, translation quality assessment, and translation technologies. She has recently designed and carried out the LeMaTTT research project, an empirical investigation into the potential effects of machine translation on the acquisition of legal thematic and info-mining competence in trainee translators. The first results of this project are about to be published.

Chenqing Song is currently an associate professor at Binghamton University, State University of New York, USA, a position she has held since 2008. As the Director of the Translation Research and Instructional Program and the Coordinator of the Chinese Language Program at Binghamton University, USA, she works closely with linguists and language pedagogy specialists university-wide and in New York State. Dr. Song received her PhD in Chinese Linguistics from the University of Wisconsin–Madison, USA, in 2008. Her research interest lies in phonology, both historical and synchronic. As a language pedagogist, her research focuses on tonal acquisition and the integration of culture into language teaching. Recently, she has extended her research to the field of translation studies, including community translation and translation in language teaching. She is currently the treasurer and a member of the Executive Committee of the International Association of Chinese Linguistics (IACL).

Shani Tobias is a lecturer in Translation Studies and Education Coordinator of the Monash Intercultural Lab at Monash University, Australia. She has published in the fields of literary and cultural translation, as well as translator and interpreter pedagogy and professional development. Her current research projects include collaborations with researchers from the University of Warwick, UK, and the University of Leeds, UK, in the area of international telecollaboration/COIL in translator training, a project with Pennsylvania State University, USA, focussing on developing a toolkit for capacity building in online intercultural exchange, and an Australian government funded project on the Chinese translation of Australian children's literature. Shani is also a NAATI-certified translator (Japanese-English) with over 20 years of professional translation experience.

Callum Walker is an associate professor of Translation Technology and Director of the Centre for Translation Studies at the University of Leeds, UK, where he teaches computer-assisted translation technology, project management, translation theory, and specialised translation. He has previously lectured at Durham University, UK, Goldsmiths University of London, UK, and University College London, UK. Alongside his academic roles, he has worked as a freelance translator since 2009 (French and Russian into English) and small translation business owner, as well as being a Chartered Linguist, Member of the CIOL, and Member of the ITI. His research interests relate to translation industry studies, with a specific focus on project management (culminating in the Routledge textbook *Translation Project Management*), micro- and information economics, and the interaction between technology and translation workflows.

Martin Ward is an associate professor of Chinese and Japanese Translation at the University of Leeds, UK. He has had published several China- and Japan-related translations from Chinese and Japanese into English of historical documents, political discourse, and literature, and also conducts research into the translation of Chinese political discourse, the situating of the translation of wartime Japanese military documents within Sino-Japanese relations, translation pedagogy and international telecollaboration. At time of writing he is a fellow of the Leeds Institute for Teaching Excellence (LITE), with a research focus on COIL-type interventions. He also employs international telecollaboration in all areas of his translation teaching. He is the founder of the East Asian Translation Pedagogy Advance (EATPA) network, bringing together academics teaching East Asian language translation at higher education institutions across the globe to share best practice, and the East Asian Translation research satellite at the University of Leeds.

Tong Wu is currently working on her PhD in translation studies at Binghamton University, State University of New York, USA. Her research interests lie in translation pedagogy, especially the training of translators' teamwork skills.

1

INTRODUCTION

Martin Ward

The field of translation and interpreting (T&I) training has been undergoing rapid and far-reaching transformation in recent years, significantly as a result of technological advances, but also as a result of sweeping shifts in the international environment within which T&I seeks to mediate. Within this shifting context, the COVID-19 pandemic then also appeared at the outset to be mainly disruptive to traditional and gradually-evolving forms of T&I training and led many a translator trainer to urgently develop almost overnight new pedagogical approaches to respond to the new normal and support the continuity and sustainability of programmes. It can be argued that many of the changes to come about were going to happen eventually anyway, and that the pandemic merely sped up that process, but translator trainers and scholars continue to pick through both traditional pedagogies and new models to identify enduring as well as innovative approaches to T&I training which can serve the discipline well into the future.

In the aftermath of the pandemic, the Association of Programmes in Translation and Interpreting Studies (APTIS) 2022 Conference *Translation and Interpreting Pedagogy in a Post-pandemic World: New Opportunities and Challenges* was held at the University of Leeds on 18–19 November 2022.[1] Bringing together over a hundred higher education translation and interpreting trainers from around the world, this conference proved to be a dynamic space for post-crisis networking and dissemination of valuable research findings. It was the enduring inspiration of this conference which motivated the editors to bring together the present volume and its partner volume, *Teaching Interpreting and Live Subtitling: Contexts, Modes, and Technologies*, in the hope that T&I trainers the world over will derive valuable insights and new approaches they may adapt and adopt to further

DOI: 10.4324/9781003440970-1

enhance the quality of T&I provision, above all for the benefit of translator trainees and the success of their work for the good of humanity in a world of crisis.

This volume provides a cross-section of perspectives on teaching various dimensions of translation both within dedicated programmes and as part of individual modules on translation-adjacent programmes, drawing on research findings across several countries and continents. Following this introduction, we proceed with an exploration by Yves Gambier in Chapter 2 of the development of translator training programmes over the past two decades and beyond. Gambier's cross-cutting review of current teaching practices and blind spots in translator training begins by highlighting the rapidly changing context in the academic and professional world of translation. In a world where technological advancement is proceeding at an exponential speed, Gambier sounds a warning bell for the dangers of placing technology at the forefront of translator training and draws the reader's attention to some of the implications of technology and ethical concerns little discussed in translation studies. He urges translator trainers to rethink the links between technology and culture and proposes the frameworks of Technopoly, Mediology and Social Construction of Technology Studies to help understand the way T&I can be seen as interacting with technology.

Following this, the book is then divided into three thematic parts, exploring in Part I the interplay between translator training inside the classroom and the complex and changing world outside the classroom which professional translators must learn to navigate, in Part II the scope and value of collaborative pedagogies and other methods of supporting trainee translators, and in Part III the voices of translator trainees as they adjust to new realities and contexts in translator training.

We begin Part I, *Inside the classroom, outside the classroom*, with Callum Walker and Joseph Lambert's examination in Chapter 3 of the hitherto somewhat "elephant in the room" topic of the place of money in the classroom. Aiming to facilitate a more confident and ambitious transition for trainee translators into a working world where they are paid fairly for the work they do, the authors' wide-reaching survey of more than two dozen Masters-level programmes in the UK and Ireland leads to several innovative recommendations for pedagogic practice. In Chapter 4, Luz Belenguer Cortés presents the results of a project (MIGPRO) implemented in the context of translator training aimed at helping migrants develop the skills required to live their daily lives. Based on service-learning and employing the *learn it, link it* process (Oakley et al., 2021), this project is shown to facilitate translation students' development of linguistic and communicative competence, as well as be beneficial for migrants outside the walls of academia. In Chapter 5, Peter J. Freeth presents critical reflections on approaches to teaching ethics in the translation classroom. Using the controversies and debates surrounding the Dutch translation of Amanda Gorman's *The Hill We Climb*, Freeth explores the purpose of broaching such topics in an appropriate manner in the context of translator training. Cautioning against the mistaken framing of this particular debate through a white racial lens, he crucially highlights the importance of avoiding further marginalization of Black voices. We conclude Part I in Chapter 6 with Maria Teresa Musacchio and Carla Quinci's analysis on the main applications and value of translationQ, proposing an approach to the analysis and revision of terminological and phraseological errors in the field of astronomy. Examining these errors in a corpus of almost two hundred translations of popular science articles, their work demonstrates how multiple translations of one source text can be simultaneously revised and assessed and how errors can be retrieved from the revision memory for analysis and teaching purposes.

In Part II, we move on yet link with the theme from Part I as we explore *Collaborative pedagogies*, beginning with an evaluation by Xijinyan Chen, Qifei Kao, Chenqing Song, Tong Wu, and Lulu Lun in Chapter 7 of the effectiveness of integrating Project-Based Learning (PjBL) in translation classrooms to bridge the gap between translation training and professional translation careers. The authors' findings point to the valuable role of PjBL in preparing students for translation careers, but also note lingering concerns around other aspects of the approach, not least increased workload for instructors. Continuing with the theme of collaboration, in Chapter 8 Barbara Guidarelli, D. Carole Moore, and Cristina Peligra examine how the cross-disciplinary collaborative *Newcastle Calls* Project, in which translation students interviewed prominent Italian figures and produced subtitled documentaries, was used to support the transition of translation students from academia to future professions through technology-facilitated professional simulation. Their work provides insights into the various benefits of projects of this nature and recommendations on the application of such projects in translation pedagogy. In Chapter 9, JC Penet explores the implications of students' emotional experiences in the context of collaborative Simulated Translation Bureaus (STBs) and how group-coaching interventions could support the self-management of their emotions. Penet also points to how these interventions could potentially support the development of empathy in trainee translators in the longer term. We conclude this part of the volume in Chapter 10 with a case study by Martin Ward and Shani Tobias, who explore the benefits of international telecollaboration in translator training, in this case in Japanese to English specialised translation. In a scenario where students from the University of Leeds in the UK and Monash University in Australia work together in online intercultural environments across time zones to complete a translation project, the authors interviewed students to examine their soft skills development and identify how such pedagogies can help students prepare for future challenges in their professional lives. Findings point to the broader, unexplored potential of such interventions.

Finally, in Part III, *Trainee translators' voices on new modes of training*, we conclude with two chapters which investigate the voices of the trainee translators themselves as they navigate a rapidly evolving translator training environment. In Chapter 11, José Ramón Calvo-Ferrer investigates students' perceptions of teaching methodologies during the pandemic. Findings point to a preference for traditional, face-to-face instruction, as well as a willingness to embrace blended learning. Whilst challenges with virtual learning remain, Calvo-Ferrer suggests that online learning may have inadvertently motivated students to pursue more hands-on approaches to translation. In Chapter 12, we conclude the volume with Yu Hao's case study into motivations of Chinese students studying translation at an Australian university during the pandemic. Various push, pull, and discipline-specific factors were identified, with pull factors coming out as the most influential. Hao observed no significant difference in career prospects between trainees who returned to campus after the pandemic and those who remained online and points to the need for more in-depth research into motivational factors impacting the choices of would-be translator trainees.

Note

1   See www.aptis-translation-interpreting.org/aptis-2022-university-of-leeds

2

BLIND SPOTS IN THE TRAINING OF TRANSLATORS AND INTERPRETERS

Yves Gambier

Keywords: ethics; machine translation; technology and culture; types of translation; types of translators

For several decades, mainly in the last 30 years in many European countries, there has been an attempt to reform, adapt, and change university programmes in translation/interpretation towards more professionalisation. During this period, methods and means as computer-assisted translation (CAT) software have begun to transform practices. The following reflections do not pretend to make an overview of the different questions raised by the proposals launched here and there, regarding for instance the competences, the types of CAT to be used. After a reminder of the current context, the directions that will be addressed in this chapter are a selection of 40 years of training provided at university and the many meetings held on different occasions and at multiple places.[1] They are not, of course, intended to cover all challenges posed by multilingual communication education; I will not discuss, for instance, interactive online teaching in the audiovisual classroom or the opportunities offered by the Net for collaborative learning. I will, instead, focus on the rapid changing context today but also at the beginning of training (the past throwing light on the future), the impact of technologies on practices (including the status of the translators and the diversity of denominations for "translation"), and the ethical dimension of research. These will help identifying the blind spots in the training of translators and interpreters.

DOI: 10.4324/9781003440970-2

1. A rapidly changing context

In the 1980s and 1990s, the number of training programmes in translation and interpretation (T&I) grew rapidly, particularly in Europe. The main focus at the time was content. Then, in the early 2000s, efforts were made to create convergences between these programmes and the industry, in spite of the institutional, legal, financial, pedagogical, technical constraints which often blocked these efforts. In the 2010s, universities began to follow the model of private businesses and programme design started to move their focus on the skills to be acquired, rather than on the content to be taught (see section 4.1 later in this chapter).

In parallel with this development, since the 1990s programmes have multiplied the tools, methods, and support available for online learning (e-learning), Open and Distance Learning (ODL), alongside the concepts of the knowledge society and lifelong learning. Servers and online applications have been set up behind acronyms such as CMS (Content Management System), LMS (Learning Management System), VLE (Virtual Learning Environment), MOOC (Massive Open Online Courses), amongst others. At the same time, technology service companies have increased the ways to control certain means of training, such as software to use, by starting closer and closer partnerships with universities. By perceiving the training exclusively as a list of tools to master, this has turned the training into a sort of formatting, with students learning how to use tools that would no longer be useful after 10–15 years.

On top of this, the 2020 COVID-19 pandemic-imposed teleworking and distance teaching, which has exposed the upheavals, tensions, and fractures of the technologised world, favouring multinationals hosting the learning platforms, and revealing the inequalities in access to the digital world.

The question here is not one of analysing in detail the recent challenges in the training of translators and interpreters or of studying the novelty of "digital workspaces" but instead focuses on pointing out some unspoken directions of reflection to revisit the question of the purpose of education, according to several directions:

- to recall certain sources or motivations for the training;
- to sketch out the gap, as regards the signals of professionalisation, between translators' associations and portals of offers and requests in translation, technical writing, and terminology;
- to question the current division between various disciplines referring to communication;
- to reconsider technology within a cultural frame and the ethics of a scholar in our discipline.

The whole may seem disjointed. This is done on purpose, so as to feed the debate on the ins and outs of training, which is an open field of potential, requirements and regulations.

2.   Historical beginnings of training: a military challenge

The Cold War marked international relations and favoured industrial espionage and intelligence services. It is in this context that machine translation (MT) came into being around the end of the 1940s (Hutchins, 1986), meaning well before the question of training was even raised. For both the USSR and the USA it was a question of knowing more and as quickly as possible about the enemy's industrial and military innovations. In the years 1955–1960, experts in formal linguistics, computer linguistics, cybernetics and cryptography started testing MT in Moscow, Tokyo, Grenoble (GETA group), Seattle, Los Angeles, at MIT/Cambridge in Massachusetts, Washington (Georgetown University and IBM carried out the first computer experiment in January 1954) and Italy (under the aegis of the Euratom/1957 project). The first MT conference was held in London in 1956. The first book on translation in the series *Que sais-je?* connects directly to *La machine à traduire* (The machine that translates) (Delavenay, 1959). The Association for MT and Computational Linguistics was formed in the USA in 1962. In 1970–1972, during the Vietnam War, Logos offered the MT of military manuals. Today, particularly since 11 September 2001, the Pentagon, the FBI, the CIA, and the DGSI (General Directorate of International Security, under the French Ministry of the Interior) are recruiting specialists in information systems, cyber-security, big data, and translation (Arabic, Persian, Chinese/Mandarin, Russian, African dialects, etc.). The DGSI announced on 8 November 2019, that it would have to employ 1,200 more of these specialists by 2024.

For the past 20 years, there have been phenomena that are too little questioned in translation. For example, who funds work in artificial intelligence (AI) and neural MT (NMT)? Thus, the research unit of the North American intelligence services, including the CIA (IARPA, Intelligence Advanced Research Projects Activities), finances academic and industrial work, particularly in linguistics and cognitive psychology; it also supervises the *Material program* which includes MT and the search via English for information available in many languages, so as to improve the machine learning of computers to solve certain problems without being specially programmed for this task (e.g., translating, summarising data from different languages). IARPA also leads the *Babel* project, which consists of developing speech recognition tools capable of transcribing any language. Recall here that *Google Translate* is now working (August 2022) with and in 133 languages at various levels and *Bing Translator* (Microsoft) supports 103 languages.

Nonetheless, we are very far from addressing the 7,000 languages or so that exist in the world, including the 4,000 with a writing system. This means that most languages are treated very little or not at all by AI or ad hoc algorithms. A country like Nigeria has more than 500 languages on its territory.

Consider Amazon: some reduce it to e-commerce alone, while it is in fact an important player in the defense and security forces sector via the Amazon Web Service (AWS). According to data related to 2022 (https://aws.amazon. com/marketplace), AWS represents 34% of the world market of the cloud, more than 10% of the turnover of the multinational, thanks to data storage, services sold to immigration services, facial recognition software, connected videophones for the police (via its subsidiary *Ring*), the surveillance business, and others. This immediately raises the question of the link between armies, companies, and universities in the 27 EU member countries, given that certain software used in certain research and teaching programmes are sponsored by these multinationals.

This short overview makes it possible to establish the relations between the orders of the armies and the secret services,[2] the digital technologies developed by the multinationals,[3] meaning and machine translation. Also, it shows that the history of MT is far from being reduced to international cooperation and the promotion of peace: it has also made it possible to transmit sensitive information on agricultural production, medicine, technologies, armaments, and so on. Finally, it sheds light on the first training programmes for translators and interpreters, which were linked to the needs, demands, and functions of the military authorities. This contradicts, or at least partially alters, the idea that reflections on translation are always and almost exclusively based on literature and sacred texts. Before exemplifying this phenomenon, it should be briefly recalled that it has been so for a long time in various cultural areas, like the Abbasid empire (from the 8th century), the so-called Toledo school (12–13th century), the *Collège Royal* founded by Francis I of France (16th century), the Jesuit programmes (from the beginning of the 17th century) set up from Scotland to Portugal, from Spain to Constantinople and İzmir, from the School of Children of Languages (18th century) to the Al-Alsum Translation School in Egypt (1835), from the Yangwu group in China (early 19th century), calling for the training of translators for shipbuilding and arms manufacturing, to the Tongwen Guan in Beijing/School of Common Languages (in the 1860s), promoted by the Office of Qing Foreign Affairs. In all these cases, political, diplomatic, and military powers have always interfered in the design of programmes.

What about the 20th century, before the wave of the 1980s and 1990s? It was in 1928 that we find the first structured programme in interpretation (made of mock conferences), established by the International Labor Organization (ILO), which had already developed the use of interpretation by telephone in the 1920s. In 1929, the Moscow Military Institute of Foreign Languages officially launched a military interpreter position. Kiev (Ukraine), in 1932–1933, set up academic training of translators within its Institute of Language Education while the Soviet regime questioned multilingualism on its territory. In 1935, the State Pedagogical Institute for Foreign Languages opened in Moscow, which in 1964 became the Maurice Thorez Institute, recognised for its training of interpreters (especially for the Global South), and which in turn was transformed in 1990 into a University of Linguistics. Several schools were opened in the same period, without it being necessary here to recall the historical context of their creation: Heidelberg (1933), Geneva (1941), Vienna (1943), and Germersheim (1947) – the latter settling in the premises of the Allies, a bit like the ESIT in Paris being inaugurated in 1957 in the premises of the NATO headquarters while the institute preceding it, created in 1951, had just been attached to the university, thus becoming a School. In Canada, before official bilingualism (1969), the Ottawa (1936), McGill (1943), and Université de Montréal (1951) were established. In Brazil, the Pan American Conference of 1947 could be held thanks to the English-Portuguese interpretation organised by the military attaché of the American Embassy in Rio de Janeiro. Many programmes were therefore launched before the start of many international organisations (UN, 1945; OECD, 1948; Comecon, 1949; NATO, 1949; Common Market, 1957).

At the end of this section, two questions remain unanswered:

1. Who funds research in neural MT and AI?
2. What are the interests of the language industries regarding offering programmes in CAT and MT, with or without certification?

Given the role of electronic tools in practice, in the organisation of work, in the production, circulation, and reception of translated materials, it is undoubtedly relevant for the entities that select translators to acknowledge the importance of these tools.

3. Multiple practices: on the future of "translation"

Three points will be addressed here regarding the impact of technologies on practices: first, the transition from a production-centered approach to a user-centered approach (section 3.1), then the variety of names recently used for different types of "translation" (section 3.2), and finally the features of a professional translator (section 3.3). In this set, does translation become a specific term or a generic to be redefined?

3.1 New types of translators

Different users, or prosumers, have now the chance to translate, thanks to CAT and MT tools facilitating localisation, subtitling, post-editing, etc., without necessarily having appropriate training, background experience, or even a precise awareness of what translating can mean, thus reproducing a certain mechanical, literalist vision of work. Against this background, at least five types of translators can be differentiated:

1. Ordinary users of the MT, who have access to the software available on the Net (*Google Translate, Microsoft Translate, Systran,* etc.), and who use it to obtain the gist of a document, without concern for the quality of the product offered or concern to archive it. However, we cannot forget the human factor in the development of MT, which always needs more translated data in order to be more efficient.
2. Fans who translate, localise, subtitle, dub, etc., their favourite movies, TV series, video games, comics, and websites, usually in an organised, though not officially recognised, network.
3. Volunteers of collective translation, involving crowdsourcing, who are often unpaid, anonymous, and with very diverse motivations. They are encouraged by platforms, e.g., to create collective subtitles for Amara, TED (Technology, Entertainment, Design conferences), YouTube, etc. They work on translation, localisation, revision projects, software, websites, articles, conferences, reports, etc.
4. Translators, who collaborate in teams, tandems, and pairs, and other formats. They can be professional or amateur; they share resources and activities (revision, terminology, proofreading) to translate the same content or document, 24 hours a day, 7 days a week, from various workplaces. These jobs, these projects can be auctioned on platforms like *Proz, Translators Café*. The qualifications requested and the requirements of the order can be on the Net.
5. Volunteers, networked translators, such as *Babel, Translators without Borders*. These translators, including professionals, are activists at the service of an altruistic, humanitarian, and political cause.

Do all these practices (Olohan, 2020) disqualify these people? Do they de-professionalise professional full-time translators? That translation does not belong only to translators who claim to be such is not new in history (see for example Paloposki, 2016). What is certain, however, is that collaboration, participation, collective project management, and technologies that facilitate these practices change the working conditions of all translators, regardless of their status (see for instance Jiménez-Crespo, 2017, 2021; Monti and Schnyder, 2018; Cadwell et al., 2022; Yu, 2022; Zwischenberger, 2022; Gough et al., 2023; Martin-Larcata, 2024). In addition, the use of MT involves a new type of literacy: digital literacy (*MT literacy*) (see the works by Lynne Bowker, between 2019 and today).

In addition to the variety of types of translators, alternative terminology to refer to what has been traditionally referred to as translation is today in use, also due to the development of technologies, markets, and the diversification of demand. These new translation names certainly appear at different speeds in different societies and languages. I am not thinking here of traditional subdivisions such as literary and specialised translation (technical, commercial, medical, legal), or conference and public service interpreting, nor of classifications related to the text genre (novels, poems, theater plays, etc.). These divisions still form strong oppositions, particularly in training: literary translation vs pragmatic translation, translation for publishing vs translation for information, natural translation vs professional translation, translation vs adaptation, etc. To understand such oppositions, I will now proceed with an illustration of the alternative names used to refer to translation, and their impact on the profession.

3.2   New names: new types of translation?

By the time, various professional sectors (business, industry, media, information technology, etc.), sponsors of translations, refusing the word "translation", have imposed alternative names to refer to translation such as:

- *Localisation*, a term first launched in the computer industry, concerning software and websites, then in the video game industry, and now in audiovisual translation (Schäler, 2010).
- *Adaptation*, long in competition with translation, while the emphasis moved from source text accuracy to receivers needs and expectations. Such adaptations (or sometimes translations) refer to texts with static images or music, such as comics, plays, children's books, advertisements, tourist brochures, etc. (Cattrysse, 2014).
- *Transcreation*, a term more and more used in marketing and the advertising industry, especially to highlight the creativity of international campaigns. Some use it to bring translation and writing closer together (Katan, 2021).
- *Language mediation*, or how, under diffcrent multilingual and multicultural conditions, a change of languages appears, a kind of *code-switching* alternative that is not always controlled by a formally qualified translator or interpreter.
- *Translanguaging, or* the transition from one language to another, can be similar to language mediation when multilingual speakers navigate between complex social and cognitive demands, thanks to their strategic use of their languages, for example, at school, in bi- or plurilingual families, or in marketplaces in a multilingual city (see, for instance, the work appearing in the journal *Translation and Translanguaging in Multilingual contexts*).

- *Transediting*, a term used in some written media to make it clear that journalists do not "translate" but seek to deliver information beyond fidelity to the source text, because they always have in mind their readers and are concerned about the readability of their article (Stetting, 1989).
- *Multilingual technical writing*, a phrase used when writing documents in multiple languages from comparable data. It is more than the design of technical manuals. This could include multilingual *documentation*, written from notes in English for example, and not from a fully-fledged source text.
- *Co-drafting*, for example, of legal texts that are also legally valid (Dullion, 2022).
- *Versioning* or audiovisual translation with its different modes (subtitling, dubbing, voice over, etc.); the term is also used in information technology, applied to software, web services, referring to creation and management of multiple product releases.
- *Revision* of a translated text (Mossop, 2011), including MT *post-editing*, which is becoming the main workflow in the industry (O'Brien, 2021).

Current denominative varieties cannot make us forget the varieties in the past, such as *mimesis, appropriation, imitation, comment,* or the various concepts defined today in other cultural areas: Indian, Chinese, Arab, Turkish, Malaysian, etc. (Reversal, transmigration, metamorphosis, substitution, and so on) (Chesterman, 2006; Gambier, 2018: 19–38; Gambier and Stecconi, 2019). This list is not exhaustive and does not apply everywhere at the same time. Nevertheless, it confirms that translation cannot be conceptualised in a monolithic and permanent way. It is a polymorphic concept, always to be negotiated, while being a global, universal practice. Nevertheless, discrepancies in names can be confusing and difficult to overcome, especially since when working with certain terminology databases, translation memory software or MT software, which rely on a more or less word-for-word process. The popular assumption that translation is a linear substitution of words testifies that traditional perceptions of "translation" and "translator" continue among those who have inherited these perceptions and continue to propagate such archetypes. This is strictly related to the assumption that language is a static rather than dynamic, envisioning communication, a mere sequence of information rather than as a sequence of interactions.

There is also a plural practice between interpreters, depending on whether one is focusing on conference interpreters, diplomatic interpreters, court interpreters, media interpreters, and community (or public service) interpreters. Thus, interpretation in the media, such as radio, television, festivals, etc., can take place in simultaneous or consecutive mode or in sign language (Pöchhacker, 2018). Also, communication can be mediated by an interpreter on site or remotely, and content can be made accessible to the audience of a channel through a pre-recorded or live interpretation. Another distinction is feasible, whether the interpretation is made on the screen or not, with the physical presence of the interpreter, or their voice only. Press conferences, interviews included in the news, shows, sports programmes, live reports of special events (such as election results, public funerals, an earthquake in a distant country, etc.) are further examples that call for relatively new practices. In such a diverse translation landscape, how can professional, qualified, competent translators be identified, and how can they be trained?

3.3 Professionalisation

Professionalisation means bringing together individual and collective efforts to promote a status, best practices, a code of conduct, or access to the profession in order to organise training courses, a certification system, or to filter classified ads. All these are what I call signals, or socio-professional parameters, reflecting a given professional self-image, with which a professional identifies, or according to which is identified, as a professional translator. In other words, what is the public position of professionals and non-professionals (or amateurs) in the hierarchy of translation professions, knowing that translation has never been a protected profession as have, for example, other liberal professions (lawyer, notary, doctor, accountant)? How and by what distinctive features are translators recognised as such? Two sources of observation are possible for this purpose: associations of translators and interpreters, and portals that form an online marketplace.

There are almost 130 national associations of translators and/or interpreters in the EU. Not to mention the 24 member associations of the European Union of Associations of Translation Agencies (EUATC), whose translators are not necessarily affiliated to a national entity. It must be said that not all associations of individuals always send clear signals to employers, or clients, for example on the possible ways of selecting a competent translator for a given task. Nevertheless, in general, national groupings send signals about formal qualification (university degree), work experience, the acceptance of a code of ethics, or the passing of a test or selection examination. Understandably, the criteria that apply to each of these signals often differ, though slightly, from one country to another, in terms of number of years of experience, nature of these experiences, formulation of ethical rules, type of test, etc.

Portals, such as *Proz.com*, *Aquarius*, and *Translators Café* bring together several thousand translators, revisers, subtitlers, and localisers from almost 150 countries. They are places of employment in the translation industries, information forums, directories of translation services, places of contact between agencies and clients, users, and translators. They also offer training modules, without neglecting the mass of help and advice, translational suggestions, and terminological proposals. They partly disturb traditional signals by being a market where offers and requests, tenders, price negotiations, and customer feedback interact, where members invest their time, knowledge, and skills in the online community. In this set, formal qualifications and the diploma acquired play only a minor role, confirming a prediction formulated recently by almost 650 experts in education working within the framework of the World Innovation Summit for Education (WISE), in Rochester, Minnesota (3–4 June 2021): in less than 20 years, peer and professional approval will begin to compete or even take the place of school certification. Could it be that we have been too much under the spell of institutional certification, in particular under the EU requirements? It is not too late to compare non-trained and trained translators, and consider again the validity of our training programmes especially if and when students have worked previously as amateurs. We should also note the rather limited effect of the mastery of technological tools among the signals of professionalisation in portals: it is not an asset as such, it is rather taken both as obvious and/or related to the added value offered by this or that translator compared to other members – a bit like working languages. Knowing languages and certain software are obvious, but having Chinese or Japanese, mastering a certain CAT tool or even a programming language can be elements of valorisation in a hyper-competitive market.

In short, online portals, fans and amateurs, MT and collective translation are altering traditional signals, such as control systems, access to the profession, and selection criteria. This means that the explicit emphasis on a diploma, for example, could undermine all recent efforts to improve university education. In fact, because validation of a translator's capacity to professionally carry out a translation task depends, today, on the experience and commitment of the translator – as transferred from an established corporation, that requires a regular contribution, to a transitional online community, that requires active participation.

4.   Research: indiscipline and ethics

After considering rapid changes in translation industry practices, let me now turn to research in TS, and particular on two main issues: the competitive division of disciplines, and ethics for the researchers.

4.1   Disciplinary divisions: Translation Studies as indiscipline?

To better understand the current academic landscape, one must apprehend the inner neoliberal logic of T&I universities, prevalent in the EU and the US. In this context, the current financial stage of our economy is changing the terms of competition to such an extent that it not just overcomes borders, it also risks of leading to fewer ethical rules being adopted, as well as short-term views when it comes to planning. Academic research finds itself in the same process, increasingly dominated by market forces, subjected to marketisation, corporatisation, liberalisation, and privatisation, keywords of the management of most of the universities today (Delabastita, 2013). This apparently strong claim, is based on the observation of the main values of the market of Higher Education institutions, which can be grouped as follows:

- Rankings, such as the Shanghai classification, the QS World University rankings, the *Times Higher Education* rankings, and the EU U-Multirank.
- Competition between universities to attract the best students, obliged to compare training opportunities and offers.
- Audits and different types of evaluation.
- Productivity requirements in research and degrees awarded.
- Ability to attract external funding in job adverts and applications for promotion.
- Partnership between universities and the private sector.
- Impact of research and innovation on the local environment.

Such an entrepreneurial system adopted by universities increasingly replaces the Humboldtian model of higher education, where the focus was on research and studies, and on students becoming autonomous individuals and world citizens. Universities, as extensions (or instruments) of the neoliberal corporate order, follow market-based rules and exert pressure on students, while teachers and scholars are supposed to be more and more innovative, productive, and better in communication. Some of the results of this competition include the use of different types of publication, the emergence of scientific fraud, and the use of English as a *lingua franca*.

What is the impact of such a landscape on TS as a discipline? Faced with these ongoing transformations, how appropriate is the object of the research/teaching field, the content of the work, or the openness of reflections? Without retracing the history of TS as a relatively recent discipline, its internationalisation, and its institutionalisation (D'hulst & Gambier, 2018: Part 3), let me simply stress that the name and nature of TS were initially specified in the 1970s (Holmes, 1972), and from the outset it always appeared as a poly-discipline (Morin, 1986), at the crossroads of and thanks to the contributions of various disciplines (initially formal, contrastive or applied linguistics, semiotics, poetics, comparative literature, philosophy).

Any discipline – if linked to the notions of knowledge, representations, and borders – is made up of two sets of elements: epistemic elements (apriorisms, presuppositions, concepts, problematisations in relation to needs and practices), and socio-institutional elements (operational standards, procedures via conferences, journals, associations, departments, etc.). This double constitution allows the said discipline to function and to be identified as such: a discipline as part of an architecture of knowledge production that integrates and continuously exceeds it at the same time. This means that TS – if we accept it is a discipline linked to the notions of knowledge, representations, and borders – is not, from the outset, a universal, permanent, static category. And because its disciplinarisation had been preceded by a multitude of discourses on translation for more than 2,000 years, from Europe to China, Iran, and the Arab world, its evolution has often been perceived through the notion of turn. However, this presupposes that the TS community has been moving linearly and in the same direction (Snell-Hornby, 2006), with some thematic (cultural, feminist, postcolonial, sociological, etc.), and methodological (functional, empirical, pragmatic, cognitive, etc.) turning points along the road. This reductionist vision says less about the conditions of the historical evolution of TS than about the conditions of production and circulation of translation research. And above all, it says nothing about the nature of relations with other disciplines (Gambier & van Doorslaer, 2016), or about the internationalisation of TS work. This is because TS is clearly not uniform or stable: it is divided between a hyper-specialisation, a compartmentalisation that is the delight of publishers (*Audiovisual Translation Studies, Localization Studies, Cognitive Translatology, Translation in Society*), and a convergence that finds it hard to defining its common denominators (is language transfer part of them?), its polymorphic object (is intersemiotic translation part of it?), its presuppositions (what is a text?), its methodological orientations. Under these circumstances, what is the future of TS and therefore of training programmes in T&I?

As long as translation studies was focused on texts, with their conventions (such as contracts, patents, articles, instructions, and novels), in circumscribed and recognised fields (such as economics, agriculture, defense, science, energy, machinery, and literature), and for specific needs, there were no insurmountable translation problems since most textual genres are strictly conventional and regulated by norms. Today, with the digitised world, the hegemony of English in publications, the number of objects and practices in translation have exploded (see sections 3.1 and 3.2). This brings to questioning the term itself: does translation encompass them all or does it only refer to a specific mode? Are all forms of translation subject to the competition of systematic automation and amateur workforce?

What can be easily ascertained is that TS is, today, financially and institutionally competing also with other disciplines, like Adaptation Studies, Intercultural Studies, Transfer Studies, Media Studies, Knowledge Management, Internet Studies, Web Science, Globalization Studies, Usability Studies, Accessibility Studies, Human-Computer Interaction Studies, Social Semiotics. As academic subjects, these competitors of TS have in common the complexity of interactive communication and behaviour but ignore or do not take into account linguistic diversity, language contact, cultural interference, T&I, which are all specific aspects of TS.

In this context, a transversal discipline it could be envisaged, capable of dealing with how groups, individuals, and cultures manage, value, negotiate, and mean "differences" and connections. However, for the moment being, TS still has to think about its "external" relations (with other disciplines and language industries, Gambier and van Doorslaer, 2016), its "internal" relations (cooperation with practitioners, professional or not, and experts), the social reception of its work (towards translators, the general public, the media, and publishers) (Koskinen, 2010), its academic status (often fragile or weakened by other disciplines also in conflict with their disputed status, such as linguistics, which still seeks to chaperone TS in various European countries, or comparative literature in the United States). TS must also think about its place in the current division of disciplines, as its teaching remains confined to the Humanities (languages, literature), while translation as a profession is, on the one hand, questioned in medicine, law, business, and social sciences; on the other hand, some would like to restrict TS to jobs and the effects of technologies.

4.2 Researchers in translation and ethics

Ethics-related issues have been widely discussed in translation research. However, the major focus of such issues has usually been on T&I practices, while the ethical issues of translation researchers have rarely been analysed. Research papers and publications on this topic are very scarce (Hekkanen, 2007; Mellinger & Hanson, 2017; Tiselius, 2019). However, the ways in which research today is used and reported in the different media and in different industries, the challenging digital technologies, the development of big data, the financial constraints on the universities, etc., raise sensible questions about ethics for researchers in our field, such as:

- the social relevance of research;
- the criteria for selection of the scientific literature as the framework of the research and for choosing examples, textual excerpts, interpreted speeches;
- awareness about how and by whom projects are funded;
- control of the human, technical and logistics resources to be used;
- the informed consent of the participants involved in gathering data;
- the types of sampling (recruiting available students, inviting participants, possible payment involved, etc.);
- awareness about the data provided in memory translation software, in neuronal MT, and the related questions of their ownership, their distribution, and the biases they represent and convey;

- the way data, examples, and archives are handled, and the way they are introduced, and translated in publications;
- the conflict of interest in peer-reviewing;
- the ways comments and suggestions are dealt with in a revision, and after a peer-review;
- awareness about affects when making decisions, interpreting data, and co-authoring a paper;
- the relationship between productivity and gender (during the pandemic, women submitted much fewer articles than men);
- the definition of fairness, responsibility, trust, confidentiality.

A discipline like TS, which is in transit, and with a broad object of investigation, and no clear-cut borders with other disciplines, needs to question the ethical values used implicitly by its members. This should be addressed to all the students in T&I. But for the time being, it remains a blind spot in the training, even though the question of data is raised more frequently when dealing with AI.

5.   By way of conclusion: seven open questions

From all that has been said – everything is in motion; everything is in transition – it would be difficult and reckless to draw confident conclusions. Prudence therefore invites us to recapitulate – not to capitulate! – a few open-ended questions related to T&I training. Some have not been discussed above, but are strictly related to those and have consequences for T&I training:

1. Not all societies, even those with a common language (e.g., French-speaking societies), have the same resources to develop CAT, MT, NMT, AI tools. Thus, English and Lithuanian do not share the same technical and financial resources. As a consequence, TS and universities, such as those of the European Master's in Translation network, should not forget this to prevent new digital divides in the same institutional body.
2. Where do the grants (institutional, state, and private) that fund ongoing research in AI and NMT come from? What should be the approach of T&I universities when using them in either research or teaching?
3. What are we talking about when we refer to "translation"? If T&I universities ignore or neglect what the word encompasses in terms of practices, professions, how can they consolidate and develop training programmes?
4. Can the gap between university education and portals and language industries be bridged if academic qualifications have a lower value on the labor markets? In wanting to ape the dominant model, are not universities mistaken? What happens when commercial companies offer online courses?

5. Are not TS currently succumbing to both the risk of fragmentation within it and arduous competition with other disciplines? Therefore, does this not make its recognition as a field of research, of knowledge, more difficult, as well as apprehension of its role in education in general, beyond the mere learning of languages?
6. Is it important to reintroduce reflections on the purposes and philosophies of education? If so, it cannot be an instrument of economic policy alone.
7. Automation can be a factor of emancipation if it is thought out and regulated. The example of social media today, however, does not allow for great optimism, and the decline in the attractiveness of Humanities and social sciences should give us pause. At the training level, the "all technology or nothing" dilemma is a trap if technology's complex links to culture and ethics are not rethought. How can such a dialogue be framed?

One aspect that these questions have in common is the technological revolution, which implies that nothing will be the same as before. In fact, after the pocket calculator, we will never return to the abacus, and after electromagnetic detection, we will never return to the water-divining rod. In this context, firms, universities, and public opinion subscribe to the myth of permanent technological change, through the concept of innovation (disruptive innovation, of course). In fairs, institutions and services, innovation is always top-down and without history. What seems to be missing in this new promise of a brighter future is culture, meant as ways technology can be integrated into behaviours, ways to give value to technology, ways to think of the relevance and efficiency of the new technology. And yet technology and culture are considered as separate from one another. In most European and American countries, there is a Ministry of Science and Technology, and a Ministry of Education and Culture; a Faculty of Science and Technology, and a Faculty of Humanities. This opposition has very distant roots since, for instance, ancient Greek philosophy was formed by marginalising the question of *techne,* that is, production, material making, efficient action, as if technology was not constituent of the philosophical truth. This has a number of implications for developing T&I curricula.[4]

The coronavirus pandemic has revealed the extent to which we could not think of health only in terms of technical devices, but we had also to take into account individual and collective behaviours, emotions and values, as if suddenly we realised we are not "Man a Machine", or automatons derived from Descartes's notion of the mechanical philosophy as "Animal Machine".

The solution is then to work together, which can allow us to avoid falling into the traps of "solutionism", the belief that technology can solve all our problems, from pollution to crime, from corruption to safety, from obesity to social relationship; and "web centrism", the belief that today's technology disruption, with its predictive algorithms, is somehow unique in history.

How to think about technology and culture, then, if we want to progress beyond the illusions of technology's omnipotence? A fair number of writers and scholars have investigated the impact of technology, but very often the argument is Manichaean, binary: the techno-optimists, or cheerleaders of progress at any cost, opposed to the techno-sceptics, prophets of doom. The result is that both camps frame questions in such a way that technology remains central, sidestepping the social and cultural structures in which we are embedded, and our technologies are shaped (Leonhard, 2016).

To this extent, three frameworks seem important to me to understand the way T&I can be seen as interacting with technology: *technopoly*, mediology and Social Construction of Technology Studies (SCOT).

"Technopoly" is a concept developed by the American media theorist Neil Postman (1931–2003) in a book published in 1992, when the Arpanet was the only packet-network (operational from the 1970s) and the precursor of the Internet (1980s). For Postman, technophiles are unable to understand the effects of their innovations. The history of technological advancements is the history of the relations between technology and culture – with three main periods: the first being tool-using cultures, when techniques like water-mills solved physical problems and served the symbolic power of religion, art, and politics; the second being technocracy, during the era of Copernicus, Kepler, Galileo Galilei, Bacon, etc., when techno-scientific rationality was in conflict with religion. In this context, society has remained under social and religious traditions; the third period being technopoly, emerging in the 20th century with Taylorism, bureaucracy, expertise, and submitting all forms of cultural life to the exclusive dominion of technology. Little by little, computers and information technology speed up the change. Information (data) has become the means and the end of human creativity: medical tests, IQ tests, and opinion polls, are examples of excessive faith and trust in technology and quantification. Regardless of one's views on Postman's position, new tools are creating new environments but do not necessarily exclude other older beliefs, as we can see with the role of religions in today's policies across the world.

"Mediology" (mediation between the production of signs and production of events, Debray, 1994: 29) is the other multidisciplinary approach trying to reconnect technology and culture. elaborated by the French philosopher and journalist Regis Debray (Debray, 1991, 1994, 1997). In studying methods used to store, transmit, pass down and disseminate cultural knowledge, this media philosophy, much more than a simple sociology of mass media, sets out to demonstrate how media (as techno-typical and ethno-cultural vectors of transmission) do not only serve to conserve data, information, and knowledge, but are also constitutive: they shape our mind-set, our beliefs, our social organisation. The material act of transmitting between individuals, groups, organisations, and societies is different from "communication", monopolised, according to Debray, by language theoreticians and university programmes or departments. Hence, mediology studies the interplay between three interdependent aspects of culture: the symbolic forms (religion, system/doctrine, and arts), the collective organisations (such as church or school), and technical systems of communication (to understand, memorise, archive, and disseminate cultural knowledge and traces). In other words, information, ideas, and cultures do not travel isolated, free of the ground, but through media over time and over spaces.

SCOT, social construction of technology (Olohan, 2017), is opposed to technological determinism (as if technology is the source of changes in human behaviours and social life) and offers three key concepts to help understanding the role of technology in our society: "relevant social groups" or how different social groups develop, use technology in such a way that they give different meaning to the artefact; "interpretive flexibility" or how different understandings of the artefact coexist across various social groups; and "closure and stabilisation" or how an artefact becomes a dominant form of the technology, leading to one understanding becoming dominant.

Regardless of the framework used to see the interrelation between culture and technology, an obvious conclusion seems to be that considering technology and culture together is a way to empower again students, trainers, translators, and all users of e-tools.

For T&I universities, knowing the sources of their finances, the interplay between investment and sustainable development, the diversity of the practices, the ethical dimension of the research, the challenges of interdisciplinarity, the impacts of technology in our daily behaviour remain too often than not blind spots, as if a fast application of technical tools was the only way to prove that the training (the curriculum, the methodology, the evaluation) is relevant, as if keeping up to the latest tools was the only meaningful way to train the future translators/interpreters. Technology can solve problems but create also new problems, and nobody knows what technology our students will cope with in ten, twenty years. Our students need to be trained in critical learning, not as automats able to use certain tools available today and obsolete tomorrow. They need to be trained with a critical mind, not as robots able to apply certain rules, ignoring the consequences of their acts on their environment (in a broad meaning).

Notes

1   I trained translators in Turku (Finland) (1973–2014), organised seminars for training teachers in different universities in Europe (1997–2012), through the Baltic Sea Region University Network (2006 2010); I was a member of the consortium for the European Master in conference interpreting (EMCI) (1997–2011), and participated in EMT/European Master's in Translation (2006–2014).

2 See, for example, the bibliometric analysis of the so-called military translation in China by S. Xu, 2019.
3 Here the reference is in particular to the Big Five, or GAFAM, meaning Google (which has opened in June 2022 a new "campus" in Zurich for 5,000 researchers), Apple, Facebook, Amazon, and Microsoft.
4 The place and the role of technology is quite different between societies (with low or high technological resources) and between universities (with a different division of the disciplines). A curriculum is constrained by different factors (institutional, pedagogical, financial, etc.). It is not within the scope of this chapter to suggest ways to integrate thoughts about technology and its relationship to culture. This is a topic to be discussed by trainers in each case; there is no universal solution.

References

Cadwell, P., Federico, F. and O'Brien, B. 2022. Communities of practices and translation: An introduction. *The Journal of Specialized Translation*, **37** (1), pp. 1–4.

Cattrysse, P. 2014. *Descriptive Adaptation Studies*. Epistemological and Methodological Issues. Antwerp: Garant.

Chesterman, A. 2006. Interpreting the meaning of translation. In: Suominen, M., Arppe, A., Airola, A., Heinämäki, O., Miestamo, M., Määttä, U., Niemi, J., Pitkänen, K.K. and Sinnemäki, K. eds. *A Man of Measure: Festschrift in Homage of Fred Karlsson on His 60th Birthday*. Helsinki: University of Helsinki, pp. 3–11.

Debray, R. 1991. *Cours de médiologie générale*. Paris: Gallimard.

Debray, R. 1994. *Manifestes médiologiques*. Paris: Gallimard.

Debray, R. 1997. *Transmettre*. Paris: Le Seuil.

Delabastita, D. 2013. B2B in translation studies: Business to business or back to basics. *The Translator*, **19** (1), pp. 1–23.

Delavenay, E. 1959. *The Translating Machine*. Que sais-je? 834. Paris: PUF

D'hulst, L. and Gambier, Y. eds. 2018. *A History of Modern Translation Knowledge. Sources, Concepts, Effects*. Amsterdam and Philadelphia: John Benjamins.

Dullion, V. 2022. When was co-drafting "invented"? On history and concepts in legal translation. *Perspectives*, **31** (6), pp. 1127–1141.

Gambier, Y. 2018. Concepts of translation. In: D'hulst H. and Gambier Y. eds. *A History of Modern Translation Knowledge. Sources, Concepts, Effects*. Amsterdam and Philadelphia: John Benjamins, pp. 19–38.

Gambier, Y. and Stecconi, U. eds. 2019. *A World Atlas of Translation*. Amsterdam and Philadelphia: John Benjamins.

Gambier, Y. and van Doorslaer, L. eds. 2016. *Border Crossings. Translation Studies and Other Disciplines*. Amsterdam and Philadelphia: John Benjamins.

Gough, J., Özlem, T., Graham, H. and Zilio, L. 2023. Concurrent translation on collaborative platforms. *Translation Spaces*, **12** (1), pp. 45–72.

Hekkanen, R. 2007. The role of ethics in translation and in Translation Studies research. *Across Languages and Cultures*, **8** (2), pp. 231–247.

Holmes, J. 1972. The name and nature of translation studies. In: Holmes J. ed. *Translated! Papers in Literary Translation and Translation Studies*. Amsterdam: Rodopi, pp. 67–80.

Hutchins, W.J. 1986. *Machine Translation: Past, Present, Future*. Chichester: Ellis Horwood.

Jimenéz-Crespo, M. 2017. *Crowdsourcing and Online Collaborative Translations.* Amsterdam and Philadelphia: John Benjamins.

Jimenéz-Crespo, M. 2021. The impact of crowdsourcing and online collaboration in professional translation. Charting the future of translation? *Babel,* **67** (4), pp. 395–417.

Katan, D. 2021. Transcreation. In: Gambier, Y. and van Doorslaer, L. eds. *Handbook of Translation Studies.* 5. Amsterdam and Philadelphia: John Benjamins, pp. 221–225.

Koskinen, K. 2010. What matters to Translation Studies? On the role of public Translation Studies. In: Gile, D., Hansen, G. and Pokorn, N. eds. *Why Translation Studies Matters?* Amsterdam and Philadelphia: John Benjamins, pp. 15–26.

Leonhard, G. 2016. *Technology vs Humanity: The Coming Clash Between Man and Machine.* London: Fast Future Publishing.

Martin-Larcata, M. 2024. Charting literary translator collaboration in digital contexts. *Translation in Society,* **12**, pp 1–26.

Mellinger, C.D. and Hanson, T.A. 2017. *Quantitative Research Methods in Translation and Interpreting Studies.* London: Routledge.

Monti, E. and Schnyder, P. eds. 2018. *Traduire à plusieurs. Collaborative translation.* Paris: Orizons.

Morin, E. 1986. *La méthode 3. La connaissance de la connaissance.* Paris: Le Seuil.

Mossop, B. 2011. Revision. In: Gambier, Y. and van Doorslaer, Y. eds. *Handbook of Translation Studies.* 2. Amsterdam and Philadelphia: John Benjamins, pp. 135–139.

O'Brien, S. 2021. Post-editing. In: Gambier, Y. and van Doorslaer, Y. eds. *Handbook of Translation Studies.* 2. Amsterdam and Philadelphia: John Benjamins, pp. 177–183.

Olohan, M. 2017. Technology, translation and society: A constructivist, critical theory approach. *Target,* **29** (2), pp. 264–283.

Olohan, M. 2020. *Translation and Practice Theory.* London: Routledge.

Paloposki, O. 2016. Translating and translators before the professional project. *The Journal of Specialised Translation,* **25**, pp. 15–32.

Pöchhacker, F. 2018. Media interpreting: From user expectations to audience comprehension. In: Di Giovanni, E. and Gambier, Y. eds. *Reception Studies and Audiovisual Translation.* Amsterdam and Philadelphia: John Benjamins, pp. 253–276.

Postman, N. 1992. *Technopoly: The Surrender of Culture to Technology.* New York: Vintage Books.

Schäler, R. 2010. Localization and translation. In: Gambier, Y. and van Doorslaer, Y. eds. *Handbook of Translation Studies.* 2. Amsterdam and Philadelphia: John Benjamins, pp. 209–214.

Snell-Hornby, M. 2006. *The Turns of Translation Studies. New Paradigms or Shifting Viewpoints?* Amsterdam and Philadelphia: John Benjamins.

Stetting, K. 1989. Transediting, A new term for coping with the grey area between editing and translating. In: Caie, G. ed. *Proceedings of the Fourth Nordic Conference for English Studies.* Copenhagen: University of Copenhagen, pp. 371–382.

Tiselius, E. 2019. The (un-) ethical interpreting researcher: Ethics, voice and discretionary power in interpreting research. *Perspectives,* **27** (5), pp. 747–760.

Xu, S. 2019. A bibliometrical analysis of Journal articles on military translation studies in China. In: Han Z. and Li, D. eds. *Translation Studies in China*. Singapore: Springer, pp. 215–228.

Yu, C. 2022. *Online Collaborative Translation in China and Beyond: Community, Practice, and Identity*. London: Routledge.

Zwischenberger, C. 2022. Online collaborative translation: Its ethical, social, and conceptual conditions and consequences. *Perspectives,* 30 (1), pp. 1–18.

PART I

Inside the classroom, outside the classroom

3

SHOW ME THE MONEY

Bringing pay, rate-setting, and financial sustainability into the translation classroom

Callum Walker and Joseph Lambert

Keywords: money; rates of pay; translator training; translation industry; financial sustainability

1. The great divide(s)

Money matters. In a survey of approximately 1,500 freelance translators, low rates of pay was by far the biggest challenge facing translators (59% of respondents, Inbox Translation, 2020). And yet, wider forecasts show sustained growth in the language industry, reaching $64.7 billion in 2022 and forecast to grow to $90.8 by 2027 (Nimdzi, 2023). This stark contrast in outlooks gives cause for concern, given that translation and localization make up 43% of the market.[1] Although disruptors such as new technologies and platforms, and issues of status are among key factors exacerbating this contrast, Translation Studies (TS) and translator training still have a part to play.

In an illuminating account of the "great divide" between TS and professional practice, David Jemiellity contends that a "[lack of institutional awareness] may explain an often insufficiently ambitious and insufficiently demanding pedagogical approach to specialized premium-market competencies like deep subject-matter knowledge" (2018, p. 546). Beyond freelance translators' predilection for working alone, which he argues "doesn't always align very well with the business world's focus on 'relationships'" (ibid. 535), Jemiellity cites prominent translators and observers who point to "poverty cults" in the translation world. Here, he argues, "an excessively frugal, economically unambitious, arguably anti-capitalist approach" prevails, putting translators "both behaviorally and ideologically at odds with many of their business

DOI: 10.4324/9781003440970-4

clients, ultimately reducing their chances for economic prosperity in the profession" (ibid.). These striking observations oblige us to question the role that translation trainers play in establishing, perpetuating, or challenging industry norms.

In this chapter, we explore money's place in the translation classroom, examining the space it has (or, perhaps, has not) occupied to the present day, before considering the ways in which it is now starting to be represented, and potential ways to consolidate its place. We do so with a view to instilling a greater sense of ambition among increasingly nervous translation graduates, a stronger understanding of their agency and control over their own fortunes (both literally and metaphorically), and, importantly, better job satisfaction in the short and longer term. We believe that this will help to support sustainability on an individual freelancer level and on the wider level of the profession as a whole.

2. In search of (a) literature (review)

The most apparent problems in reviewing literature in this area are also likely to be encountered by those devising reading lists for relevant modules: (1) pedagogical literature on "teaching money" is virtually non-existent in TS and in other disciplines, as best we can tell; (2) research on money in the translation profession is scarce, despite recent interest; and (3) most industry sources are anecdotal, with much of the idiosyncratic advice dependent on the author's background, experience, and client base. Mitigation comes in part through the challenges facing anyone tackling this area: the fragmented, dynamic, and heterogeneous nature of the industry means that advice is necessarily partial and contingent, while additional barriers such as pervasive taboos against discussing money or antitrust regulations further complicate matters (Lambert & Walker, 2022, pp. 10–11). Nonetheless, this is a vital topic that warrants our attention.

When we talk about money, we are typically dealing with micro-economics: the economics of decision-making by individuals and companies, often with a focus on pricing mechanisms. For all the successes of the translation industry outlined above, economics has only started to draw limited attention more recently. In 2014, Yves Gambier laid down a manifesto for economics-driven research as the basis for an "economic turn" in TS on the back of radical transformations in the industry. He highlighted, not surprisingly, the role of technology, heightened demand for translation, public awareness, and the short supply of translators, all of which feed directly into questions of money (Gambier, 2014). Three years later, Łucja Biel and Vilelmini Sosoni's special issue on economics (2017) made a noble effort to foreground this domain, bringing together articles on different economic facets of the translation industry: the economics of languages and translation as risk management (Pym, 2017), the precarity and limited agency of freelance translators amid growing technologisation (Moorkens, 2017), and the impact of crowdsourcing on translation quality (Jiménez-Crespo, 2017). These articles, which differ widely in their focus, address the *status quo* of pricing and costs from different perspectives, adopting descriptive, empirically-informed accounts of current trends and issues. Karen Bennett's special issue (2022) also picks up on monetary concerns, but largely skirts around the crux of professionals' monetary realities, instead collating a number of disparate articles on different themes. Only two articles are particularly noteworthy in our current context: Peter Sandrini's (2022) discussion of the economic impact of technology and automation on translators' expertise, and Armando Magaia's (2022) account of the financial challenges faced by translators and interpreters in Mozambique. All of the sources above address the current reality, but – naturally – do not offer guidance that may be of direct use to students studying on a translation programme. We have reviewed these articles in these terms not to be critical – they are incredibly valuable contributions to the gap in literature – but rather to clarify that it was never the authors' intention to provide practical guidance to aspiring translators on rate-setting, and this is the reality facing lecturers, on the one hand, and students, on the other.

The only scholarly contribution to break this mould is Sabrina Girletti and Marie-Aude Lefer's publication *Introducing MTPE Pricing in Translator Training* (2024), which takes a similar tack to this chapter in noting that "despite [post-editing's] crucial importance, especially for young graduates entering the translation market, the topic of PE pricing is rarely discussed in training programmes" (ibid., p. 2). Girletti and Lefer's aim is similar to ours, in that they too seek to present pedagogical proposals and bring pricing training into translation programmes, to develop awareness, and to help students to face up to market challenges. Interestingly, in their article they comment – in a similarly named sub-section to ours, entitled "The quest for information on MTPE pricing" – on the dearth of materials available to students on how much to charge for such services. Drawing on data from task edit times, modification edit metrics, prior conceptions of rates, and reflecting on the pros and cons of word-based, time-based, and edit-rate-based pricing models, they convincingly argue for the importance of such training "before students graduate and enter the market[, allowing] them to become game-changing actors in the language industry" (ibid., 13). In conjunction with our account below, this publication could mark a shift in scholarly and pedagogical interest in this subject, which can only improve the offering of many universities' translation programmes.

Nonetheless, if we view the problem of the lack of dedicated literature from another perspective, a growing number of researchers have at least started to explore translators' working conditions, often with a focus on pay and income. Among others, articles by Dunne (2012), Doherty (2016), do Carmo (2020), and Nunes Vieira (2020), in addition to our own publication on the topic (Lambert & Walker, 2022), have all tackled different dimensions of the effects of recent far-reaching changes in the industry on rates of pay and the value of translation and its perception by different parties. A small number of sources have looked at price formation, but this is typically from the project manager's or LSP's perspective (Walker, 2022, pp. 129–143), or looking specifically at fair MTPE pricing models (Sakamoto & Bawa Mason, 2024). The bottom-up perspective – how translators set their prices – is mostly neglected, with JC Penet's textbook (2024) a notable exception in adapting price formation principles into guidance for future translators.

When we consider the employability skills of translation graduates, questions of money, negotiation, and pricing are notably absent (Hao & Pym, 2021; Schnell & Rodríguez, 2017). Indeed, just as money is a blind spot in the classroom, despite increasing calls for transparency within translation and beyond,[2] rates of pay are a blind spot in such employability studies. An analysis of industry needs (i.e., the skills and competences required to work in translation) is necessarily from an employer's perspective, and this precludes calls for or better supply-side understanding of what constitutes better rates of pay. There are no job advertisements for freelance translators or tightly-regulated bodies calling for certain rates of pay as there might be in other professions, in addition to various other factors complicating regulation of rates of pay (see Lambert & Walker, 2022).

Herein lies the crux of the problem. Students are faced with a growing number of (typically academic) sources which provide often top-down data on trends in the contemporary translation industry, and even detailed insights into earning potential in different segments or countries. A recent surge in articles in association magazines (Jackson, 2022; Kreuzer, 2023; Raymond, 2023; Willis-Lee & Jackson, 2023; Worrall, 2023) and books such as Jenner and Jenner's *The Entrepreneurial Linguist* (2010), a mainstay on many programmes' reading lists, also provide well-meaning advice from experienced professionals. But the recommendations are vague and the pricing practices discussed are often related to the unique circumstances in which that translator works. One unique and enlightening book worth mentioning here, which very much breaks with these characteristics, is Chris Durban and Eugene Seidel's agony-aunt-style *The Prosperous Translator* (Durban, 2010), with almost 40 pages of pointed advice on "Pricing and value" (pp. 90–127). Nonetheless, learning what others charge and how they determine their rates (which are dependent on a range of factors, as discussed below) is different to learning how to determine one's own rates. Recommending specific prices – which does happen in rare cases – could raise question marks under competition law (Lambert, 2023a, p. 46). However, one recent example where rates are discussed directly can be found in our report (Walker et al., 2024) – and forthcoming reports – comparing rates between members and non-members of the UK Institute of Translation and Interpreting (ITI), which bypasses competition law restrictions by presenting objective historic data. Such reports can be useful to lecturers and to students alike, but such data are still hard to come by. Nonetheless, the lack of such data makes it difficult for lecturers to guide students on pricing beyond merely making them aware of current realities, which can be alarming for newcomers to the profession. Even then, the realities that are presented to students may be skewed or not representative of the range in the industry as a whole, as we discuss in section 4.

Translators have even posted on social media and in blogs about the lack of guidance on rate-setting in translation curricula.[3] Li et al. (2023) and Jääskeläinen et al. (2011) convincingly argue that translation education should meet certain market realities and that there is gap between these two worlds. If the market reality is indeed that translators are all talking about pay issues, then it follows that we should teach our students about this. Magaia echoes this view, arguing that "an effective translator and interpreter training model should, among other things, equip students to be self-employed" (2022, p. 86), and part of self-employment is being an effective businessperson.

One final way in which rates of pay has entered recent debates in TS is within the context of ethics, and specifically sustainability. While some scholars argue that money is not an ethical issue, Lambert (2023b) contends that since rates of pay regularly feature among the most pressing ethical issues facing translators, this means that the topic must be taken seriously. A productive perspective from which to approach this is sustainability, which has received considerable attention recently, in both academic and industry contexts. The ubiquitous three-pillar, triple bottom line conception of sustainability popularised by Elkington affords a central place to finance within his interdependent, porous, and dynamic pillars of "economic prosperity, environmental quality, and social justice" (Elkington, 1997, p. vii). In a TS context, these concerns for financial and human capital take on vital importance in the contemporary industry context (Lambert & Walker, 2024; see also Moorkens et al., 2024). Moorkens (2020), for instance, contends that economic and human resource sustainability is foundational to the development and sustainability of whole societies "and is indivisible from environmental sustainability", while the ELIS Survey in 2023 commented that "the sustainability of freelance activity [...] needs to be investigated more in-depth." (ELIS Survey 2023, p. 46).

3. Money in the translation classroom

In this section, we consider the place that discussions of money occupy in the translation classroom in UK and Irish HEIs. Given the heterogeneity of translation training even within this geographical profile, this is not an easy task, nor one that we can hope to complete in an entirely comprehensive manner. Nevertheless, by combining readily available information from prominent UK and Irish translation postgraduate programmes, the EMT Competence Framework (European Commission, 2022), and our experience of working across a range of HEIs, we have endeavoured to sketch a snapshot of the information on offer to students now, gaps in current provision, and the potential for further prominence for these crucial issues within current frameworks.

For our review, we consulted the websites of the 24 current members of the Association of Programmes in Translation and Interpreting Studies UK and Ireland (APTIS) and compiled programme and module data on 31 Masters-level programmes.[4] While APTIS member institutions offer a larger number of programmes in total, we discounted interpreting-only, language-specific, literary translation-specific, and undergraduate programmes with a view to ensuring consistency, comparability, and fairness. Using the EMT Competence Framework's industry-oriented areas of competence as a scaffold ("Language and Culture", "Translation", "Technology", "Personal and Interpersonal", and "Service Provision"),[5] we tabulated a range of common module types that could feasibly incorporate a focus on rates and money, and classified each university's offering according to whether such content was part of a compulsory or optional module, an extra-curricular activity, or not present at all. We also checked for explicit mention of the words "rates", "money", "quotation", and indirect references to rate-setting. We compiled this information separately first, before comparing notes to ensure agreement, and to mitigate against missing key information. Throughout the process, we relied only on publicly-available programme and module descriptions and discounted personal knowledge of the programmes and modules, either through direct experience, conversations with colleagues, or external examiner roles. The rationale for this approach was that these websites are the materials that prospective students encounter when exploring programmes and, if rates and money were more prominent a feature on our programmes, would be the best place to signal such a focus. We also recognise the limitations of this approach: such catalogues and websites are necessarily concise, meaning that detailed in-class content is omitted. Materials can also be obsolete or purposefully vague to allow flexibility.[6] Conversely, mere mention of rates in the catalogues does not guarantee comprehensive coverage. Despite these shortcomings, the results offer an important indicator of the centrality of rates of pay in programmes, and provide an insight into potential platforms for development, as explored below.

3.1 Established practices

Within our review of UK and Irish programmes (see Table 3.1), only six of 31 (19.4%) programmes specifically mentioned rates. The University of

Aberdeen's MSc Translation Studies optional module "Professional Skills for Translators" covers "fee structures and pricing for freelance translators". The University of Birmingham's optional "Professional Development" module covers how to "set your rates". The University of East Anglia's core "Professional Translation Work Experience" module covers "pricing, marketing, career development and ethical behaviour". At the University of Edinburgh, their optional module "Technology and Translation in the Workplace" mentions coverage of "remuneration". At the University of Leeds, both programmes specifically mention "pricing" and "quoting" in core translation technology modules.

In the classroom, students typically research rates of pay in order to bid for jobs or provide quotes to their tutors when engaging in simulated translation bureaus, case-study projects, and work placements. This research will often lead to easily-accessible online materials such as ProZ.com's "Average rates charged for translators",[7] which provides an aggregated view of rates that users have entered on their profiles, and covers an impressive range of language pairs and specialisms.[8] Resources such as the aforementioned ITI rates report (Walker et al., 2024) and forthcoming reports in this series will also prove useful to students for ballpark figures. In our experience, students also contact LSPs when preparing quotes, though this *ad hoc* method leads to rather erratic results. Students also call upon (relatively anecdotal) advice from tutors with varying degrees of industry experience. Guest talks from industry professionals, meanwhile, can (and sometimes do) cover rates of pay, though the aforementioned issues of secrecy around rates, taboos around money, and the heterogeneity of the profession are important limitations to note.

Ultimately, these resources regularly result in students gaining a rough grasp of the range of "standard" per-word prices, but do not expose them to the wider pressures on rates as outlined above. Nor do they encourage them to critique this *status quo* or to expand their horizons beyond the "standard". In terms of feedback, we find that students are often told that their prices are " 'too high/low' or '(un)realistic', or that they are 'underselling themselves', and yet [...] specific examples of appropriate pricing levels are rarely offered" (Lambert & Walker, 2022, pp. 8–9). Of course, this is not intended to critique trainers, who are working in a hugely constrained context. As Table 3.1 shows, these discussions of rates are taking place within modules that focus elsewhere (e.g., technology), with a huge amount of material to be covered in a short space of time. While rates of pay are a vital area of discussion, translator training covers a vast array of topics (as suggested by the range of EMT framework competences; postgraduate study also typically aims to do more than simply prepare graduates for industry) and fitting required content into such dense programmes is already a challenge without adding dedicated sessions on money. When we consider the social taboo around discussing rates of pay, the paucity of academic and industry resources to call

TABLE 3.1 Sites for embedding rates education in APTIS member translation programmes

Note: Key • = Covered on core module; o = Covered on optional module; # = Extra-curricular

University	Programme	Rates/money/ pricing explicitly mentioned	Practical translation	Technology	Ethics	Translation profession/ business skills	Simulated translation bureau	Work placement	Guest speakers	Notes on mentions of or allusions to rates and pricing
Cardiff University	MA Translation Studies	N	•	•		•		o	#	
Dublin City University	MA Translation Studies	N	o	•		•	•	o	•	
	MSc Translation Technology	N	o	•		•		o		
Goldsmiths University of London	MA Translation	N	•	•	•	•		•		
Heriot-Watt University	MSc Translating	N	•	•		•				
Queens University Belfast	MA Translation	N	o	•		•		o	#	
Swansea University	MA Translation and Interpreting	N	•	•	•	•	o	o	o	
	MA Professional Translation	N	•	•	•	•	o	o	o	
The Open University	MA Translation	N	•	•	•	•			•	

(Continued)

Institution	Programme							Notes
University College London	MA Translation Studies	N	○	○	•	○	#	
	MA Translation and Culture	N	○	•	•	○	#	
	MSc Translation and Tech. (Sci., Tech. & Med.)	N	•	•	•	○	#	
	MSc Translation and Tech. (Audiovisual)	N	•	•	•	○	#	
University College Cork	MA Translation Studies	N	•	•	•	○		
University of Aberdeen	MSc Translation Studies	Y	•	○	○	○		"Professional Skills for Translators" module: "Topics [...] are likely to include [...] marketing one's services as a freelance translator; [...] fee structures and pricing for freelance translators; [...]".
	MSc Translating and Interpreting Studies	N	•	○				

TABLE 3.1 (Continued)

University	Programme	Rates/money/pricing explicitly mentioned	Practical translation	Technology	Ethics	Translation profession/business skills	Simulated translation bureau	Work placement	Guest speakers	Notes on mentions of or allusions to rates and pricing
University of Birmingham	MA Translation Studies	Y	•	•		○			#	"Professional Development" module: "sessions will [...] support you in understanding how to market yourself, set your rates, interact with clients and so on".
University of Bristol	MA Translation (Online)	N	•	○	○	○			#	
University of Chester	MA Language, Cultures and Translation	N	•							
University of East Anglia	MA Applied Translation Studies	Y	•	•	•	•	•	•		Mention of "pricing" on the "Technological Tools for Translators" and "Professional Translation Work Experience" modules.

University	Programme								Notes
University of Edinburgh	MSc Translation Studies	Y	•	○	○			#	Mention of "remuneration" on the "Technology and Translation in the Workplace" optional module.
University of Leeds	MA Applied Translation Studies	Y	•	•		•	•	#	Mention of "pricing" and "quoting" on two technology modules, and "quote and invoice" on "Localisation and Project Management" module.
	MA Audiovisual Translation and Localisation	Y	•	•		•	•	#	
University of Manchester	MA Translation and Interpreting Studies	N	○	○		○			
University of Portsmouth	MA Translation Studies	N	•	○		○			
University of Sheffield	MA Translation Studies	N	•	•		○			
University of Surrey	MA Translation	N	•	•	•	○			
	MA Translation and Interpreting	N	•	○	•	○			

(Continued)

TABLE 3.1 (Continued)

University	Programme	Rates/money/pricing explicitly mentioned	Practical translation	Technology	Ethics	Translation profession/business skills	Simulated translation bureau	Work placement	Guest speakers	Notes on mentions of or allusions to rates and pricing
University of Warwick	MA Translation and Cultures	N	•	○	•	•		#	•	Mention of "negotiat[ing] ethical working conditions enabling social, economic and environmental sustainability in the profession" and the "neoliberal economics of translation and non-hegemonic alternatives for a sustainable profession" on "Critical Skills for the Translation Profession" module.
University of Westminster	MA Specialised Translation	N	•	•	•	•	•		•	
	MA Translation and Interpreting	N	•	•	•	•	•		•	

upon, and the heterogeneity of translation cohorts, the task becomes even more challenging. However, while acknowledging these barriers, we argue that coverage of rates of pay should occupy a higher place in the hierarchy than at present. Consider, as noted above, that industry surveys regularly find issues with pay to be more important to translators than everything else. In both iterations of Inbox Translation's freelance translator surveys (2020, 2023), 59% of respondents cited low rates of pay as the main challenge they currently experience as freelance translators. Surely this means that this topic merits a dedicated space in the translation curriculum, even if these conversations are hard and they come at the expense of something else?

3.2 Emerging perspectives

Besides indicating the relative dearth of (explicit) acknowledgements of discussions of rates of pay in translator training, our review above also hints at places in which rates of pay could be discussed. Indeed, the modules in which rates are mentioned allude to the variety of contexts where this topic is relevant.[9] With the above time and space constraints in mind, we now consider where these discussions could realistically (and often seamlessly) be integrated into existing provision, based on our knowledge of typical postgraduate translation programmes and our review summarised in Table 3.1. As well as listing modules, we also offer cursory examples of ways in which rates could be embedded, to illustrate the plethora of potential entry points. The range of modules covered in our review demonstrates that every programme has the potential for discussions of rates and the vast majority have multiple opportunities to do so:

- The most obvious place to discuss rates is within **modules aiming to develop industry skills**. Learning how to price your services, how to negotiate with clients, or how to budget for projects, for example, are key skills in the translation industry, and any module on the topic could justifiably add sessions on pay.
- **Translation technology modules**: Given the interconnectedness of translation technology and rates of pay, these modules provide a perfect venue to discuss payment practices, and to critically engage with emerging industry practices, addressing discounts for TM matches or rates offered for MT post-editing, for instance. Depending on the module's reach, this could also include quoting for jobs using project/file analysis statistics within CAT tools, enabling students to approach the issue of rates from a range of perspectives, i.e., as a "linguist" or PM, and how perspectives and priorities might differ between these agents.
- Next are **simulated translation bureaus** (STB), in which "students create and run their own fictitious translation agencies for course credit" (Penet

& Fernandez-Parra, 2023, p. 332). These modules are increasingly popular given that they enable students to develop the "adaptive expertise" (Angelone, 2022) required by the contemporary translator's multi-faceted practice. A common element within these modules is coverage of translation project management, which again opens up channels to discussing rates, quotations, invoicing, payment practices, and complex relationships between agents in a translation project. Many of these modules include discussions of rates and quotations in various ways. Indeed, price formation is explicitly mentioned as a component by INSTB,[10] for example (see Buysschaert et al., 2018, p. 129). However, it is worth reiterating the potential for discussions of rates to be added to these sessions across the board to further democratise these practices.

- **Case study projects**: these are a lighter-touch version of a STB, where students are required to bid for a project and produce a quotation, often as part of the assessment for the module. Attention should be paid to explaining price formation practices, the industry context, and different market sectors (see below), and different client types, needs, and expectations, to deepen students' contextual awareness and feed into their decision-making.
- **Guest speakers**: Sessions led by professionals from the translation industry are a regular feature of programmes, with the aim of discussing industry realities and offering students an authentic, first-hand perspective. While industry professionals sometimes shy away from discussing rates, programme leaders can encourage them to openly discuss the topic.
- **Business skills modules**: Rate-setting coverage can also be embedded within general business skills modules, which are sometimes co-convened between translation departments and careers services. These modules regularly require students to complete reflective reports, which can provide an opportunity to engage critically with payment practices, industry realia, financial aspirations, or the behavioural disconnect between translators' mindsets and businessperson culture. Such modules could also invite discussions of micro-economic and socio-economic factors governing price formation.
- **Sessions on ethics and sustainability**: An emerging strand of thought within discussions of ethics is financial sustainability. Warwick University's newly-designed core module "Critical Skills for the Translation Profession" intriguingly mentions coverage of "negotiat[ing] ethical working conditions enabling social, economic and environmental sustainability in the profession" and the "neoliberal economics of translation and non-hegemonic alternatives for a sustainable profession". This kind of module hints at the potential for discussions of ethics and rates of pay to co-exist. Sessions on ethics generally are a common feature within translator training programmes and can easily be designed to include critical engagement

with prevailing (yet questionable) industry practices. In addition, the use of real-life case studies makes them particularly suitable for the task (see, for instance, Drugan and Megone (2014) for a range of case studies, or Lambert (2023b, pp. 147–150) for a discussion of rates of pay and ethics, and suggestions for in-class discussion points). These sessions on ethics often fall within wider "Translation Theory" modules (which, while not featured in our survey, feature in some form on most programmes) and show that it is possible to marry these supposedly disparate themes, challenging TS' typical theory-practice divide. While not a typically "academic" topic, coverage of rates of pay can easily invite critical engagement with academic literature, reflection on industry reports, and the incorporation of qualitative and quantitative research methods.

- **Work placement modules** represent another area in which rates of pay can be discussed. Though placements are often voluntary, students can nevertheless address these topics with providers, and coverage can easily be embedded within the "general" sessions that are typically offered to students on such modules.
- Finally, rates could be discussed in **practical translation modules**, where students can be introduced to the wider context of translation service provision rather than simply the process of translation. In some contexts, these modules are led by translation professionals, allowing students to draw upon first-hand industry experience and bringing in language specificity in terms of rates, allowing for more tailored discussions.

4.   Future perspectives

While the above highlights multiple forums to discuss rates in translator training contexts and sketches an array of pertinent topics to address, a number of emerging perspectives are growing in prominence and can add further sophistication to coverage of rates, wherever it is embedded.

4.1   Market segments, added value, and risk

One clear area for improvement in pedagogical practice, from our experience, is to better highlight and teach on the range and diversity of market segments and roles within the translation industry (a market reality highlighted by Gouadec, 2007, p. xiv; see also Zetzsche, 2023). The oft-cited distinction between the "bulk" and "premium" markets is a widely acknowledged delineation of the industry context, but there is considerably more nuance within this binary cline. Not merely the inclusion of a "middle market'" (however defined), but also an extension of the scale to what might be called the "super-premium" segment. As Jemiely observes (2018, p. 537), these segments of the industry "tend to be in highly specialized technical, industrial and financial areas, niches that translation-studies academics generally don't work in, publish on or know much about". Durban (2022, p. 15), meanwhile, divides the industry into three segments: bulk markets, with "high volumes, texts with short shelf life, prices low, quality less important", and "where MT is already used for most work"; added-value segments, "where quality is more important than in bulk, but budgets are under severe price pressure and the role of PEMT is on the rise"; and premium markets, "where deadlines can be tight but quality is key, underpinned by subject-matter expertise. Prices here are attractive, and risk—perceived or genuine—is a determining factor", a concept we cover further below.

It is across this heterogeneous landscape where differentiation between thriving as translators and merely surviving (which we discuss in Lambert & Walker, 2024) becomes most acute. Durban (2022, p. 15) argues, "as technology improves, genuinely expert practitioners should be doing everything they can to position themselves higher up the food chain". It is clear to many top-end practitioners that the client mix and knowing your client are important factors in progressing beyond the "threshold" into the premium market. Those working in the bulk market likely have almost exclusively LSPs as their clients and few or no direct clients; conversely, at the super-premium end of the market, this position is completely inverted. The premium market relies on trusting relationships with, typically, fewer clients, but those dealings are founded on high-quality, intensely specialist services. While an oversimplification, client mix is a key determinant of the prospect for more sustainable and better paying jobs from more respecting clients.

Reading between the lines of various translator association surveys broadly supports this heavy right-tailed modelling of the direct client proportion across the bulk–premium spectrum, especially since association surveys often fail to capture data from the very top end of the market, thereby "resulting in a picture of the industry where the best-compensated work is largely invisible" (Jemielity, 2018, p. 545). Nonetheless, we should reflect further on why premium translators have more direct clients than those in the middle market or lower down the scale. There are a number of factors at play here, but in simple terms it boils down to specialisation, creativity, added-value services (Zetzsche, 2023), and risk (Durban, 2022).

Deep specialisation, as Zetzsche argues (2023, p. 125), and creating, satisfying, and frequently exceeding quality expectations, are essential to the premium market segment. These facets stem, in particular, from extremely well-refined target language skills, often involving highly creative solutions departing some way from the source text, as well as (controversially, for some) translating only into one's native language. The clash with basic quality assessment criteria in pedagogical settings becomes quite apparent here. Those at the top of the industry have the confidence and freedom to be bold with their choices, and this is where the added value is highlighted most evidently in the translation itself. In the classroom, while creativity is encouraged in principle, there are instances where such radical departures from the source text can be penalised, as creative solutions – including omission and restructuring – will often clash with traditional expectations in terms of accuracy, which are necessarily enshrined in university learning criteria. But there are also other paths, veering away from the premium market segment, including becoming a high-output, detail-driven, technology-supported bulk-market practitioner. Indeed, some graduates choose to hone their skills in such a way that they "become very fast and efficient as an MT posteditor", and others shift their focus to transcreation and copywriting (Esselink, 2022, p. 92).

Of course, with continually-improving MT and AI solutions – something of which many clients are increasingly aware – showcasing the added value of high-quality human translation is an important skill for new translators amid progressively automated production processes (Massey, Piotrowska, & Marczak, 2023, p. 328), and this is essential if our students want to succeed in their chosen market segment. As Massey et al. (2023) argue, we need to consider how we "(re-)positi[on] human language mediators to maximise their value-adding potential, and educat[e] them to do so" (also echoed by Massey & Ehrensberger-Dow, 2017). It is clear from leading figures in the industry that the premium market is not well sold to students on many programmes. Echoing Jemielity's "poverty cult" comment discussed earlier in this chapter, do lecturers "discourag[e] students from aiming high by giving them the mistaken impression that there is nothing high to aim for" and portraying an "overly 'Grub Street' image of the profession", as Jemielity argues (2018, pp. 546–547)? He would argue that this is the case, and that this is largely down to "institutional ignorance of specialized niche markets" (ibid.). The spectre of Great Divide continues to loom large, it would appear. Perhaps we lecturers are the ones propagating Jemielity's aforementioned "disconnect" between translator and businessperson culture, and need to challenge our own economic ambitions so that we can, in turn, challenge our students to aim higher. Perhaps our pedagogical inquiry in the classroom ought to undergo a complete shift from *how much should we charge?* (a common question and point of discussion among students) to *what* or *how much does translation enable for our clients?* in economic and financial terms. The value of translation can of course be conceived in purely economic terms, via indicators such as return on investment, but such metrics can be difficult to access and interpret. Nonetheless, this line of thinking should feed into our understandings (as lecturers) and our students' understandings of the worth of a translator, the most obvious, front-line expression of which lies in their rates. But this is somewhat simplistic, and therefore flawed, for there are other dimensions to value beyond money alone.

Another way to conceptualise these perspectives on value mirrors a growing interest among TS scholars and certain practitioners in risk (see, for instance, notions of "credibility risk" and "communicative risk" in Pym, 2015). High-end translators frequently discuss risk and the importance of guiding their clients to an understanding of the risk of a low-quality translation, use of machine translation, etc. (see Durban, 2022). In some contexts, it may be a case of encouraging clients to consider the trade-off between a high-cost, high-quality translation from an experienced and highly specialised translator, and the potential lost profits or – worse – damaged reputation that could result from clunky, ill-conceived, and poorly-worded translations (see "cost of quality", in Walker, 2022, p. 187ff). In essence, we should prompt students to consider how much they are worth to manage – or better, mitigate – such risks for their clients. The disastrous human effects of machine translations in the processing of asylum applications in the US has been well documented in the media,[11] and offer a stark reminder of the value of expert intervention in high-risk cases. But with risk also comes reward, as Durban rightly acknowledges (2022, p. 15): "the riskier the situation/problem you're tackling, the higher your reward (intellectual satisfaction, social recognition, remuneration)", a view also shared by Pym (2020, p. 152) when discussing the value of establishing trust and the interrelatedness of trust, risk, and cost.

4.2 Value, calculating rates, and perspectives on the translation industry

In short, lecturers should undergo a (in some cases, radical) reappraisal of how we understand and teach students about the value of translation. First and foremost, we need to understand, from the abundant literature on information economics, that the digital document produced by translators, and more specifically each individual word within that document, has no intrinsic value. The value of translation resides in the information, knowledge, and craft embodied by the translator in that document, which may, in turn, result in a tangible or, more likely, intangible value for the client (e.g., commercial gain). But the word and the document have no easily quantifiable value in the same way that a piece of gold does. This notion needs to be better understood, as it helps students, in particular, to detach themselves from the naïve idea that the per-word rate is the only option, when, in reality, it is a poor proxy for the value of translation services. When charging per word, for most, this is a deeply-imperfect stand-in for time: the word and time share a very weak connection given that certain words demand far more of our time than others, to offer one simple example.

Some would counter this argument by stating that they have different per-word rates for general and specialised texts, for example. But this argument still misses the point. Dogmatic persistence with per-word pricing in all contexts is frankly indolent; just because its reach is so pervasive in the industry, this does not mean it cannot be challenged, even if, in certain instances (e.g., working with LSPs), such practices persist for now. Conversations with premium-market translators suggest that few premium translators charge per word, and there are continued calls to re-think this pricing model; *a minima*, they charge per hour for their work, but in many cases they charge on a project-by-project basis. Per-word pricing is reductive and unhelpful to the wider valorisation of translation as a professional service – which includes more than just translation alone, let us not forget – and this is particularly the case in direct-client relationships where it can be argued that per-word prices could even be harmful to one's professional image.[12]

If we are to move forward, however, we must consider how these points translate in practice into a classroom environment. We have already seen from the brief review presented in section 3 that the necessary infrastructure for embedding "money matters" in our curricula is largely in place. One area in which we consider academia to be lacking in the context of rates, however, is the availability of realistic case studies from the industry (a rare exception being Drugan & Megone, 2014, pp. 195–197). Case studies, involving real events and effects, are one of the most influential ways to highlight to students the potential for creativity in choices, ethical uses of technology, and what could go wrong, for instance. This is an area where industry and academia could collaborate better to produce such case studies, and such case studies could be from a wide range of perspectives (freelancer, LSP, project manager, end client, software developer) with a view to prompting discussion on a plethora of practical and ethical issues and agendas, and even to "re-running" certain scenarios in simulated translation bureau environments.

The other key dimension is to ensure that students are not introduced to "the industry" as monolith. As Zetzsche's article rightly notes (2023), translation is "very, very diverse". But a new translator does not remain fixed at the point of entry to the profession; where they enter the market will not be where they ultimately want to be (or end up) in future. To progress to this metaphorical light at the end of the tunnel is not an easy task, admittedly, but it is far from an insurmountable challenge. Students have to see their progress on this path as a process of continuous development. This can, of course, take the form of CPD, work experience in other industries, and dedicated non-translation qualifications to specialise in an increasingly narrow number of domains and sub-domains. But here we refer to continuous development in a more holistic and ontological sense. It requires time, confidence, and experience to enhance skills in negotiation, refine the ability to on-board, network, and build relationships with direct clients, adopt a stronger sense of business acumen (including on-going reviews of rates, pricing practices, income versus outgoings, etc.), and much more besides.

For our part, Jemielity suggests that lecturers should be more prescriptive in teaching industry realities (2018, p. 548). While the sentiment is noble, we disagree in part, for TS has a complex relationship with its prescriptivist past. We argue, instead, that the descriptive approach works, but needs a radical shift so as to encompass the *wide-ranging* realities of the industry. We need to better start students on this path of self-discovery by ensuring that we represent and open students' eyes to upper-middle and premium segments of the market, and exciting, innovative opportunities to diversify and add value in the current climate. In addition, we can ensure that students are equipped with the necessary insights into industry realities to give them the best possible chance of success in already saturated market segments, which, at present are increasingly precarious and unsustainable without a fundamental shift in mindset, but still likely one of the segments in which most new graduates will begin their career.

We can also try to change this situation on a macro-level by shifting our overall priorities. The general tendency for translators to be drawn towards the craft of translation to the detriment of economic realities, calls to mind the aforementioned ideological and behavioural "disconnect" between general translator culture and businessperson culture (see Jemielity, 2018, p. 535). A potential means of resituating this in the classroom could be to adopt principles from business ethics and corporate social responsibility (CSR). In Carroll's fundamental CSR pyramid (see Figure 3.1), we see economic responsibilities placed as a foundational element, as "society expects, indeed requires, business organizations to be able to sustain themselves ... by being profitable" (2016, p. 3). Profit is seen not only as perfectly legitimate, but societally required. In the context of translation, rethinking the way we

FIGURE 3.1 Carroll's pyramid of corporate social responsibility (Carroll, 2016)

approach certain topics could be a way to plot a different course in the future. That said, the burden of addressing pay issues should not just fall on translators of the present and future. Powerful LSPs have greater agency when it comes to setting prices and adopting ethical, and sustainable, pricing practices. Returning to Elkington's economic sustainability considered in section 2, a lack of access to financial capital in the short-term risks leading to catastrophic human capital shortages for the industry in the longer term. Indeed, reports of "talent shortages" abound in recent years in the UK context (CIOL, 2020; Nimdzi, 2022; RWS, 2023); pricing models that enable the retention of talent in a longer-term are crucial, and these conversations necessarily have to continue beyond the classroom.

5.   Recommendations for embedding rates and money: a way to go

Given the fundamental monetary concerns that exist among professionals today, we consider the lack of coverage of rates of pay in the translation classroom particularly problematic, and even symptomatic of a wider (misplaced) lack of concern around the value of translators and translation. In the UK, this narrative has even fed into the questioning of the value of translation degrees, which risks undermining the longer-term health not only of the translation profession, but also the place of translation in higher education institutions.

In light of our discussion throughout this chapter and the imperatives outlined in the paragraph above, and in conjunction with the agenda laid down in Girletti and Lefer (2024), we delineate below a number of overlapping recommendations for practice. We do so with a view to proposing what a component of a professional practice-oriented module on rates and money could include and how we might prepare students to achieve a sustainable professional income upon completion of their training and entry into the profession.

- **Break down the taboos around discussing money by setting up spaces and appropriate classroom exercises to talk about rates in different contexts.** As shown in section 3, all universities already have the pedagogical infrastructure in place to accommodate such content on their programmes. We should not discount the merits of discussing rates in practical translation classes, or indeed in other forums where technology or ethics are the main focus. While there is a risk of alarming aspiring translators, we have a moral duty to paint a realistic image of the industry landscape *in its entirety* (from the bulk market right up to the premium). This vision has already seen positive steps within the industry, with calls for transparency over rates of pay appearing with growing regularity in UK industry publications, as noted earlier.

- **Teach and encourage discussion about the value of translation.** What is it that translators do that create value? And how does this value reflect the inherent limitations in the industry's deeply entrenched per-word pricing model? Within such discussions, invite critical reflection on payment practices such as discounts for TM fuzzy matches and repetitions, and post-editing, as well as critical reflection on the limitations (and agendas) of macro-level industry publications on the translation market, its value, profits, and prices.
- **Enhance our emphasis on specialisation as a translator.** True specialisation – in a limited number of domains – takes time, but this path can begin during training and can manifest itself through specialist modules (e.g., legal translation, medical translation) and through text selections in independent assessments (e.g., extended translation projects). A point related to specialisation is reinforcing the importance of core translation competences, including source language comprehension, but – equally, if not more importantly – target language mastery. Mastery of one's target language is more important than ever with the growth in post-editing, for those who pursue this line of work within their wider portfolio of services.
- **Add a focus on business skills and business mindedness.** In a parallel publication, we argue that students need a better grasp of business skills and price formation in particular, as part of a wider awareness of financial sustainability (Lambert & Walker, 2024). In class, we should expose students to wider models of business and sustainability (CSR, micro-economics, and the triple-bottom line) to ensure that they are able to critically consider how their interests and needs relate to wider market forces. Confidence, not just in their skills and value, but also their ability to advocate for this in negotiation with industry stakeholders (and in the face of competing interests and pressures) as emerging professionals is key.
- **Establishing assessment frameworks that encourage creativity** and "deviation" from the source text in line with practices that might be expected of a premium-market translator (or, if such frameworks already exist, reinforcing their implementation). In some cases, this might require training for colleagues involved in teaching or assessing translation who may be less familiar with the translation market (see, for instance, Durban 2022 for concrete examples of the forms this creativity and premium differentiation can take).
- Across translation programmes in a range of different classroom environments (practical translation, simulated translation bureaus, etc.), **acknowledge the dominance of the per-word pricing model, but challenge students to actively explore other pricing models** (e.g., per hour or per project) that more accurately reflect the value of what they do as translators.
- **Include financial literacy and price formation more explicitly in pedagogical frameworks** such as the EMT Competence Framework.

Chiefly, and above all else, we believe that there is an urgent need to break the silence around rates in the classroom and beyond, and to make time for these discussions, even within the already highly-condensed schedules of postgraduate translator training. Rethinking rates training in the short term can build towards tackling the medium- to long-term financial sustainability challenges facing the predominantly freelance, global translation industry.

Notes

1 www.nimdzi.com/language-industry-services-market-split-by-service-and-segm ent-leaders-in-2023
2 See, for instance, cases like those reported in: www.theguardian.com/world/2023/ aug/31/they-were-earning-10000-more-than-me-what-happens-when-colleag ues-come-clean-about-pay
3 See, for instance, www.linkedin.com/pulse/what-ma-translation-doesnt-teach-you-jennifer-o-donnell/ and www.iti.org.uk/resource/things-to-know-before-start ing-as-freelance-translator.html
4 www.aptis-translation-interpreting.org
5 All mentions of rates in the framework fall within the "Service Provision" area of competence. Skill 30 references "rates/invoicing", Skill 31 "budget", and Skill 32 notions of "fair competition". The scant mention of money and finance in the framework overall serves to further highlight the relative neglect of this topic, and the fact that rate-setting should probably feature more prominently in the framework.
6 As a case in point, rates of pay and finances are covered on various occasions on the MA Translation Studies at Cardiff University, but this is not reflected in the material online.
7 www.proz.com/?sp=pfe/rates
8 In a hint towards the pervasiveness of this method even beyond the classroom, Willis-Lee and Jackson (2023, p. 12) note that "the overwhelming majority of translators I speak to set their rates by looking at 'average' industry rates published on platforms like ProZ.com" before going on to outline the flaws in this approach.
9 As reiterated in the EMT framework (2022, p. 11): Skill 32 in particular, which focuses primarily on ethical issues, points out the embeddedness of these concepts.
10 The International Network of Simulated Translation Bureaus: www.instb.eu
11 See, for instance, www.theguardian.com/us-news/2023/sep/07/asylum-seekers-ai-translation-apps
12 The shortcomings of per word pricing have come under informal scrutiny in industry sources in recent years, such as a Slator podcast (2023), which labelled per-word pricing models in translation "outdated".

References

Angelone, E. (2022). Weaving Adaptive Expertise into Translator Training. In G. Massey, E. Huertas-Barros, & D. Katan (Eds.), *The Human Translator in the 2020s* (pp. 60–73). Abingdon: Routledge.

Bennett, K. (2022). Translation and Money: A Meaningful Symbiosis. *Translation Matters, 4*(2), 1–4.

Biel, Ł., & Sosoni, V. (2017). The Translation of Economics and the Economics of Translation. *Perspectives, 25*(3), 351–361. doi:10.1080/0907676X.2017.1313281

Buysschaert, J., Fernández-Parra, M., Kerremans, K., Koponen, M., & van Egdom, G.-W. (2018). Embracing Digitial Disruption in Translator Training: Technology Immersion in Simulated Translation Bureaus. *Revista Tradumàtica, 16*, 125–133. doi:10.5565/rev/tradumatica.209

Carroll, A.B. (2016). Carroll's Pyramid of CSR: Taking Another Look. *International Journal of Corporate Social Responsibility, 1*(3). doi:10.1186/s40991-016-0004-6

CIOL. (2020). BEIS Call for Evidence: The Recognition of Professional Qualifications and Regulation of Professions: October 2020. Available from: www.ciol.org.uk/beis-call-evidence-recognition-professional-qualifications-and-regulation-professions-october-2020

do Carmo, F. (2020). 'Time is Money' and the Value of Translation. *Translation Spaces, 9*(1), 35–57. doi:10.1075/ts.00020.car

Doherty, S. (2016). The Impact of Translation Technologies on the Process and Product of Translation. *International Journal of Communication, 10*, 947–969.

Drugan, J., & Megone, C. (2014). Bringing Ethics into Translator Training: An Integrated, Inter-disciplinary Approach. *The Interpreter and Translator Trainer, 5*(1), 183–211. doi:10.1080/13556509.2011.10798817

Dunne, K.J. (2012). The Industrialization of Translation: Causes, Consequences and Challenges. *Translation Spaces, 1*, 143–168. doi:10.1075/ts.1.07dun

Durban, C. (2022). Translation, Time, Technology – Who's Counting? In M. Kubánek, O. Klabal, & O. Molnár (Eds.), *Teaching Translation vs. Training Translators* (pp. 11–20). Olomouc: Palacký University.

Durban, C. (Ed.) (2010). *The Prosperous Translator: Advice from Fire Ant and Worker Bee.* FA&WB Press.

Elkington, J. (1997). *Cannibals With Forks: The Triple Bottom Line of 21st Century Business.* Oxford: Capstone.

Esselink, B. (2022). Thirty Years and Counting: A Global Industry Growing Up. *The Journal of Internationalization and Localization, 9*(1), 85–93. doi:10.1075/jial.00020.ess

European Commission. (2022). European Master's in Translation: Competence Framework 2022. Available from: www.commission.europa.eu/system/files/2022-11/emt_competence_fwk_2022_en.pdf

Gambier, Y. (2014). Changing Landscape in Translation. *International Journal of Society, Culture and Language, 2*(2), 1–12.

Girletti, S., & Lefer, M.-A. (2024). Introducing MTPE Pricing in Translator Training: A Concrete Proposal for MT Instructors. *The Interpreter and Translator Trainer.* doi:10.1080/1750399X.2023.2299914

Gouadec, D. (2007). *Translation as a Profession.* Amsterdam: John Benjamins.

Hao, Y., & Pym, A. (2021). Translation Skills Required by Master's Graduates for Employment: Which Are Needed, Which Are Not? *Across Languages and Cultures, 22*(2), 158–175. doi:10.1556/084.2021.00012

Inbox Translation. (2020). Freelance Translator Survey 2020. Available from: www.inboxtranslation.com/resources/research/freelance-translator-survey-2020/

Inbox Translation. (2023). Freelance Translator Survey 2023. Available from: www. inboxtranslation.com/resources/research/freelance-translator-survey-2023/

Jääskeläinen, R., Kujamäki, P., & Mäkisalo, J. (2011). Towards Professionalism – Or Against It? Dealing With the Changing World in Translation Research and Translator Education. *Across Languages and Cultures, 12*(2), 143–156. doi:10.1556/Acr.12.2011.2.1

Jackson, S. (2022). Money Matters. *ITI Bulletin, November-December*, 36–37.

Jemiely, D. (2018). Translation in Intercultural Business and Economic Environments. In S.-A. Harding & O. Carbonell Cortés (Eds.), *The Routledge Handbook of Translation and Culture* (pp. 533–557). Abingdon: Routledge.

Jenner, J.A., & Jenner, D.V. (2010). *The Entrepreneurial Linguist: The Business-School Approach to Freelance Translation*. Las Vegas: EL Press.

Jiménez-Crespo, M.A. (2017). How Much Would You Like to Pay? Reframing and Expanding the Notion of Translation Quality through Crowdsourcing and Volunteer Approaches. *Perspectives: Studies in Translation Theory and Practice, 25*(3), 478–491. doi:10.1080/0907676X.2017.1285948

Kreuzer, D. (2023). Money Matters. *ITI Bulletin, July-August*, 28–29.

Lambert, J. (2023a). From Stagnation to Innovation: Codes of Ethics and the Profession Today. In J. Bourne, M. Fernández Sánchez, J. Gutiérrez Artacho, T. Portnova, E.M. Pradas Macías, & E. Quero Gervilla (Eds.), *Reflexiones sobre ética profesional de traductores e intérpretes y buenas prácticas* (pp. 39–56). Granada: Comares.

Lambert, J. (2023b). *Translation Ethics*. Abingdon: Routledge.

Lambert, J., & Walker, C. (2022). Because We're Worth It: Disentangling Freelance Translation, Status, and Rate-Setting in the United Kingdom. *Translation Spaces, 11*(2), 277–302. doi:10.1075/ts.21030.lam

Lambert, J., & Walker, C. (2024). Thriving or Surviving: Motivation, Satisfaction, and Existential Sustainability in the Translation Profession. *Mikael, 17*(1), 89–104. doi:10.61200/mikael.136209

Li, L., Dang, Q., & Zhao, K. (2023). Embracing Transdisciplinarity to Prepare for the Future: Revisiting the Gap Between the Labour Market and Translator Education. *The Interpreter and Translator Trainer, 17*(3), 454–478. doi:10.1080/1750399X.2023.2237324

Magaia, A. (2022). Financial Matters Affecting Mozambican Professional Translators and Interpreters: A Survey. *Translation Matters, 4*(2), 78–89.

Massey, G., & Ehrensberger-Dow, M. (2017). Machine Learning: Implications for Translator Education. *Lebende Sprachen, 62*(2), 300–312. doi:10.1515/les-2017-0021

Massey, G., Piotrowska, M., & Marczak, M. (2023). Meeting Evolution with Innovation: An Introduction to (Re-)Profiling T&I Education. *The Interpreter and Translator Trainer, 17*(3), 325–331. doi:10.1080/1750399X.2023.2237321

Moorkens, J. (2017). Under Pressure: Translation in Times of Austerity. *Perspectives, 25*(3), 464–477. doi:10.1080/0907676X.2017.1285331

Moorkens, J. (2020). "A Tiny Cog in a Large Machine": Digital Taylorism in the Translation Industry. *Translation Spaces, 9*(1), 12–34. doi:10.1075/ts.00019.moo

Moorkens, J., Castilho, S., Gaspari, F., Toral, A., & Popvić, M. (2024). Proposal for a Triple Bottom Line for Translation Automation and Sustainability: An Editorial Position Paper. *The Journal of Specialised Translation, 41*, 2–25.

Nimdzi. (2022). The Nimdzi 100. Available from: www.nimdzi.com/nimdzi-100-top-lsp/

Nimdzi. (2023). The Nimdzi 100. Available from: www.nimdzi.com/nimdzi-100-top-lsp/

Nunes Vieira, L. (2020). Automation anxiety and translators. *Translation Studies, 13*(1), 1–21. doi:10.1080/14781700.2018.1543613

Penet, J.C. (2024). *Working as a Professional Translator*. Abingdon: Routledge.

Penet, J.C., & Fernandez-Parra, M. (2023). Dealing with Students' Emotions: Exploring Trait EI Theory in Translator Education. *The Interpreter and Translator Trainer, 17*(3), 332–352. doi:10.1080/1750399X.2023.2237327

Pym, A. (2015). Translating as Risk Management. *Journal of Pragmatics, 85*, 67–80. doi:10.1016/j.pragma.2015.06.010

Pym, A. (2017). Translation and Economics: Inclusive Communication or Language Diversity? *Perspectives: Studies in Translation Theory and Practice, 25*(3), 362–377. doi:10.1080/0907676X.2017.1287208

Pym, A. (2020). Translator Ethics. In: K. Koskinen, & N. Pokorn (Eds.), *The Routledge Handbook of Translation and Ethics* (pp. 147–161). Abingdon: Routledge.

Raymond, J. (2023). We Need to Talk About Money. *The Linguist, Spring*, 7–9.

RWS. (2023). Translation Technology Insights 2023. Available from: www.trados.com/download/translation-technology-insights-2023-report/215294/

Sakamoto, A., & Bawa Mason, S. (2024). In Search of a Fair MTPE Pricing Model: LSPs' Reflections and the Implications for Translators. *Perspectives*. doi:10.1080/0907676X.2023.2292572

Sandrini, P. (2022). "It's the Economy, Stupid": Discussing the Translator's Business Against the Background of a Changing Techno-Economic Landscape. *Translation Matters, 4*(2), 49–62.

Schnell, B., & Rodríguez, N. (2017). Ivory Tower vs. Workplace Reality: Employability and the T&I Curriculum – Balancing Academic Education and Vocational Requirements: A Study from the Employers' Perspective. *The Interpreter and Translator Trainer, 11*(2–3), 160–186. doi:10.1080/1750399X.2017.1344920

Slator. (2023). Why Cost Per Word in Translation Is Outdated. Available from: www.youtube.com/watch?v=9NL7nExJgaE

Walker, C. (2022). *Translation Project Management*. Abingdon: Routledge.

Walker, C., Ivins, C., & Lambert, J. (2024). *Freelance Translator Rates: The Value of ITI Membership*. Milton Keynes: Institute of Translation and Interpreting. Available from: www.iti.org.uk/resource/value-iti-membership-freelance-translator-rates.html

Willis-Lee, J., & Jackson, S. (2023). Price Points. *ITI Bulletin, March–April*, 12–13.

Worrall, J. (2023). Time for Transparency? *ITI Bulletin, January–February*, 36–37.

Zetzsche, J. (2023). The Very, Very Diverse World of Translators. *Digital Translation, 10*(1), 121–127. doi:10.1075/dt.00003.zet

4

TEACHING FRENCH TO SPANISH TRANSLATION IN CONTEXT

Service-learning as a means to develop translation competence

Luz Belenguer Cortés

Keywords: service-learning; translation competence; translation training; language teaching; higher education

1. Introduction

Second language and translation learning, instruction, and teaching strategies have been ripe for adaptation to the learners that educators have in their classrooms (Flores, 2015, p. 33). Despite translator training research encouraging specific language training to meet the needs of aspiring translators and interpreters, few have attempted to identify and provide specific approaches that guide the teaching of this newly established discipline "Languages for Specific Purposes" (Carrasco Flores, 2019, p. 121). In fact, general education theory and practice have had a greater impact on the educational direction of in-service language teacher education (Crandall, 2000). Despite the recent trends of using machine translation in training students in translation and interpreting degrees (Mejías Climent and De los Reyes Lozano, 2023), machine translation systems are not replacing human mediators since translation competence is something that must be intrinsic to trained professional translators. Despite that, it is time for university to leave its academic bubble – i.e., to bridge the gap between academia and the profession (Jemielity, 2018) – to acquire the different translation competences and, as we can see over the past decades, growing numbers of universities are incorporating community service-learning into the curriculum (Prentice and Robinson, 2010, p. 1; Maginn, 2019).

As Steinke and Fitch (2007, p. 24) state, "virtually all definitions of service-learning refer to an organized educational experience that both meets

DOI: 10.4324/9781003440970-5

needs of the community and fulfils learning objectives." When it comes to our field of interest, translation training should go beyond the coursebook to ensure students understand the reality in which they live so as to help them develop a broader understanding of social issues, diversity, and social justice (Salgado-Robles and Thompson, 2022). Furthermore, it is key to improving the linguistic competencies learners will need in their future professional careers, and community service-learning is "emerging as a central component of efforts to connect both disciplinary learning and general education with this historic and increasingly salient commitment to public purposes" (Felten and Clayton, 2011, p. 75). When we say "community service-learning", we refer to the pedagogical strategy where students become recipients and providers from the activities carried out to seek their learning (Furco, 1996).

The present chapter aims to introduce a project whose goal was to educate students about the reality of French-speaking migrants arriving in Spain in a "vulnerable state" due to different causes (Belenguer Cortés, 2024, pp. 17–21) and encourage those students to take action using their linguistic competence and translation competence. The primary objective was to boost students' proficiency in French and French-Spanish translation competences using service-learning as a pedagogical strategy. To encourage performance assessment (Fernández, 2010) and authentic assessment (Brown, 2015) based on the service-learning methodology, a MIGrant PROject was developed (MIGPRO, Belenguer Cortés, 2022, 2024). In the aforementioned project, 28 students in their twenties were exposed to community service-learning through a collaboration with the Red Cross Castellón and Universitat Jaume I (UJI, Castellón, Spain) to help migrants develop the skills required to live their daily lives.

This pilot study aimed to provide students on the Translation and Interpreting degree programme at UJI – with French and Spanish as working languages – with an opportunity to leave the academic cocoon to guarantee translation competences learning. Hence, our goal was to help these students acquire the skills they would need in French-to-Spanish translation with service-learning as a significant instructional strategy. Surveys were employed as an additional pedagogical research technique, which were distributed before the learning process. In this chapter, we present the following research questions (found in Belenguer Cortés, 2022):

I. Is there any improvement in participants' competences with the service-learning strategy?
II. When given the option, which educational task and resources do students choose?
III. Has Spanish and French language proficiency among students improved?
IV. During the community service-learning tasks, do they veer toward glossary creation or syllabus creation?

V. Is there any difference in materials created by participants with (or without) a migrant background?

This chapter analyses the procedure and the results obtained in the early stages of the aforementioned project, but we will focus on research question II and on students' perception in terms of their translation competences acquisition before and after the project. To do so, we will describe the theoretical platform of MIGPRO (Belenguer Cortés, 2022, 2024) and we contrast the replies from the first survey with the glossaries and instructional materials made by the students.

2. Translator training

Munday (2012) defines the process of translation between written languages as "the changing of an original written text (the source text) in the original verbal language (the source language) into a written text (the target text) in a different verbal language (the target language)" (in Bugel, 2013, p. 371). Both translation practice and translation studies have seen considerable innovation in recent decades (Dam et al., 2019, p. 248). In fact, the interest in translation's nature has become a very complex specific area due to its interdisciplinarity (Pintado Gutiérrez, 2012, p. 322). Some of the most important concepts developed resulting from the link between communication and translation are translation as a communicative, interlinguistic and intercultural process at the textual level (García Izquierdo, 2000); translation as a linguistic action, which, from a pragmatic angle, acquires a cognitive and a psycholinguistic interest (Riedermann, 1996, p. 114); the implications of communication in translation – since translation is an act of communication when working with the concept of translation equivalence originated in a linguistic material (Kiraly, 2000) – and the need of the communicative competence beyond the linguistic knowledge and the linguistic manipulation abilities available (Firth, 1957).

When we refer to communicative competence, we refer to linguistic competence (Chomsky, 1965): the knowledge the speaker has of the language and its real use of the language depending on the situation. Hence, competence is related to knowledge and ability (Pintado Gutiérrez, 2012, p. 323). Cenoz Iragui (2004, pp. 460–462) explains that communicative competence has direct implications in the learning goals, the teaching strategies, the learning autonomy and assessment. Nevertheless, nowadays translation competence and translation training are computer-based (Sikora and Walczynski, 2015, p. 130):

Modern translation and interpreting industry cannot function properly, offering high quality services, without computers, the Internet and technology. [...] Therefore, the competent use of translation technologies has become a prerequisite for anyone wishing to join the translator's profession. CAT tools literacy seems to increase translators' chances to find employment, as more and more translation agencies outsource to translators or project managers under the condition that they are able to use a specific CAT tool.

Cronin (2013) provides a detailed explanation of certain developments in translation technology, and Kenny (2019) offers detailed research of its impact on translation training. The Computer Assisted Translation (CAT) tools are normally made up of four major parts available to translators, including translation memory, terminology management, concordance, and alignment programs (Peng, 2018). Nevertheless, whereas certain schools of translation studies are ready to accept all new developments, others tend to disregard them as unnecessary or prefer implementing traditional practices. In fact, translation training can take many forms (Pym, 2009) and, given its rapid evolution (Yan et al., 2015, p. 264), a reflection on its progress is required to guide further research in this area (Yan et al., 2013). Hence, a balance should be found in the "translator-computer interaction" (O'Brien, 2012), especially when referring to students and their translation training (Çetiner, 2018).

2.1 Translation competences

Hurtado Albir (2017) asserts that, like any procedural knowledge, translation competence is fundamentally an operational knowledge in which strategies are important and automated processes are pervasive. The PACTE research group (Process in Acquisition of Translation Competence and Evaluation) has presented their translation competence model, which has evolved over the years, using empirical-experimental research. The following are its fundamental tenets (PACTE, 2003, 2005, found in Carrasco Flores, 2019, p. 124):

• Translation competence and multilingual competence are qualitatively different. The fundamental body of knowledge required to translate is known as translation competence.
• Translation competence is expert knowledge, including procedural knowledge (which is the more prevalent type) and declarative knowledge.
• Translation competence is made up of a system of interconnected, hierarchical, and variable sub-competences.

The system of knowledge and abilities that underlies communication in two languages – more particularly, comprehension of the source language and production in the target language – is known as the bilingual sub-competence. Encyclopaedic knowledge, bicultural understanding, and subject-specific knowledge are all included in the extra-linguistic sub-competence. The understanding of documentation materials and ICT used in translation are included in the instrumental sub-competence. The sub-competence for knowledge about translation covers translation methods and tactics as well as information on the labour market, including laws governing taxes and labour, among others. The strategic sub-competence entails the specific methods used to direct the translation process by triggering all the other sub-competences, forging connections between them, and resolving any issues that could come up. The capacity to engage all psychomotor mechanisms, as well as cognitive and attitudinal resources that may be involved in the translation process is referred to as one of the psychophysiological components.

Apart from PACTE (2003, 2005; Hurtado Albir, 2017), Pym (2014, 2023), and Kelly (2014) are the most cited in terms of proposed translation competence models, among many others. Nevertheless, "while these scholars' models differ, each assumes – either explicitly or implicitly – that competent translators have three skills that students should develop through community service-learning: (1) resolving challenges, (2) organising their work, and (3) assessing their performance" (Thomson and Dague, 2018, p. 90). In MIGPRO, we aimed to help students develop these skills through community service-learning since undergraduates would be able to face real-life challenges in the safety of the classroom. Hence, service-learning was thought to be the most suitable for the context of translation training and foreign language learning.

2.2   Community service-learning

The employment of translation and language technology in translation courses is still resisted by educational institutions and translation teachers (Pym et al., 2006; Varela-Salinas, 2007; Dwivedi, 2019). As Bugel explains (2013, p. 369), "Translating for the sake of training and practice was the way I was taught and subsequently used to teach translation, over time that approach started to feel artificial in the absence of an actual client." Thus, different approaches could be considered. Community Service-learning is "a type of experiential learning where students apply academic course content to real-life situations as they provide service to community organizations" (Thomson and Hague, 2018, p. 88) and it establishes a mutually beneficial connection where the service and learning components of the experience are reciprocal (Jacoby, 1996).

The impact of community service-learning on language acquisition and cultural understanding as a method for teaching language and culture seems a natural step towards adequately preparing migrants to be future citizens to join the current society. Therefore, community service-learning requires students' engagement by understanding the mission and goals of the organisation with which they are preparing to work (Cress et al., 2023) and should fulfil a genuine community need, must be integrated with other instructional materials, and activities and must involve reflection (Lowther Pereira, 2018, p. 6).

Learning languages "very specifically calls for the culturally contextualized communicative practice available through service-learning" (Bugel, 2013, p. 371). Hence, it appears logical that teaching language and culture using community service-learning would have an influence on students' ability to acquire new languages and comprehend different cultures and, in addition, improve their negative self-perceptions of their language abilities (Beaudrie, 2020). Thus, community service-learning could be also considered a motivational strategy of translation training and foreign language learning tool (Pak, 2007).

3. MIGPRO: a MIGrant PROject

Since translators need to develop an ability to stand back and reflect on what they do and how they do it (Baker, 2011), MIGPRO was contextualised and presented from the very beginning of the academic year (2021–2022) so students could bear in mind the learning goals, the teaching strategies, and the learning autonomy, as we mentioned earlier in section 2. Hence, we will first start with the teaching methodology followed during the entire project.

3.1 The "learn it, link it" methodology

To introduce the project and its methodology, we will first provide our approach based on the following premise: different learners need different approaches to succeed (Oakley et al., 2021, p. 21). Hence, in order to avoid a mismatch between teaching strategies and learning styles since it can have a negative impact on academic achievement and course attendance (Felder and Henriques, 1995), translation training should also consider this when applying different pedagogical tools and teaching strategies.

In addition, there are two distinct categories of learners, according to Oakley et al. (2021, p. 16): *race-car learners*, also known as *fast thinkers* – students who are quick with their answers and with making connections to new information – and *hiker learners*, who benefit more from a flexible way of thinking. The main difference between these types is how they learn something and how they put the theory they have learnt into practice. We call this procedure *learn it, link it* (Oakley et al., 2021, p. 3). Thus, considering the application of the *learn it, link it* methodology in community service-learning in translation training, a suitable and flexible proposal was needed to be created to attend to every student's needs whilst meeting the translation training goals.

To apply community service-learning and still make it suitable for any type of learner (Felder and Brent, 2005; Fitzgerald, 2009) – given the learning autonomy we want students to achieve – while helping students reach the goals explained in the course syllabus (UJI, 2023), MIGPRO was developed to adapt to *fast thinkers* and *hiker learners* as explained in section 3.2.

3.2   Stages and methodology

MIGPRO was the result of a collaboration between UJI (Spain) and Red Cross Castellón (Spain) to facilitate the provision of a learning service by translation and interpreting undergraduates. In the present study, 28 students with French as a Second Language who were enrolled in *TI0936 – Translation C-A1 (French-Spanish) (I)*, UJI, 2023) during the 2021–2022 academic year were our MIGPRO participants, in which students had to translate from their C language (French) into their A language (Spanish). In this subject, students learn upper-intermediate French, which is used for both communication and language mediation. Hence, these students could train their abilities in a real-life context.

This project sought to assist French-speaking migrants in acquiring basic Spanish whilst helping students improve their French and Spanish competencies and their translation competence. To integrate community service-learning as a pedagogical tool in translation training, MIGPRO was developed so students were exposed to an upper-intermediate level of French that is used for both communication and language mediation (Belenguer Cortés, 2022, p. 664).

Since we find pure and applied research in translation and interpreting pedagogy (Colina and Angelelli, 2015, p. 108; Laviosa, 2014, 2016), we consider the present study as applied research since is conducted directly on issues related to teaching, learning, or testing, in classrooms or virtual environments, on persons, materials, or activities, with the goal of having a direct impact on pedagogical practice. As Ruggiero already suggested in her study, "particular emphasis is given to student perceptions of the field as a result of undergoing a significant learning experience" (2018, p. 27). Thus, in the present paper, community service-learning will be tested by analysing the results obtained from the materials created and the answers provided in the survey.

In the present study, if we analyse the course syllabus of French-Spanish Translation (originally called *TI0936 – Translation C-A1 (French-Spanish)*

(I), UJI, 2023), the expected translation competence in the subject are the following (UJI, 2023):

- increasing theoretical knowledge with regard to the language combination in question;
- developing problem-solving skills;
- consolidating the use of electronic resources for documentation;
- consolidating and extending skills in the use of basic reference works and other documentation resources;
- assimilating the factors to be considered in decision making;
- ability to identify and understand how the different text types work in languages C and A, as well as their impact on translation;
- ability to apply the theoretical knowledge acquired in language B subjects;
- ability to apply different strategies to reading comprehension and the identification of translation problems; ability to apply autonomous work methods;
- ability to apply appropriate translation techniques and strategies.

Thus, if we recall Cenoz Iragui's words mentioned earlier (2004, pp. 460–462), the learning goals, the teaching strategies, the learning autonomy, and the assessment are intrinsically involved with the objectives present in the course syllabus. Together with service-learning, resolving challenges, organising their work, and assessing their performance will be achieved, as mentioned previously (Thomson and Dague, 2018, p. 90).

To apply the community service-learning strategy in the current project, we sought to turn students into providers and content producers: to do so, the main goal was to create French-to-Spanish glossaries and Spanish as a second language didactic tool for French-speaking migrants who were not able to speak Spanish. This enabled them to create materials and reflect on related competences (the *learn it* phase) while also allowing them to absorb basic knowledge of French and Spanish language and how it is applied to its learning as a foreign language and its translation (the *link it* phase). The reason for making students create Spanish as a Second Language materials was to help them develop the habit of creating French-to-Spanish glossaries – a practice they lacked due to the constant use of bilingual dictionaries and CAT tools – and activities that required dedication in terms of accuracy and bearing in mind the client's requirements – in this case, the Red Cross migrants – who had specific profiles and needs concerning their language acquisition.

To cover the needs of these two learner types, they could create a glossary that included the most essential French and Spanish terms the migrants needed or, alternatively, create a lesson plan to help migrants develop the skills required to live their daily lives. To combine the Spanish glossaries and lesson plans presented in the created learning materials, the glossaries and lessons were divided into units. The content of the aforementioned units focused on A1 foreign language content were based on CEFR (Alexiou and Stathopoulou, 2021; Runnels, 2021, p. 235).

By giving students two ways to pursue the *learn it, link it* circle, we helped improve the conditions for developing and reinforcing foreign language competencies (Garret-Rucks, 2016), which is undoubtedly crucial to learning, together with motivation and peer-to-peer collaboration. In fact, they become more aware of their learning process and their strengths and weaknesses (De Higes Andino and Cerezo Merchán, 2018, p. 69).

The project spanned four months, during which the students produced materials for Spanish as a second language learners under the lecturer's supervision. Students were given activities that reflected the challenges encountered in a real professional setting, i.e., preparation of terminology, adaptation to the presented instructions, and design of the proper strategy and methodology for both designing glossaries and lesson plans. The project was undertaken as a course activity and at the end, students were able to decide whether to donate the created materials to the Red Cross through informed consent to express explicit agreement with the sharing of their answers of the survey (and subsequent materials) with the Red Cross.

Students were urged to select the type of proactive task they deemed most appropriate in working with Red Cross migrants after receiving basic information in MIGPRO. The community service-learning strategy was used in the *link it* phase, in which the acquisition of language and culture mediation strategies were targeted, since the learning resources are co-created based on refugees' needs. The stages in MIGPRO were (Belenguer Cortés, 2022, p. 666):

1. An initial survey.
2. Getting to know MIGPRO.
3. Examining the demographics of immigrants (18–21 years old).
4. Deciding on a subject and a working approach.
5. Examining preventative action.
6. Exchanging proactive action.
7. Using general comments to improve results.

As mentioned, the project began with an initial survey after introducing 28 students in their twenties to the reality of migration and outlining the goal and stages of MIGPRO. Students voluntarily consented to the Red Cross using the materials and the author publishing their responses and related information by signing an informed consent approved by the ethical review board of UJI.[1] The survey contained the following open questions related to language acquisition:

- Do you think your level of French is good enough for the current course?
- Do you speak or practice French outside the classroom? How do you practice it?
- Do you think practicing French outside the classroom is needed?
- Do you think the French language needs more time allocated on the degree programme to improve your linguistic skills?

Students received background information on the project and instruction in the foundations for creating glossaries and lesson plans were offered. Students needed to plan the goals they had for the migrants and how they planned to reach them (i.e., content and methodology). Hence, students were asked to reflect on goals, content, and methodology before designing learning materials. In addition, undergraduates were required to send the final version of their glossary or lesson plan to the lecturer (i.e., we assessed how they *link* their learning). Since students were creating lesson plans for the first time, the objectives and techniques were not evaluated, but rather the resulting material and the procedure during MIGPRO.

The concept of glossaries was then presented to the students. Alternatively, they could design a course to deal with extremely challenging language and cultural factors that migrants face in their every-day lives. The project ended with reflection, surveys, and feedback exercises. As mentioned previously, these steps were carried out in the classroom individually, under the lecturer's ongoing supervision and subsequent feedback.

Finally, we compared the responses from the initial survey with the glossaries and educational resources the students produced as a result in order to answer the research questions. To do so, we quantified the number of glossaries or lesson plans created since most of the data in the materials created were qualitative.

4. Results

One of the unexpected results coming from MIGPRO was the commitment shown by students, since every participant decided to create both a glossary and a lesson plan to improve their skills, which led to a remarkable engagement in the project but did not allow us to make a distinction between *race-cars* and *hikers* in terms of learning (research questions II and IV) or in terms of migrant background (research question V, where only 8% of students had a migrant background, i.e., three participants). According to the survey (see Figure 4.1), 21 participants (75%) feel that practicing French outside the classroom is needed, whereas 19 (67.8%) suggest French as a

SURVEY

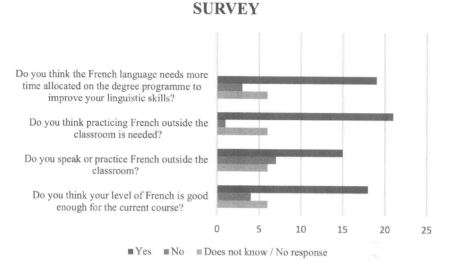

Do you think the French language needs more time allocated on the degree programme to improve your linguistic skills?

Do you think practicing French outside the classroom is needed?

Do you speak or practice French outside the classroom?

Do you think your level of French is good enough for the current course?

0 5 10 15 20 25

■ Yes ■ No ■ Does not know / No response

FIGURE 4.1   Results found in the MIGPRO survey in terms of language acquisition

Second Language needs more focus on the degree programme. In contrast, only seven students (25%) practice French as a Second Language outside the classroom. Hence, students manifest an urgent need to use other strategies to be exposed to the foreign language outside the classroom (research question I) to achieve language competence to boost engagement and participation of students when it comes to more practical aspects of language.

Based on the materials that are created, we can observe that activities including community service-learning can lead to an improvement in their engagement in their French and Spanish language competence to boost translation competence (research question I) due to the resulting created materials, in which participants produced both glossaries and lesson plans when they were only required to choose one of them (research questions II and IV). Most participants noticed an improvement in their linguistic skills considering the participation in MIGPRO as well as the answers to the surveys (see Figure 4.1), which was the main goal of this project (research questions I and III). Participants were able to develop their glossaries and lesson plans by themselves (i.e., learning autonomy in communicative competence; Cenoz Iragui, 2004), teaching strategies were adapted to the student's profile, and learning goals were met by the created materials (i.e., assessment). Furthermore, community service-learning worked as a motivation whereby students resolved challenges, organised their work and had their performance assessed, as explained earlier (Thomson and Dague, 2018, p. 90). Students reflected on how they wanted to meet these goals, for bilingual, extralinguistic, instrumental, strategic sub-competences sought in TI0936 (UJI, 2023) were also achieved in translator training by the *learn it, link it* methodology (Oakley et al., 2021), together with other psychophysiological components (PACTE, 2003, 2005), with direct implications on learning goals, teaching strategies, learning autonomy, and assessment.

It is worth noting that students were responsible for their learning (Latorre Beltrán, 2004), which makes the study centred on participants and, therefore, provides results in our study that are very limited (Suárez Pazos, 2002; Belenguer Cortés, 2024). Nevertheless, even if surveys or any empirical data cannot show students' improvement quantitatively speaking (research question III), interest in the project through empathy (Belenguer Cortés, 2024) and language improvement was manifested (see Figure 4.1). Limitations can be found in the fact that there is no connection between the materials created and the surveys since they are anonymous, and parity was applied to the students enrolled on the 2021–2022 course. Results are tied to the context (UJI) and the community for which the service was conducted (Red Cross migrants). Nevertheless, the initial findings are promising and hint cultural awareness in terms of participation and empathy (Belenguer Cortés, 2024). This reinforces the value of service-learning as a significant learning approach in translation and interpreting degrees and calls for future research in MIGPRO.

5. Conclusions

For the research questions, we can conclude by saying a noticeable engagement is found in most participants noticed to improve their language competence considering the participation in MIGPRO as well as the answers to the surveys (research question I). Research in community service-learning has shown positive effects in students' participation in foreign language learning and social awareness, since students have duplicated their efforts by designing both glossaries and lesson plans (research question II). MIGPRO aimed to educate future translators about migration issues and promoting a proactive mindset towards both personal and societal realities while improving their translation competence and language competence. As mentioned earlier, students were encouraged to select their learning route in accordance with their learning (*race-car/hiker*) profile to improve their French to Spanish translation competence and language competence by improving their knowledge of French as a second language knowledge. MIGPRO provided students with a stimulating and cutting-edge chance to experience real-world learning. Thus, continued research in this field is expected. One important outcome would be that students in subsequent academic years imitate this behaviour and participate, allowing migrants and students to ultimately benefit from the experience. Hence, plans are to replicate this pilot study in subsequent years to observe the results across different courses with service-learning as the pedagogical tool. As mentioned in previous papers (Belenguer Cortés, 2022, p. 669), the initiative is expected to have a wider reach where students may instruct and introduce the major ideas to Red Cross refugees. The chance to empower both students and refugees will be provided by this project, which may include lectures or other educational activities.

Note

1 Ethical approval no. CD/38/2022, granted on 18/03/2022 by the Ethical Review Board of UJI.

References

Alexiou, T. and Stathopoulou, M. 2021. The pre-A1 level in the companion volume of the common European framework of reference for languages. *Research Papers in Language Teaching and Learning* 11(1), pp. 11–29.

Baker, M. 2011. *In Other Words: A Coursebook on Translation*. New York: Routledge.

Beaudrie, S.M. 2020. Towards growth for Spanish heritage programs in the United States: Key markers of success. *Foreign Language Annals* 53(3), pp. 416–437.

Belenguer Cortés, L. 2022. French-Spanish service-learning as a pedagogical tool: An overview of the MIGPRO Project. In Domenech, J. (ed.), *Eight International Conference on Higher Education Advances (HEAd'22)*. València: Universitat Politècnica de València, pp. 663–670.

Belenguer Cortés, L. 2024. La integración de la realidad migratoria en traductores e intérpretes en formación con la empatía como hilo conductor. *Alfinge, revista de filología* 35, pp. 14–35.

Brown, S. 2015. La evaluación auténtica: el uso de la evaluación para ayudar a los estudiantes a aprender. *Relieve* 21(2), pp. 1–10.

Bugel, T. 2013. Translation as a multilingual and multicultural mirror framed by service-learning. *Hispania* 96(2), pp. 369–382.

Carrasco Flores, J. 2019. Teaching English for translation and interpreting: A framework of reference for developing the translator's bilingual sub-competence. *Complutense Journal of English Studies* 27, pp. 121–137.

Cenoz Iragui, J. 2004. El concepto de competencia comunicativa. In Sánchez Lobato J. and Santos Gargallo, I. (eds.), *Vademécum para la formación de profesores*. Madrid: SGEL, pp. 449–465.

Çetiner, C. 2018. Analyzing the attitudes of translation students towards cat (computer-aided translation) tools. *Journal of Language and Linguistic Studies* 14, pp. 153–161.

Chomsky, N. 1965. *Aspects of the Theory of Syntax*. Cambridge, MA: MIT Press.

Colina, S. and Angelelli, C. V. 2015. Translation and interpreting pedagogy. In Angelelli, C.V. and Baer, B.J. (eds.), *Researching Translation and Interpreting*. London: Routledge, pp. 108–117.

Crandall, J.J. 2000. Language teacher education. *Annual Review of Applied Linguistics* 20, pp. 34–55.

Cress, C.M., Collier, P.J. and Reitenauer, V.L. 2023. *Learning through Serving: A Student Guidebook for Service-Learning and Civic Engagement Across Academic Disciplines and Cultural Communities*. New York: Taylor & Francis.

Cronin, M. 2013. *Translation in a Digital Age*. London & New York: Routledge.

Dam, H.V., Brøgger, M.N. and Zethsen, K.K. 2019. *Moving Boundaries in Translation Studies*. New York: Taylor & Francis.

De Higes Andino, I. and Cerezo Merchán, B. 2018. Using evaluation criteria and rubrics as learning tools in subtitling for the D/deaf and the hard of hearing. *The Interpreter and Translator Trainer* 12(1), pp. 68–88.

Dwivedi, N. 2019. *Exploring Institutional Logics for Technology-Mediated Higher Education*. New York: Taylor & Francis.

Felder, R.M. and Brent, R. 2005. Understanding student differences. *Journal of Engineering Education* 94(1), pp. 57–72.

Felder, R.M. and Henriques, E.R. 1995. Learning and teaching styles in foreign and second language education. *Foreign Language Annals* 28(1), pp. 21–31.

Felten, P. and Clayton, P.H. 2011. Service-learning. *New Directions for Teaching and Learning* 2011(128), pp. 75–84.

Fernández, A. 2010. La evaluación orientada al aprendizaje en un modelo de formación por competencias en la educación universitaria. *Revista de docencia universitaria* 8(1). Available from: www.dialnet.unirioja.es/descarga/articulo/3996629.pdf

Firth, J.R. 1957. *Papers in Linguistics*. Oxford: Oxford University Press.

Fitzgerald, C.M. 2009. Language and community: Using service-learning to reconfigure the multicultural classroom. *Language and Education* 23(3), pp. 217–231.

Flores, J.F.F. 2015. Using gamification to enhance second language learning. *Digital Education Review* 27, pp. 32–54.

Furco, A. 1996. *Service-Learning: A Balanced Approach to Experiential Education*. Washington, DC: Corporation for National Service.

García Izquierdo, I. 2000. *Análisis textual aplicado a la traducción*. Valencia: Tirant Lo Blanch.

Garrett-Rucks, P. 2016. *Intercultural Competence in Instructed Language Learning: Bridging Theory and Practice*. Charlotte, NC: Information Age Publishing.

Hurtado Albir, A. 2017. *Researching Translation Competence by PACTE Group*. *Benjamins Translation Library*. Amsterdam: John Benjamins.

Jacoby, B. 1996. Service-Learning in Today's Higher Education. In Jacoby, B. (ed.), Associates *Service-Learning in Higher Education: Concepts and Practices*. San Francisco: Jossey-Bass Publishers, pp. 3–25.

Jemiety, D. 2018. Translation in intercultural business and economic environments. In Harding, S. and Carbonell Cortés, O. (eds.), *Routledge Handbook of Translation and Culture*. London: Taylor and Francis/Routledge, pp. 533–557.

Kelly, D. 2014. *A Handbook for Translator Trainers*. Routledge.

Kenny, D. 2019. Technology and translator training. In O'Hagan, M. (ed.), *The Routledge Handbook of Translation and Technology*. London: Routledge, pp. 498–515.

Kiraly, D. 2000. Translation into a non-mother tongue: From collaboration to competence. *Translation into Non-Mother Tongues in Professional Practice and Training* 8, pp. 117–123.

Latorre Beltrán, A. 2004. La investigación acción. In Bisquerra Alzina, R. (ed.), *Metodología de la investigación educativa*. Madrid: Editorial La Muralla, pp. 370–394.

Laviosa, S. 2014. *Translation and Language Education: Pedagogic Approaches Explored*. London/ New York: Routledge.

Laviosa, S. 2016. Corpus-based translanguaging in translation education. In Corpas Pastor, G. and Seghiri, M. (eds.), *Corpus-based Approaches to Translation and Interpreting: From Theory to Applications*. Frankfurt: Peter Lang, pp. 151–171.

Lowther Pereira, K. 2018. *Community Service-Learning for Spanish Heritage Learners: Making Connections and Building Identities*. Amsterdam/ Philadelphia: John Benjamins Publishing Company.

Maginn, A. 2019. Language Acquisition Through Service Learning and Community Engagement: Critical Reflection, Intercultural Competence, and Action Agency. In: Gras-Velazquez, A. (ed.), *Project-Based Learning in Second Language Acquisition*. London: Routledge, pp. 192–213.

Mejías Climent, L. and De los Reyes Lozano, J. 2023. *La traducción audiovisual a través de la traducción automática y la posedición. Prácticas actuales y futuras*. Granada: Comares.

Munday, J. 2012. *Introducing Translation Studies: Theories and Applications*. New York: Routledge.

Oakley, B., Rogowsky B. and Sejnowski, T.J. 2021. *Uncommon Sense Teaching: Practical Insights in Brain Science to Help Students Learn*. London: Penguin.

O'Brien, S. 2012. Translation as human-computer interaction, *Translation Spaces* 1(1), pp. 101–122.

PACTE. 2003. Building a translation competence model. In Alves, F. (ed.), *Triangulating Translation: Perspectives in Process Oriented Research*. Amsterdam: John Benjamins, pp. 43–66.

PACTE. 2005. Investigating translation competence: Conceptual and methodological issues. *Meta* 50(2), pp. 609–619.

Pak, C. 2007. The service-learning classroom and motivational strategies for learning Spanish: Discoveries from two interdisciplinary community-centered seminars. In Wurr, A. and J. Hellebrandt, J. (eds.), *Learning the Language of Global Citizenship: Service-Learning in Applied Linguistics*. Bolton, MA: Anker, pp. 32–57.

Peng, H. 2018. The impact of machine translation and computer-aided translation on translators. *IOP Conference Series: Materials Science and Engineering* 322(5), p. 052024.

Pintado Gutiérrez, L. 2012. Fundamentos de la traducción pedagógica: Traducción, pedagogía y comunicación. *Sendebar* 23, pp. 321–353.

Prentice, M. and Robinson, G. 2010. Improving student learning outcomes with service-learning. *Higher Education* 148. Available from: www.digitalcommons.unomaha.edu/slcehighered/148

Pym, A. 2009. Translator Training. Pre-print text written for the *Oxford Companion to Translation* Studies. Available from: https://usuaris.tinet.cat/apym/on-line/training/2009_translator_training.pdf

Pym, A. 2014. *Method in Translation History*. London: Routledge.

Pym, A. 2023. *Exploring Translation Theories*. London: Taylor & Francis.

Pym, A., Perekrestenko, A. and Starink, B. 2006. *Translation Technology and Its Teaching*. Tarragona, Spain: Intercultural Studies Group.

Riedermann Hall, K. 1996. Cognition and translation didactics. *Meta* 41(1), pp. 114–117.

Ruggiero, D. 2018. A significant learning approach to WLSP and its impact on student perceptions of the field and its definition. *CUADERNOS* 740, pp. 21–52.

Runnels, J. 2021. *Pluricultural Language Education and the CEFR*. Cambridge: Cambridge University Press.

Salgado-Robles, F. and Thompson, G.L. 2022. Language Learners and Service-Learning. In Geeslin, K. (ed.), *The Routledge Handbook of Second Language Acquisition and Sociolinguistics*, pp. 277–290.

Sikora, I. and Walczyński, M. 2015. Incorporating CAT tools and ICT in the translation and interpreting training at the undergraduate level. *The Translator and the Computer* 2, p. 119.

Steinke, P. and Fitch, P. 2007. Assessing service-learning. *Research & Practice in Assessment* 2, pp. 24–29.

Suárez Pazos, M. 2002. Algunas reflexiones sobre la investigación-acción colaboradora en la educación. *Revista Electrónica de Enseñanza de las Ciencias* 1(1), pp. 1–17.

Thompson, G. and Hague, D. 2018. Using community service-learning in the Spanish translation classroom: Challenges and opportunities. *Cuadernos de ALDEEU* 33, pp. 87–112.

Universitat Jaume I. 2023. *TI0936 – Translation C-A1 (French-Spanish) (I)* (Course syllabus). Available from: www.eujier.uji.es/pls/www/gri_www.euji22883_html?p_curso_aca=2022&p_asignatura_id=TI0936&p_idioma=en&p_titulacion=207

Varela-Salinas, M.J. 2007. How new technologies improve translation pedagogy. *Translation Journal* 11(4), pp. 1–14.

Yan, J.X., Pan, J., Wu, H. and Wang, Y. 2013. Mapping interpreting studies: The state of the field based on a database of nine major translation and interpreting Journals (2000–2010). *Perspectives: Studies in Translatology* 21(3), pp. 446–473.

5

RACE AND ETHICS IN THE TRANSLATION CLASSROOM

Reflections on teaching the Amanda Gorman's translators controversies as a white British lecturer

Peter J. Freeth

Keywords: ethics; race; translator training; Amanda Gorman; anti-racist pedagogy

1. Introduction

Ethical considerations have become an increasingly urgent topic in translation and interpreting pedagogy (Lambert, 2023, p. 7). From literary translation to public service interpreting and post-editing in supranational institutions, students need to graduate from training courses with a clear understanding of the various codes of conduct and moral responsibilities that govern not only the labour of translation but also how the role of the translator or interpreter is understood by the clients, service users, and audiences they serve. Indeed, as noted by Baker and Maier, "practically all decisions they [the students] make as professionals will potentially have ethical implications" (2011, p. 4) and so there is a need for educators to engage "far more directly and explicitly with the issue of ethics" across translation curricula. Given that teaching on ethics usually comprises a limited number of specific sessions within broader theoretical or professionalisation focussed modules (Lambert, 2023, p. 7), ethical discussions within the classroom often link to issues surrounding fidelity, agency, and translator visibility – particularly in the case of courses focussing on written forms of translation. In such cases, the hypothetical nature of discussing these topics in general terms can make it difficult for students to understand what is at stake or the relevance of these issues to their work. A key challenge in translator training thus becomes how we make relevant often abstract and hypothetical ethical discussions to meet this urgent need for further training.

DOI: 10.4324/9781003440970-6

In this chapter, I present critical reflections on my attempts to make relevant the teaching of one specific ethical issue, race and representation, through my inclusion of the Amanda Gorman's translators controversies in practical, language-specific translation classes. In doing so, I aim to: (1) encourage colleagues to embed discussions of ethics in pedagogy far beyond theoretical modules and discussions; (2) inspire reflexivity from others who choose to use the debate as a case study in the classroom; and (3) contribute to increasingly important debates surrounding race within translation studies in the UK. I will begin by providing contextual information on Gorman and the Dutch translation of her poem *The Hill We Climb* before discussing my own background and the pedagogic context in which I taught the translation controversies. Subsequently, I will reflect on my own pedagogic practice and will use these reflections to highlight four main ethical considerations that I argue must be taken into account when using the Gorman's translators controversies as a case study in any translation classroom: which aspects of the controversies do we highlight; how do we frame the controversies; what kinds of classes do we teach them in; and how do we handle the Dutch source materials. I then conclude with some suggestions for further ways in which white colleagues in translation studies can support anti-racist work as we seek to decolonise and diversify our discipline.

2. Amanda Gorman, *The Hill We Climb* and its Dutch translation

In January 2021, the Black American poet Amanda Gorman performed her spoken-word poem *The Hill We Climb* at the inauguration of President Joe Biden. Gorman was invited to perform by First Lady Jill Biden and, in an interview with the *New York Times*, Gorman reports being given an open brief with no direction other than the event's theme of "America United" (Alter, 2021). In the same interview, Gorman describes how she had struggled to finish the poem and had felt "worried she wasn't up to the monumental task she faced". Following a year of politically divisive COVID lockdowns and the #BlackLivesMatter movement sparked by the murder of George Floyd by a white police officer in Minneapolis, Gorman had struggled to write more than a few lines per day. However, after watching pro-Trump rioters storming into the US Capitol Building on 6 January 2021 on the news, Gorman completed the poem that same night (ibid.).

Consequently, like many pieces of great art and literature, the socio-political contexts that informed *The Hill We Climb* and in which it was performed are integral to understanding the significance of the piece and the origins of the controversy surrounding its translation. For instance, the issues of race and racial justice at the poem's core are not only linked to Gorman's own experiences as a Black woman in 21st-century America, but also to the systems of power and privilege that allowed (and continues to allow) Black Americans to be killed by those who are meant to represent and uphold national law and order, whilst armed white rioters were able to force their way into heart of the US government, assault approximately 140 police officers (one of whom died) and then simply walk away.[1] Furthermore, during her performance Gorman wore a ring featuring a caged bird as a tribute to previous inaugural poet Maya Angelou. Whilst this again makes explicit reference to the continued struggles faced by Black communities in the US and the voices of Black poets before her, Gorman has also noted that it references Angelou's "issues with speech" and connects with her own experiences growing up with a speech impediment (Brisco, 2021). As such, the medium of the spoken-word poem not only draws on a rich history of Black poetry but also serves as an act of defiance pertaining to Gorman's own experiences and struggles. Finally, when discussing her performance on Twitter, Gorman made explicit links to the feminism at the heart of her work, stating "I would be nowhere without the women whose footsteps I dance in […] Here's to the women who have climbed my hills before" (Gorman, 2021). Given the importance of the #MeToo movement prior to and during the beginning of Donald Trump's presidency just four years prior to Biden's inauguration, then, Gorman's feminism and the platform given to her to share this message are also significant in understanding the socio-political significance of her poem, performance, and visibility at Biden's inauguration.

The significance of *The Hill We Climb* and the context in which it was written, performed, and received therefore presents a clear case for translating the text into other languages. In a Dutch context, the translation rights were bought by publisher Meulenhoff, who announced in a press release on 23 February 2021 that the white author Lucas Rijneveld had been commissioned as translator (Meulenhoff, 2021a). Following this announcement, an opinion piece by Surinamese-Dutch journalist and activist Janice Deul was published in the newspaper *De Volkskrant*. In this article, Deul argued that Rijneveld constituted an "incomprehensible choice" as the translator for Gorman's work (Deul, 2021), instead arguing that the appointment of Rijneveld was a missed opportunity to commission a translator who is "a spoken word artist, young, female, *and:* unapologetically Black" (emphasis in original).[2] What followed was described by Kotze and Strowe as a "media furore over the suitability of the translators of Amanda Gorman's poem" (2021), beginning first in the original Dutch context and then spreading out internationally through both the mainstream press and social media. Indeed, British outlets including the BBC and *The Guardian* published articles on the initial controversy surrounding the choice of Rijneveld as the translator (see, for example, Holligan, 2021; Flood, 2021; and Michallon, 2021) and the consequences of this debate in other linguistic and cultural contexts, such as Catalan publisher Univers' later decision to not publish an already completed translation of the poem by white translator Víctor Obiols (BBC, 2021; AFP in Barcelona, 2021).

3. My pedagogic practice

As noted by Kotze (2021), the sudden shoving of translation and translators "into the spotlight" as a topic of controversy "in an unprecedented slew of newspaper opinion pieces and tweet-skirmishes" is an unusual position for our discipline and profession. In Anglophone and European contexts, translation is generally understood as an invisible practice, with translated texts being presented as though they are original texts written in the target language. This argument is most famously ascribed to the work of Lawrence Venuti (1995 [2008/2018]) and whilst recent critiques of his work have questioned the validity of his argument across all facets of our contemporary, digitally connected world (such as Freeth, 2024), continued endeavours for more explicit recognition of translators and their work such as campaigns like the Translators Association's *#TranslatorsOnTheCover* (Society of Authors, 2021) or Gameloc Gathering's *#TranslatorsInTheCredits* (Whyte, 2022) demonstrate the ever-present invisibility of translation and translators.

Thus, upon seeing a public debate about ethical issues such as race and representation in translation being covered in major British newspapers, I immediately scrambled to both make my students aware of this sudden societal visibility for translation and to engage pedagogically with the situation as it was happening. Having spoken to colleagues at several institutions during this period and at subsequent networking events such as the APTIS 2022 conference, it has become clear to me that I was not the only one to do so. In my case, the primary teaching I was undertaking at the time (spring 2021) was a block of German-to-English literary translation within a specialised translation module on the MA Applied Translation Studies at the University of Leeds.[3] As such, I was able to follow Drugan and Megone's recommendation for an integrated approach to teaching ethics (2011) by using the Gorman debate as a case study within a practical translation module. Doing so allowed me to open up "a space for critical reflection" (Baker and Maier, 2011, p. 4) on both the students' translations and their own privileges, prejudices, or experiences.

Based on the success of my teaching, which received "the highest praise" for "the topical nature of some of the work (e.g., feeding into the Amanda Gorman ethical debates)" at a course committee meeting in April 2021, I then reran the exact same session on the same module during the following academic year. However, without the immediacy of discussing the controversy as it was unfolding, I noticed a shift in both how my students responded to the debate as a case study and my own feelings about using the controversy in isolation as a vehicle to discuss translator ethics and issues of race and representation more generally. Where I felt that I had a clear rationale for its initial inclusion in the 2020/2021 academic year, I began to question why I was singling out this specific case study, what the implications of doing so were given the whiteness of my classroom, and whether I was even the right person to be teaching this content in the first place.[4] All of these questions culminated into the development of two primary fears. The first was that I was reductively using one case study to exemplify a far more complex issue that requires more time and nuance to adequately cover in a pedagogical context, whilst the second was if many white scholars such as myself were using the Gorman's translators controversy as a case study in isolation, this could result in the fetishisation of the debate.[5] Indeed, hearing about a postgraduate teaching assistant being asked to run a one-off seminar on the "ethics of the Gorman controversy" in the context of an non-language-specific, MA-level theory module with almost no other guidance not only served to justify my fears but also demonstrates the continued need to expand discussions of ethics beyond isolated sessions within general theory modules (Drugan and Megone, 2011; Lambert, 2023).

Another elephant in the room that I feel must be addressed at this stage is both my own positionality as a white, male, and cis academic and the whiteness of the academic institutions and student bodies with whom I have worked. Race cannot be decoupled from the poem or poet at the heart of this debate, not only in terms of the symbolic visibility given to Gorman as a young, Black, female, spoken-word poet through her performance at President Joe Biden's inauguration but also because it was Deul's dismay that Dutch publisher Meulenhoff had not entrusted or granted such visibility upon a "young, female, *and* unapologetically Black" translator that sparked the media debates and subsequent controversy. According to Higher Education Statistics Agency's most recent staff statistics, only 17% of UK academic staff were Black and minority ethnic (BME) in the 2020/2021 academic year, whilst only 11% of Professors were BME (HESA, 2022).[6] Furthermore, as noted by Tachtiris and Layne, Black scholars working in translation studies at institutions located in the Global North are "few and far between" (2023, p. 1), a situation that has resulted in what Tachtiris describes as "the unbearable whiteness of translation in the West" (Tachtiris, 2024, p. 2). Thus, both British academia and translation studies more specifically remain predominantly white spaces and the systems of power that underlie academic research and teaching in Britain privilege white members of staff such as myself. I argue that my decision to include a Black German author, a decision that predated the controversies, and the Gorman's translators controversy within my teaching can be seen as act of "allyship" (Carlson et al., 2020) through which I sought to give more visibility to Black voices within my classroom and institution more broadly, thereby supporting increasing calls to decolonise our classrooms and enact education for social justice across higher education institutions in the UK. Nevertheless, I must acknowledge that all such attempts are refracted through the prism of my own privileges and biases, despite my best intentions and attempts to mitigate against them.

I would also like to acknowledge that although Rijneveld's non-binary gender identity was not an active factor in the debate surrounding the translation of Gorman's work, I was keen to ensure that all mentions of him during classroom activities or discussions used the correct pronouns. At the time of the debate, Rijneveld identified as non-binary and so used they/them pronouns, which were the pronouns used by all participants in the pedagogic context given as an example throughout this chapter. At the time of writing this chapter (December 2023), however, Rijneveld is now known as Lucas Rijneveld and has chosen to be addressed by male pronouns (see Rijneveld, 2022). As such, I will be using Rijneveld's chosen pronouns of he/him in this chapter and caution should be taken in classroom environments either when discussing Rijneveld and his work, or when utilising news articles from the time as primary sources that discuss him using different pronouns.

4.   Ethical considerations when teaching the Gorman's translators controversies

Now that I have introduced Gorman and her work, provided a brief overview of the controversy surrounding the Dutch translation of *The Hill We Climb*, and outlined my own personal and pedagogic backgrounds, the following sections reflect on four significant questions that, based on my own pedagogic experience, I think must be considered when using the Gorman's translators controversies as an ethics case study within the translation classroom.

4.1   Just the one controversy?

As noted in section 2, the cultural and political significance of *The Hill We Climb* presented a clear case for translating Gorman's poem into other languages. In a Dutch context, the translation rights were bought by publisher Meulenhoff, who then announced in a press release on 23 February 2021 that the white author Lucas Rijneveld had been commissioned as translator (Meulenhoff, 2021a). The press release noted the many accolades Rijneveld had won for his poetry and literature, including the 2020 International Booker Prize for the English translation of his novel *The Discomfort of Evening*. As such, Meulenhoff seemingly justified the selection of Rijneveld as translator based on his prestige and literary achievements both in Dutch and in English translation. Furthermore, according to the press release, Gorman had been "direct enthousiast" [immediately enthusiastic] about the selection of Rijneveld, who had been publisher Meulenhoff's "gedroomde vertaler" [dream translator] during the auction for translation rights. Following his own sharing of the news, Rijneveld also claimed in a Facebook comment that he had been Gorman's own choice as translator.[7]

However, immediate responses on social media and in the Dutch press made it clear that Rijneveld was not the dream translator for everyone. One of the first notable responses came from the Surinamese-Dutch spoken-word poet Zaïre Krieger on the day of Meulenhoff's press release (2021a), who noted the names of several female, spoken-word artists of colour who "beter hadden kunnen doen" [could have done better] (2021b) – including herself – before stating that when she had previously mentioned there was "geen ruimte" [no room] for spoken-word artists of colour, "this is exactly what I meant" (2021c). For such critics, the commissioning of Rijneveld therefore served as concrete evidence of the marginalisation of Black voices in the Dutch literary space, even when they possessed the requisite language skills and poetry acumen to undertake the translation. In such cases, social media criticisms of the selection of Rijneveld all pertained to the question of why a translator who more closely matched Gorman's own profile was not given the opportunity, rather than a suggestion that Rijneveld could not, or should not, translate Gorman's work.

The following day, Meulenhoff published a statement responding to such criticisms (2021b) in which they highlight similarities between Gorman and Rijneveld, such as the international recognition that they received at a young age and that "zijn ze beiden niet bang om zich uit te spreken" [they are both not afraid to speak out]. Within this response, Meulenhoff also made several references to discussions held during the selection process to argue that the choice of Rijneveld matched the "zeer duidelijke eisen" [very clear requirements] set by Gorman and her team for translators of her work; that Gorman and her team had "direct positief reageerden" [immediately responded positively] to their suggestion of Rijneveld as translator; and that they had agreed with Gorman and her team that the translation would be read by "sensitivity readers" from "verschillende achtergronden" [varied backgrounds] regardless of who translated it. Here we can note several interesting points. First, the publisher's response frames the debate around Rijneveld specifically and why he would have been a suitable translator for the text, which fails to address Krieger's criticisms because arguing why Rijneveld specifically was a good choice does nothing to clarify why a Black translator was not chosen for the task. Second, the frequent references to Gorman and her team throughout the statement serve as an attempt to silence critics by legitimising their actions with the weight of Gorman's authorial voice, whilst also presenting a different account of events to Rijneveld's claim that he had been Gorman's choice (Patrick Grayham, 2021). Finally, the acknowledgement that sensitivity readers were being commissioned indicates that they were themselves already aware of potential inadequacies in Rijneveld's ability to handle the Blackness of the text on his own. This admission demonstrates the publisher's problematic willingness to engage people from "verschillende achtergronden" [varied backgrounds] to undertake this work invisibly whilst the white Rijneveld was positioned publicly as the translator of the text. From the very outset of the controversy, then, we can see a disconnect between criticisms of the choice of Rijneveld from the likes of Krieger, in which the primary argument was that it provided continuing evidence of the marginalisation (and arguably exploitation) of Black voices within Dutch literary and translational spaces, and the publisher's rebuttal, which focused solely on why Rijneveld should be permitted to undertake the translation.

The following day, Surinamese-Dutch journalist and activist Janice Deul's opinion piece on the choice of Rijneveld, which echoes many of the sentiments raised by Krieger on Twitter, was then published in the newspaper *De Volkskrant* (Deul, 2021) and the "media furore" (Kotze and Strowe, 2021) began in earnest. What followed morphed into an international debate on who can and should be allowed to translate who, with coverage in the British media coming under titles such as "Why a white poet did not translate Amanda Gorman" (Holligan, 2021) and "Amanda Gorman's white translator quits" (Flood, 2021). However, as noted by both Kotze (2021) and Kotze and Strowe (2021), as well as made clear in my discussion of Krieger's tweets above, the reduction of the controversy to such questions demonstrates a clear misunderstanding of the issues raised by critics such as Krieger and Deul, and risks developing into a narrative of white victimhood in which the focus remains on translators such as Rijneveld. Indeed, within British mainstream coverage of the controversy there was no visibility given to any of the Black, female, spoken-word artists named as potential candidates by either Krieger or Deul. Rather, the focus remains squarely on the experiences of white translators, who are framed as "victims" (Kotze, 2024, pp. 12–14), and white institutions such as Meulenhoff.

Consequently, the use of this media debate to discuss who can or should translate a text within the translation classroom similarly risks framing this debate within a narrative of white victimhood, or at least problematically frames these debates through white perspectives. Indeed, whilst news articles from institutions such as the BBC, *The Guardian* and *The Independent* (to speak only of the British coverage) may initially seem like an exciting opportunity to discuss a case study that has entered the mainstream, we also need to critically evaluate how these institutions covered the story and how this coverage prioritised the interests of white stakeholders such as Rijneveld – a clear example of white privilege (as defined by Bhopal, 2023). Taking a further look at the articles published by those three publications, for instance, *The Guardian* and *The Independent* pieces by Flood (2021) and Michallon (2021) serve only to recount the narrative of the controversy through published statements by the major parties involved (Deul, Rijneveld, and Meulenhoff) and whilst Flood mentions contacting Gorman's team for "further comment", none is given.[8] The BBC article (Holligan, 2021) does include original quotes from an interview with Deul conducted by Holligan but presents the subsection "Who is Rijneveld?" and a large photograph of him before any explicit reference to Deul, which then comes with quotes from their interview under the next heading "Why the outcry?". Notably, the by-line and introductory paragraphs similarly frame the debate in terms of Rijneveld and public outcry because "the translator is not black", which again presents the controversy in terms of white experience rather than Black. When seen through this lens, even the title of the article seems to be a reversal of what the original criticisms were addressing: rather than why a Black poet was not originally selected to translate Amanda Gorman, the article is called "Why a white poet did not translate Amanda Gorman". Finally, in the case of all three of the articles discussed here, it should be noted that they were written by white authors. As such, the specific framing of the controversy through the white lens of Rijneveld and publisher Meulenhoff demonstrates how the media "select out limited aspects of an issue in order to make it salient for mass communication", and so present this discourse through the "white racial frame" (Feagin, 2013, p. 9).[9]

What the above discussion has aimed to demonstrate is that there are actually two controversies at play here. The first pertains to what Kotze and Strowe (2021) refer to as "representativeness" and the selection of Rijneveld over a Black, female, spoken-word poet, as expressed both on social media by Krieger and in the Dutch media by Deul. The second relates to the subsequent representation of Deul's criticism and the "media furore" (Kotze and Strowe, 2021) in which the debate shifted to white-centred discourses of who can or should be allowed to translate who. Indeed, as noted by Tachtiris and Layne (2023, p. 2),

> Rarely do issues in literary translation reach so widespread an audience, but the translation community did not rise to the occasion in a sea of hyperbolic handwringing about "cancel culture" and straw-man arguments claiming that those calling for a Black translator were insisting that only Black translators should translate Black authors.

From a pedagogical perspective, then, the biggest decision we must make when teaching the Amanda Gorman's translators controversies is which of these controversies, and so which of these debates, we are choosing to bring to our classrooms – or, indeed, whether we will address both. Such a decision must not be taken lightly. As noted earlier in this chapter, as well as by Tachtiris and Layne (2023, p. 1) and Tachtiris (2024), UK higher education remains a predominantly white space and so if we are choosing to teach the first of these two options, we must be properly equipped to handle the subject matter, relevant work from Black scholars, and our students' responses.

The latter is important in terms of protecting students of colour, especially Black students, who may find such debates triggering or who risk becoming involuntary spokespeople or representatives for Blackness more generally simply from being present in the classroom, which constitutes a clear form of microaggression that prioritises the educational growth of white students over the student of colour (Sue et al., 2009, p. 188). It is also important in terms of white students who may need guidance or support in confronting their own whiteness and privilege when discussing these issues due to the fact that white privilege constitutes a "normalised" and "seemingly invisible" structural advantage that has become a "normative baseline" (Bhopal, 2023, p. 113). Consequently, such discussions can lead to a situation where white students' "entire sense of self and their social world is called into question" (Johnson, Rich, and Cargile, 2008, p. 120). As such, great care must be taken when choosing which aspects of the controversies we are highlighting when we choose to the use the topic within a translation studies classroom setting.

4.2 How to frame the controversies?

Beyond making the decision as to which aspects of the controversies to focus on within the classroom, the question of how we then present the controversies to our students is equally important. Indeed, it is key that the very introduction of this topic in module handbooks and similar overviews of module content avoids presenting the controversies through a "white racial frame" (Feagin, 2013) that perpetuates the white narratives found in the media coverage discussed in the previous section. The relevance of this question becomes clear when we think about how we refer to the controversies. For instance, was this the Amanda Gorman controversy? The Amanda Gorman translation controversy? The Amanda Gorman's translators controversy? Or even the Lucas Rijneveld translation controversy? Arguably, it is none of those things, as the controversy had very little to do with Gorman specifically outside her authorship and, in the end, Rijneveld's translation never came to fruition. The controversy belongs to us and our societies; to an inability to give visibility, space, and power to Black voices; to constantly permitting white people to dominate social and cultural spaces to the detriment of everyone else. Yet, the centrality of Gorman's identity and authorship, as well as the cultural capital surrounding Rijneveld, makes it difficult to move beyond the two of them when even choosing a name for the debate.

In naming and framing the debate throughout this chapter, I have opted for the "Amanda Gorman's translators controversies" as a title. This choice marks an attempt to keep attention focussed on translators in the plural, rather than on Rijneveld specifically, and so seeks to prevent a white-centric focus on the debate of who can or should translate who. The use of the plural "controversies" also clearly communicates the fact that there are different levels and discourses co-occurring at various levels across the original Dutch response and within a transnational context. Arguably, however, doing so fails to explicitly centre the debate around Black experiences. As such, a subtitle of "Why a Black translator was not chosen to translate Amanda Gorman" could remedy this whilst also serving as a provocative reversal of the BBC article title "Why a white poet did not translate Amanda Gorman" (Holligan, 2021). Furthermore, retaining Gorman's name but utilising it as an adjectival possessive can support independent research or flipped classroom models in which students research the discourse surrounding the controversies on their own before the primary teaching event, as much of the English-language discourse is framed around Gorman's authorship. Thus, the inclusion of her name provides necessary details and context. However, I believe the ideal solution would be to frame any teaching events in terms of the broader issues and themes of race, white privilege, and systemic injustice in translation contexts, thereby preventing any risk of fetishising or presenting the controversies as an unusual or isolated case. One potential solution would be to follow Kotze and Strowe's lead (2021) and focus on questions of representation and representativeness, though other possibilities surrounding themes such as diversity and identity politics also exist (see for instance Tachtiris' discussion in Chapter 3 of *Translation and Race*, 2024, pp. 90–117).

4.3   In what kind of classes?

As noted by Lambert, the inclusion of ethics as a single session within a broader theoretical module is "prevalent on many courses in translation" (2023, p. 7) and so the temptation when teaching the Gorman's translators controversies is to use it as a case study within such a context. However, not only have such approaches been long criticised in favour of an integrated approach that links ethics to professional practice (notably Drugan and Megone, 2011), such an approach also fails to alert our students to "the ethical implications of behaviour that they might regard as routine, unproblematic, and hence not experience as challenging from a moral point of view" (Baker and Maier, 2011, p. 3). Indeed, given the white privilege that underpins the translation industry and higher education in the UK, linking the debate to critical reflections on the students' own practice and experiences is key to fully engaging with the racial injustice at the heart the controversies.

In my own case, in-class discussion of the Amanda Gorman's translators controversies took place as part of a practical translation class that was run with a flipped approach. As such, students completed an independent translation task at home that we then workshopped in class to construct a "fair copy" translation as a group. For the class in which we discussed the controversies, students were tasked with translating a section from

1000 Serpentinen Angst, a novel by Black German author Olivia Wenzel that opens with her reaction to Donald Trump's election victory in 2016. As such, clear links could be made between Wenzel and Gorman as authors and the socio-political climates in which they wrote their respective works. This class came several weeks into the semester and the source text was presented unproblematically in the same way as all prior source texts: with no explicit references to race in the task. The only accompanying material was an optional task to read a BBC news article about Rijneveld being chosen as Gorman's translator (Holligan, 2021), which was presented as an unusual case of translation being in the news and was not linked explicitly to the Wenzel source text. Optional readings such as this were provided every week and were presented as an opportunity for the students to expand their knowledge, rather than as a necessity for in-class participation.

When it then came to the class, I simply presented the students with two questions before we began discussing their own translations:

1. Who is Olivia Wenzel?
2. How does this relate the Amanda Gorman controversy?

The ensuing discussion lasted for over 30 minutes in both instances that I ran this particular class (2020/2021 and 2021/2022) and so these simple questions worked well as a stimulus for class discussions on race and ethics in an otherwise white, German-to-English translation classroom. More specifically, the broad phrasing of these questions gave space and agency to the students to lead our exploration of these ethical questions, whilst the fact that they had already completed a translation of a text by a Black German author gave them practical experience relating to these largely hypothetical and theoretical discussions to inform and challenge their opinions. Of course, the students did not all agree with each other. Nevertheless, the classroom served as a "supportive environment" that allowed them to "rehearse both sides of an argument freely, and to think through its ethical implications from different perspectives" (Baker and Maier, 2011, p. 6).[10] As such, the students were able to use these discussions to reflect on their own practice and to explicitly discuss the ethical implications of their translation strategies and overall approaches, which had otherwise become "routine" and "unproblematic" (Baker and Maier, 2011, p. 3) over the course the module. Notably, on both occasions our classroom discussions moved towards questions of who translates who, thereby reflecting the white framing found in English-language media discourse documenting the controversy. When this happened, I sought to re-orient the debate to highlight the white privilege at the heart of both the translation industry and our educational institution by encouraging critical reflection on whiteness in our department and on the students' course thus far, which in both instances that I taught the class was also mirrored in the students' broader educational experiences prior to commencing their MA studies, as well as my own.

Finally, whilst issues of race and white privilege may be prevalent across the Global North, discussion within a language-specific translation class allowed for a level of nuance that was incredibly relevant to the students' knowledge of their working languages and would not be possible in a generic class on a mixed-language module as such specificity would risk becoming exclusionary. Indeed, the complex and varied socio-political contexts of every language almost necessitates that race and white privilege are taught at this level of specificity alongside more open discussions between broader cohorts where difference can be highlighted, lest discussions remain too general and hypothetical for students to make clear links either to their practice or experiences.

4.4   How to handle the Dutch source materials?

As noted in section 3, when I originally saw this story in the news, I excitedly decided to use this as a discussion topic in one of my classes without fully engaging with the original Dutch-language source materials. At the time, the debates were ongoing and the discourse was shifting, so it seemed like a timely topic to include and one that we could come back to in future weeks should further developments come. However, due to a lack of Dutch language skills, time, and understanding, I relied on news articles such as Flood (2021), Holligan (2021), and Michallon (2021) to inform both myself and my students as pre-class reading. Consequently, I presented the controversy from a white perspective that failed to address the deeper problems at the core of this debate pertaining to racial inequality and systemic injustices across the literary, publishing, and media fields. It was only when I read Kotze's excellent piece *Translation is the Canary in the Coalmine* (2021) and later in the year Kotze and Strowe's response to "Representing experiential knowledge" (2021) that I realised not only the extent to which the debate had mutated into a white-centred discussion of who can translate who, but also how I had also been complicit in perpetuating that narrative with my pedagogy.

Interestingly, Kotze finds that my experience is not unusual, with much of the English-language debate on social-media platform Twitter (now X) drawing "primarily on English-language media" and so English-language debate on the controversies proceeded "almost exclusively through the sharing of already 'mediated' discourse" whilst direct references to Deul's original opinion piece were scarce (2024, p. 13). Given the relatively limited presence of Dutch in translation courses across UK higher education, as well as the fact that translation theory and ethics are often taught in non-language specific classes or modules, my anecdotal suspicion is that many UK-based colleagues may also have responded similarly: relying on English-language news media or perhaps even machine translation to present this issue in classes on translation ethics – at least in the immediate aftermath. However, now that there is over three-year's distance between us and the controversies, we can no longer rest on our laurels and be complicit in perpetuating the problematic recentring of the controversy around whiteness found in English-language coverage. If we are actually interested in addressing the structural racism and white privilege that continue to dominate (literary) translation practices and policies, this then requires real engagement with the primary sources and criticisms from those such as Krieger and Deul, whilst also necessitating a discussion of how public debate on the topic reframed the issue around white victimhood. Kotze's published translation of Deul's original column is a useful resource in doing so, particularly as Kotze also provides additional comments and insights from Deul on edits made to the column by editors from the newspaper *De Volkskrant*, such as a change in the article's title and introduction (Deul, 2021).

However, other primary sources from the original debate, such as the tweets from Krieger and Meulenhoff's initial statement analysed earlier in this chapter, were also written and published in Dutch but there is no English translation available. Yet, in seeking to teach the racial injustice at the heart of these controversies, I am advocating for the critical evaluation of these primary sources in the British translation studies classroom – particularly in terms of demonstrating to students how the debate was recentred in the media to prioritise whiteness and even white victimhood. As such, students' ability to read and discuss these sources is crucial. The most obvious solution for staff without Dutch language skills (or a friendly Dutch-speaking colleague who can assist) is the use of machine translation (MT) services. Of course, the use of MT itself presents a myriad of other ethical issues that are out of scope for the present discussion (see for instance Kenny, 2011 and Moniz and Parra Escartín, 2023). Nevertheless, presenting (or asking students to generate) multiple versions from different MT engines not only provides an additional entry point into an ethical discussion of MT engines or even large language models more broadly, but also then gives students agency in going beyond accounts of the controversies as (re)written in the mainstream media. Whilst MT may not be a perfect solution, the important factor here is that students are able to trace the development of the controversies and understand the original Dutch-language debates on race and systemic injustice from which the discussions of who can or should translate who mutated.

5. Conclusions

This chapter aimed to demonstrate the need for academics who use the debates surrounding the Dutch translation of Amanda Gorman's *The Hill*

We Climb as a case study of translation ethics to confront the white privilege at the heart of the controversies and the racial re-framing they were subject to in the mainstream media. Through a critical discussion of the original Dutch controversy and how this discourse was rewritten in the (English-language) media, I have demonstrated that there are multiple controversies that require pedagogic attention and reflected on how understanding this nuance has influenced my own pedagogical practice when teaching race and ethics in the practical translation classroom. As a lone, white scholar I cannot claim that this contribution serves as a comprehensive guide; nor do I seek to present a prescriptive methodology for teaching either the controversies, or race and ethics more broadly. Given my own privileges, I am certainly in no position to attempt either. Rather, this chapter seeks to encourage critical reflection on pedagogic practice and more thorough coverage of racial injustice within translation studies programs, both in the UK and further afield. As just a few suggestions of how this may be achieved, I encourage colleagues to engage with more Black and anti-racist scholarship in theoretical modules, such as Corine Tachtiris' *Translation and Race* (2024) and John Keene's *Translating Poetry, Translating Blackness* (2016); to integrate Black "praxis of translation" into practical classes such as the work of Geri Augusto (2014) and Cibele de Guadalupe Sousa Araújo, Luciana de Mesquita Silva, and Dennys Silva-Reis (2019); or to include practical explorations into the biases, prejudices, and intolerances found in machine translation engines or large language models when teaching translation technology. Doing so is going to take considerable work given the overall whiteness of our discipline, particularly within institutions in the Global North. Nevertheless, as a white member of the UK's translation and interpreting studies community, I am convinced that it is vital that both I and others of a similar profile undertake this work as urgently, thoroughly, and sensitively as possible.

Notes

1 Whilst I acknowledge that those responsible are still being arrested and held to account over three years after these events, the fact that US law enforcement are still only now managing to track down and prosecute all of those responsible supports, rather than contradicts, my underlying point here.
2 The original article by Deul has been translated into English by Professor Haidee Kotze and published on her personal medium.com site (Deul, 2021). Where this opinion piece is quoted in English, it is therefore this version that I am quoting.
3 The specification for this module as it ran in 2020/2021 can be found at https://webprod3.leeds.ac.uk/catalogue/dynmodules.asp?Y=202021&F=P&M=MODL-5124M [Accessed 29 February 2024].
4 For the two years I designed this scheme of work and taught on the relevant module, both myself and all the students enrolled on the module were white British.
5 To be clear, the term fetishise is here used in its non-sexualised meaning.

6 I use the term "Black and minority ethnic" here as it is defined by the HESA themselves on the same webpage, as a term to collectively refer to "Black, Asian, Mixed and Other ethnicity categories" (HESA, 2022). However, it should be noted that the term is now falling out of usage in Britain as it "emphasise[s] certain ethnic minority groups (Asian and black) and exclude others (mixed, other and white ethnic minority groups)" (gov.uk, 2021).

7 The comment can be seen in a screenshot shared on Twitter (now X) (PatrickGrayham, 2021) and reads "Het is de keuze van Amanda Gorman. Denk [sic] dat zij self mag bepalen wie zi kiest om haar wekr to vertalen" [It is the choice of Amanda Gorman. Think she gets to decide herself who she chooses to translate her work].

8 See Tachtiris (2024, pp. 103–104) for a discussion of Gorman's silence on the matter.

9 A similar argument is put forward by Kotze (2024, pp. 13–14) in her analysis of Twitter discourse surrounding the controversies, where she notes that Twitter users often shared and commented on these same articles and in doing so foregrounded the figure of the "injured" translator Rijneveld and positioned him as the victim of racism, whilst Deul's opinion piece was invisibilized. In Tachtiris' words, Deul was instead "characterized as overly emotional as well as insurrectionist, reproducing the stereotype of the 'angry Black woman'" (2024, p. 99).

10 Given that this class was taught halfway through the second semester of teaching, I had developed rapport with the students and established the classroom as a safe space for respectful disagreement through our previous, lower stakes discussions. However, the use of trigger/content warnings in module handbooks or explicitly stating ground rules before discussing challenging topics such as race may be useful in establishing an environment where such pedagogic practice is both possible and productive.

References

AFP in Barcelona. 2021. *'Not suitable': Catalan translator for Amanda Gorman poem removed.* [Online]. [Accessed 24 November 2023]. Available from: www.theguardian.com/books/2021/mar/10/not-suitable-catalan-translator-for-amanda-gorman-poem-removed

Alter, A. 2021. *Amanda Gorman Captures the Moment, in Verse.* [Online]. [Accessed 4 December 2023]. Available from: www.nytimes.com/2021/01/19/books/amanda-gorman-inauguration-hill-we-climb.html

Araújo, C.G.S., de Mesquita Silva, L. and Silva-Reis, D. 2019. Translation Studies & Black Women in the Light of Feminism. Translated by John Milton. *Revista Ártemis.* **27**(1), pp. 14–24.

Augusto, G. 2014. Language Should Not Keep Us Apart! Reflections towards a Black Transnational Praxis of Translation. *Callaloo.* **37**(2), pp. 632–647.

Baker, M. and Maier, C. 2011. Ethics in Interpreter & Translator Training: Critical Perspectives. *The Interpreter and Translator Trainer.* **5**(1), pp. 1–14.

BBC. 2021. *Amanda Gorman's Catalan translator dropped because of 'profile'.* [Online]. [Accessed 24 November 2023]. Available from: www.bbc.co.uk/news/world-europe-56340162

Bhopal, K. 2023. Critical Race Theory: Confronting, Challenging, and Rethinking White Privilege. *Annual Review of Sociology.* **48**, pp. 111–128. https://doi.org/10.1146/annurev-soc-031021-123710

Brisco, E. 2021. *Amanda Gorman tells Oprah about her connection to Maya Angelou: 'It was an amazing discovery'.* [Online]. [Accessed 4 December 2023]. Available from: www.eu.usatoday.com/story/entertainment/celebrities/2021/03/26/amanda-gorman-oprah-interview-cites-angelou-morrison-inspiration/6998957002/

Carlson, J., Leek, C., Casey, E., Tolman, R. and Allen, C. 2020. What's in a Name? A Synthesis of 'Allyship' Elements from Academic and Activist Literature. *Journal of Family Violence.* 35(8), pp. 889–898.

Deul, J. 2021. *English translation: Janice Deul's opinion piece about Gorman/Rijneveld.* Translated by Kotze, H. [Online]. [Accessed 24 November 2023]. Available from: www.haidee-kotze.medium.com/english-translation-janice-deuls-opinion-piece-about-gorman-rijneveld-8165a8ef4767

Drugan, J. and Megone, C. 2011. Bringing Ethics into Translator Training: An Integrated, Inter-disciplinary Approach. *The Interpreter and Translator Trainer.* 5, pp. 183–211.

Feagin, J.R. 2013. *The White Racial Frame: Centuries of Racial Framing and Counter-Framing.* 2nd ed. London and New York: Routledge.

Flood, A. 2021 *'Shocked by the uproar': Amanda Gorman's white translator quits.* [Online]. [Accessed 24 November 2023]. Available from: www.theguardian.com/books/2021/mar/01/amanda-gorman-white-translator-quits-marieke-lucas-rijneveld

Freeth, P.J. 2024. Introduction. In: Freeth, P.J. and Treviño, R. (eds.) *Beyond the Translator's Invisibility: Critical Reflections and New Perspectives.* Leuven: Leuven University Press, pp. 7–28.

Gorman, A. 2021. *Thank you! I would be nowhere without the women whose footsteps I dance in.* [Online]. [Accessed 4 December 2023]. Available from: www.twitter.com/TheAmandaGorman/status/1351979460640317441

gov.uk. 2021. *Writing about ethnicity.* [Online]. [Accessed 24 November 2023]. Available from: www.ethnicity-facts-figures.service.gov.uk/style-guide/writing-about-ethnicity

HESA. 2022. *Higher Education Staff Statistics: UK, 2020/21.* [Online]. [Accessed 24 November 2023]. Available from: www.hesa.ac.uk/news/01-02-2022/sb261-higher-education-staff-statistics

Holligan, A. 2021. *Why a white poet did not translate Amanda Gorman.* [Online]. [Accessed 24 November 2023]. Available from: www.bbc.co.uk/news/world-europe-56334369

Johnson, J.R., Rich, M., and Cargile, A.C. 2008. 'Why Are You Shoving This Stuff Down Our Throats?' Preparing Intercultural Educators to Challenge Performances of White Racism. *Journal of International and Intercultural Communication.* 1(2), pp. 113–135. https://doi.org/10.1080/17513050801891952

Keene, J. 2016. *Translating poetry, translating blackness.* [Online]. [Accessed 29 February 2024]. Available from: www.poetryfoundation.org/harriet/2016/04/translating-poetry-translating-blackness

Kenny, D. 2011. The ethics of machine translation. In: *Proceedings of the XI NZSTI National Conference, 4/5 June 2011, Auckland.* [Online]. [Accessed 18 December 2023]. Available from: www.core.ac.uk/download/pdf/11311284.pdf

Kotze, H. 2021. *Translation is the canary in the coalmine.* [Online]. [Accessed 24 November 2023]. Available from: www.haidee-kotze.medium.com/translation-is-the-canary-in-the-coalmine-c11c75a97660

Kotze, H. 2024. Concepts of Translators and Translation in Online Social Media: Construal and Contestation. *Translation Studies*. [Online first]. https://doi.org/10.1080/14781700.2023.2282581

Kotze, H. and Strowe, A. 2021. Response by Kotze and Strowe to 'Representing Experiential Knowledge'. *Translation Studies*, 14(3), pp. 250–363.

Krieger, Z. 2021a. *Hoe salty op een level van 1 tot Dode Zee ga ik klinken als ik zeg dat tig vrouwelijke spoken word artiesten van kleur (Babs Gons, Lisette Maneza etc.) dit beter hadden kunnen doen?*. [Online]. [Accessed 4 December 2023]. Available from: www.x.com/ZaireKrieger/status/13643432 87327444998?s=20

Krieger, Z. 2021b. *(Even het feit dat ik een van de weinige spoken word artiesten ben die in beide talen vloeiend schrijft ook even achterwege latend??? Why deze keuze?????)*. [Online]. [Accessed 4 December 2023]. Available from: www.x.com/ZaireKrieger/status/1364344146161451011?s=20

Krieger, Z. 2021c. *Jullie weten toch toen ik bij Spijkers met Koppen én bij Correspondent zei dat er geen ruimte was voor spoken word artiesten van kleur? This is exactly what I meant. Lmao. Cant believe Im still surprised.* [Online]. [Accessed 4 December 2023]. Available from: www.x.com/ZaireKrieger/status/1364344893527773184?s=20

Lambert, J. 2023. *Translation Ethics*. London and New York: Routledge.

Meulenhoff. 2021a. *Booker Prize-winnaar Marieke Lucas Rijneveld vertaalt Amanda Gormans poëzie.* [Online]. [Accessed 4 December 2023]. Available from: www.news.pressmailings.com/meulenhoff/persbericht-booker-prize-winnaar-marieke-lucas-rijneveld-vertaalt-amanda-gormans-poezie

Meulenhoff. 2021b. *Uitgeverij Meulenhoff over Marieke Lucas Rijneveld als vertaler van de poëzie van Amanda Gorman.* [Online]. [Accessed 4 December 2023]. Available from: www.x.com/Meulenhoff/status/1364605334795517953?s=20

Michallon, C. 2021. *Dutch writer Marieke Lucas Rijneveld steps down from assignment to translate Amanda Gorman's work.* [Online]. [Accessed 24 November 2023]. Available from: www.independent.co.uk/arts-entertainment/books/amanda-gorman-poem-translation-dutch-b1808315.html

Moniz, H. and Parra Escartín, C. eds. 2023. *Towards Responsible Machine Translation: Ethical and Legal Considerations in Machine Translation*. Cham: Springer.

PatrickGrayham. 2021. *Ze claimt dat Gorman zelf de keuze heeft gemaakt.* [Online]. [Accessed 4 December 2023]. Available from: www.twitter.com/PatrickGrayham/status/1364486470925504514/photo/1

Rijneveld, L. 2022. *A few weeks ago I wrote a poem (Vrij van beren) about choosing to be addressed with male pronouns from now on.* [Online]. [Accessed 4 December 2023]. Available from: www.twitter.com/Lucas_Rijneveld/status/1488 795220976312320

Society of Authors. 2021. *#TranslatorsOnTheCover – sign the open letter.* [Online]. [Accessed 24 November 2023]. Available from: www2.societyofauthors.org/tran slators-on-the-cover/

Sue, D.W., Lin, A.I., Torino, G.C., Capodilupo, C.M. and Rivera, D.P. 2009. Racial Microaggressions and Difficult Dialogues on Race in the Classroom. *Cultural Diversity and Ethnic Minority Psychology*. 15(2), pp. 183–190.

Tachtiris, C. 2024. *Translation and Race*. London and New York: Routledge.

Tachtiris, C. and Layne, P. 2023. Special Focus Introduction: Centering Black Cultural Production in Translation. *Studies in 20th & 21st Century Literature*. 47(1): article no: 4 [no pagination]. https://doi.org/10.4148/2334-4415.2257

Venuti, L. 1995 [2008/2018]. *The Translator's Invisibility*. London and New York: Routledge.

Whyte, C. 2022. *Online movement pushes that translators be named in game credits*. [Online]. [Accessed 24 November 2023]. Available from: www.slator.com/online-movement-pushes-that-translators-be-named-in-game-credits/

6

ASSESSING TERMINOLOGY AND PHRASEOLOGY IN SPECIALISED TRANSLATION PEDAGOGY USING *TRANSLATIONQ*

*Maria Teresa Musacchio and Carla Quinci**

Keywords: specialised translation; terminology; phraseology; computer-assisted revision; error analysis

1. Introduction

In a description of special language or language for specific purposes (LSP), i.e., the language of communication experts in a domain or field use (ISO 1087:2019), the first feature that is usually listed is terminology, since terms are easily spotted as the words or phrases that make a special language text difficult to comprehend. Though there is much more to a special language – e.g., the conventions typical of domain-specific communication as to register, genre(s), style, and syntax (Wright, 2011, pp. 244–5) – in specialised translation and specialised translator education, terms are often seen in their discourse- and text-building/construal function. As such, they are described together with the web of relations they weave in text, starting with phraseology or the set of collocations and colligations (Stubbs, 2009, p. 124) which are either peculiar of the domain/field or part of general language: "The specific linguistic means of expression always include domain-specific terminology and phraseology and also can cover stylistic or syntactic features" (ISO 1087:2019).

Throughout their learning in specialised translation, students are supposed to:

Acquire, develop and use thematic and domain-specific knowledge relevant to translation needs (mastering systems of concepts, methods of reasoning, presentation standards, *terminology and phraseology*, specialised sources etc.).

(EMT Expert Group, 2022, p. 8, our emphasis)

DOI: 10.4324/9781003440970-7

Of all special language features, terms are traditionally regarded as largely context-independent, especially in science and technology, where the concepts they designate are considered clearly defined and taxonomically organised. However, a mere look at any evolving science or technology suggests that, just like any other features of special languages, the terms and phrases in a field or domain are ultimately chosen to meet end-users' expectations concerning different forms of communication such as peer-to-peer, scientist to skilled practitioner, skilled practitioners to technicians, specialists to lay people, science writers addressing the lay public (Wright, 2011, p. 247). Trainees thus need to acquire great flexibility in handling all special language features with a view to avoiding the so-called "inappropriateness of the merely correct" (Wright, 1993, p. 69) and translating a text in "such a way that it will be accepted by the target discourse community as recognizably belonging to a genre, conforming to the rules and conventions of the genre, fulfilling identifiable communicative purposes" (Olohan, 2016, pp. 16–17).

For trainee translators, terminology management is a complex process because they need to develop skills to identify boundaries between terms and non-terms as these are often fuzzy. Choosing a term, a synonym or variant requires careful consideration of context. In science popularisation, for example, a full term or a term whose form is transparent may be preferred to the most frequent but rather opaque term used in expert-to-expert communication. To compound the issue, terms may undergo a process of determinologisation whereby they lose some of their properties in the transfer to use in general language, or of transterminologisation (Humbley and Picton, 2017), when they are used in another field/domain and acquire new properties. In any case, at the core of terminology work lies an investigation of multiword units that can turn out to be terms or phrases in LSP or general language (LGP). Investigating LSP collocations (also called specialised collocations in LSP lexicography) as non-idiomatic phraseology with a greater or lesser degree of fixedness can contribute to identifying term boundaries and distinguish terms from phraseology: "Some authors trace a boundary between terminology and phraseology, ascribing to multi-word terms a purely naming function (…), whereas the function of specialised collocations would be the descriptions of relations" (Giacomini, 2022, p. 57).

Acquiring thematic and domain-specific knowledge involves corpus-based/driven research to extract terms and study them, but also to identify the recurrent phrases that accompany them. It can be a lengthy process that requires much effort, though it is essential in learning specialised translation as it reflects the professional translators' approach to content, which is based primarily on text analysis and ultimately on language, as opposed to field or domain experts, who focus on content behind and beyond its linguistic realisation.

In this study, we will investigate terminology and phraseology from a didactic perspective based on the data drawn from translations by first-year MA students. These were extracted by using a specific software tool – *translationQ* – developed for the revision and assessment of translations to help improve the consistency and reliability of revision and scoring in translator education. Through the empirical data it provides, we are going to analyse the translation errors made by students in order to evaluate the development of two essential sub-competences in specialised translation, that is the thematic and info-mining competences. First, we outline research on tools for translation revision as an introduction to the framework of revision and assessment parameters developed at the University of Padova to be used in *translationQ*. Then we describe how the software can be used for teaching and research purposes (section 2). We further present the study's specific objectives and design (section 3) followed by a quantitative and qualitative analysis of the terminological and collocational/colligational errors made by two cohorts of students translating popular astronomy texts (section 4). Finally, we will draw our conclusions and describe how this analysis can be used in the classroom to (further) develop thematic and info-mining competences (section 5).

2.   Revising and assessing translations

In translation studies, the introduction of industry standards (such as EN 15038:2006 and ISO 17100:2015) and the development of CAT tools and machine translation systems have given new impetus to the debate on revision quality and criteria for the assessment of target texts at professional as well as training level. New avenues of research include defining revision and related activities and developing revision parameters (most notably Mossop, 2019), especially for application in the assessment of CAT and MT outputs (e.g., TAUS). Van Egdom (2021, p. 204) notes, however, that revision standards do not cover concrete procedures and constructive feedback in translator training is still underresearched.

In university-level translation programmes, translation revision and assessment usually focus on the translation product and consider the degree of competence the translator has achieved, the quality of the translation as a function of the allocated time, and the extent to which it meets the end-users' requirements (Scarpa, 2020, p. 318). In a didactic setting, providing feedback to students – whether for formative or summative assessment – often involves a huge amount of revisions of translations of the same source text. This can adversely affect the consistency and hence the quality and fairness of revisions as large volumes to revise take a toll on the memory of the reviser and the task repetitiveness can cause frustration when the same error is found repeatedly.

Many years ago, to ensure consistency and reliability of revisions, Pym[1] suggested using *Markin*,[2] a software program originally developed to mark students' compositions, and adapting it to the needs of translation revision. *Markin* has customisable error/reward buttons with a scorecard that can be used to provide feedback to students. However, each text has to be uploaded manually and then sent back to each student with the list of errors, good solutions, comments, and scores. No revision memory is created and general feedback to the class as a whole needs to be manually collated by the instructor, thus making the process extremely time-consuming. Since 2018, the software has no longer been updated and customer support has been discontinued.

Computer-assisted translation tools can also be used by translators to revise their own or other translators' texts, but do not allow to upload several translations of the same text to compare and evaluate. CAT tools have no scoring grid or other system to keep track and evaluate errors and translation memories are maintained to ensure that they contain "correct", good-quality output. As a result, they are not envisaged to contain information that can be used to provide feedback to trainee translators.

To bridge this gap in theory and practice and help solve revision problems, especially revisions of multiple translations of the same text, KU Leuven University and the Belgian company Televic developed *translationQ*, a cloud-based software tool that creates a revision memory (RM), i.e., a database where human-generated revisions are stored, and then retrieved and proposed to the human reviser whenever a match is identified with the new segments (van Egdom, 2021; van Egdom et al., 2018).

In an attempt to reduce human effort, RMs follow the same "ecology of translation" (Cronin, 2017) inherent in the principle "revise-save-reuse". RMs are essentially databases where translation errors, i.e., revised items, are stored together with their metadata, including the revision parameter, the penalty assigned for the error or the reward for a good solution, the suggested correction or improvement and further optional feedback (cf. 4.1). This means that repeated errors – whether in the same or different translations – are detected automatically and cannot be overlooked while the same error or good solution is assigned the same penalty/reward. This eliminates any cause of frustration, which positively reflects on the correction and evaluation process. The possibility to provide constructive feedback ensures that the reasons for correction are made clear to the trainees while revisions can be used to identify areas for improvement and devise activities to that end.

2.1 Adapting and editing revision parameters: industry vs education settings?

The default revision parameters implemented in *translationQ* are drawn from error categories in the language industry, i.e., the Dynamic Quality

Framework (DQF), which largely correspond to the criteria for translation revision outlined in ISO 17100 (ISO, 2015) translation standard (van Egdom, 2021, p. 213). In terms of categories and labelling of individual translation errors, the *translationQ* revision categories are drawn from Multidimensional Quality Metrics (MQM, 2023) – terminology, accuracy, linguistic conventions, style, locale conventions, audience appropriateness, design markup, and custom – which are broadly in line with those of ISO 5060 (ISO, 2024) scorecards even if they sometimes use different labels or list a parameter as a first-level category where it is a subcategory in ISO 5060 (ISO, 2024, pp. 19–21) or vice versa.

Though criticised for failing to avoid subjective judgements in their labels (van Egdom, 2021, p. 214) in translator education, scorecards help students to acquire the necessary metalanguage for revision, foster the students' reflection on their performance and learning, and provide clear, motivated feedback. In short, revision parameters are needed in translator training, but have to be adapted to the educational setting in which they are used. For this reason, a decision was made at the University of Padova to collect data on the revision parameters and scorecards used by translator educators in the different language combinations available. The parameters and scorecards were then discussed to tailor the *translationQ* framework to learning outcomes by comparison and contrast with Mossop's revision parameters (cf. Mossop, 2019).

Considerations of space do not allow to include the whole classification developed at the University of Padova, but the relevant categories for terminology and phraseology will be described. The category *terminology* has two types of translation errors, i.e., *inconsistent use of terminology* and *inconsistent with termbase*. *LSP phraseology* is listed as a translation error under the category *sublanguage* while LGP collocations fall under *genre style* together with *rhetorical preferences*. Although listing terminology errors under a different category from LSP phraseology may be problematic as it projects the idea that terminology is sort of context-independent and not part of sublanguage, i.e., special language, constraints in the number of subcategories that can be listed under any first-level category, and more generally in the extent to which the framework could be adapted, made this distinction unavoidable. Moreover, the importance of acquiring terminology management skills in specialised translator education cannot be overemphasised.

After testing the current framework for over three years, we now feel that the time has come to consider revising the system, though we still think that, unlike the terminology category, the distinction between LSP phraseology and LGP collocations is useful to capture the different phraseological components that a LSP text may exhibit, and as such are particularly useful to develop the students' thematic competence and info-mining skills.

3. Research design: objectives and methods

The implementation of *translationQ* at the University of Padova immediately proved a time-saving practice for revisers. Yet, the extent to which this software could assist not only for revising translations, but also for determining the students' learning gaps and needs in specialised translation courses was still to be explored. We thus decided to design an investigation aimed at determining the types of data that can be extracted from the software to assess the students' acquisition of thematic competence, and possibly compare their performances contrastively, not only with reference to their final scores, but with a focus on the types and frequency of any errors concerning the use of LSP. Precisely, our research questions were the following:

a) Which data can *translationQ* provide for the analysis and assessment of students' thematic competence?
b) How can these data be analysed for determining the students' level of thematic competence?
c) Can such analysis provide a basis for contrastive studies investigating the performances of different cohorts or those of the same cohort over time? And if so, how?

In light of our objectives, we decided to select two comparable datasets, i.e., those produced in two translation assignments dealing with the same subject field and completed by the same number of students (98). The two datasets meeting these requirements were those produced by two cohorts of first-year MA translation trainees having performed a translation test at the end of the course in English-to-Italian Specialised Translation 1. The course focused on the teaching of technical and scientific translation, with special reference to astronomy and science popularisation. In both academic years (2019/2020 and 2021/2022), the final tests consisted in the translation of two popularising articles on astronomy having equal length (approximately 250 words) and were carried out under the same conditions. Specifically, the students were all allowed to access the Internet and had to complete the task within 90 minutes.

The translations produced in both tasks were revised and assessed by the same reviser, i.e., the trainer who had held the course, by using *translationQ*. The data were all saved in the same RM, from which the errors concerning terminology and phraseology were eventually extracted following the methodology outlined in section 4.1. The analysis was thus limited to these categories of errors to quantitatively determine any changes in their number and distribution across the error types, the assignments, and the cohorts, as well as their potential causes from a qualitative perspective (see section 4.2).

4. From the classroom to the lab: data extraction, analysis, and discussion

To answer our research questions, we initially had to determine the types of data that can be extracted from *translationQ* and the types of insights they provide into translation trainees' performances which can be used for research and/or didactic purposes. These are presented in section 4.1 and are then used in the analysis offered in section 4.2, in which both quantitative and qualitative considerations on the students' terminological and phraseological errors are put forward.

4.1 Data extraction and triangulation

The data that *translationQ* can provide are mainly stored in the RM(s). They can be accessed via a dedicated menu and are displayed in a table in which each row includes all the metadata saved in individual entries. The metadata are organised in columns, which are labelled as follows: (a) *item*, i.e., the target text marked as an error; (b) *correction*, i.e., an alternative acceptable target-language version of the item; (c) *language pair*, which specifies the source and target languages; (d) *category*, i.e., the error type associated with the item; (e) *score*, i.e., the bonus or penalty attributed to the item in the form of a positive or negative value; (f) *feedback*, i.e., any further comments provided by the reviser; and (g) *frequency*, i.e., the number of times the item was found in the translations revised by using that RM. No data concerning the source-language term or phrase associated with the item are available. These can only be extracted manually by opening the settings of individual entries.

From our RMs, we could thus extract both quantitative and qualitative data concerning the severity (letter *e* above) and frequency (letter *f* above) of specific errors, and the corresponding target-language unacceptable versions (letter *a* above) and error types (letter *d* above). The main challenges in data extraction were due to the manual extraction of the metadata concerning the ST items originating the error – which can only be found by opening individual entries – and the presence of datasets produced in different translation assignments in the same RM. This represented a major drawback as filtering the data by assignment – which is not supported at the time of writing – is essential for distinguishing the errors made by different cohorts of students when translating the same ST and/or the same cohort of students in different assignments and studying their performance(s). Assignment-specific data were thus extracted manually. It should be noted that this was only possible because, even though the same RM was used for revising multiple assignments, each cohort had translated a different ST. Had more cohorts translated the same ST, distinguishing between the dataset produced by one or the other cohort would have been impossible.

By triangulating these data, the trainer/researcher can obtain crucial information, both quantitative and qualitative, about the students' learning outcomes and needs. Quantitively speaking, error frequency can be analysed in combination with:

- error categories, to determine the most frequent types of errors made by the students in each task and/or compare the frequency with which specific error types were made;
- target-text items, i.e., the errors, to identify the most common unacceptable translations proposed by the class;
- ST items, to identify the source-text passages that generated the highest number of errors, thus proving the most problematic;
- the number of students, to compare the performances of different classes or the performance of the same class at different stages of the training.

The analysis of the TT items and the ST items can also provide qualitative information concerning, on the one hand, the nature of the error, and, on the other hand, the nature of specific translation problems or the level and type of difficulty of specific STs.

As this study focuses on the use of LSP by trainees, the analysis in section 4.2 will only consider the data concerning the categories of terminological and phraseological errors. These are analysed contrastively to investigate whether the two components of domain-specific language pose the same translation problems in terms of the types of errors they result in and their frequency. A further contrastive perspective is also provided by comparing the datasets produced by the two samples of trainees under consideration, i.e., the 2019/2020 cohort (Astro 1) and the 2021/2022 cohort (Astro 2).

Specifically, the analysis considers and triangulates the following indicators:

- the cumulative frequency (CF), i.e., the overall frequency of terminological and phraseological errors per task;
- the number of target-text items (NoI-TT), i.e., the number of different TT terms/phrases marked as errors;
- the number of source-text items (NoI-ST), i.e., the number of different ST terms/phrases generating the errors;
- the mean of errors per student (E/S), which is calculated as the ratio between the CF and the number of students;
- the mean of errors per target-text item (E/TtI), which indicates the average frequency with which individual target-text solutions have been adopted;

- the mean of errors per source-text item (E/StI), which indicates the average frequency with which individual source-text items have resulted in translation errors;
- the distribution of errors across ST items, i.e., the number of different TT items originated by individual ST items and their frequencies;
- the absolute frequency (AF) of errors, i.e., the frequency with which each TT item was marked as an error.

4.2 Analysis and discussion

The analysis first adopted a quantitative approach for contrastively examining any potential trends in the (average) frequencies of translation errors (Figure 6.1). The CFs of the two assignments – ASTRO 1 in dark grey and ASTRO 2 in light grey – show an interesting discrepancy between terminological and phraseological errors, with the former being substantially identical in number in both tasks (F = 159 vs 151), and the latter being instead far more frequent in ASTRO 2 (F = 245) than in ASTRO 1 (F = 81). Since the number of participants is equal in both assignments, the same trend is visible also when considering the E/S as the values concerning terminology (m = 1.62 and 1.54) are considerably lower than those of phraseology in ASTRO 2 (m = 2.50) while they almost double phraseological errors in

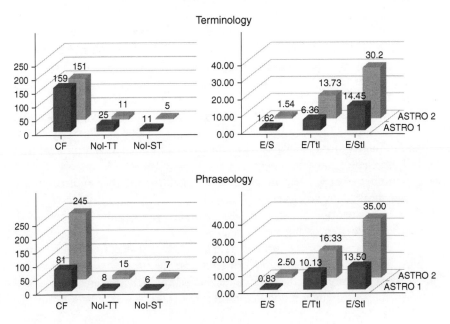

FIGURE 6.1   Quantitative contrastive analysis

ASTRO 1 (m = 0.83). This might be explained in terms of an imbalance in the cohorts' thematic competence or in the number and types of difficulties in the specific ST. The supposedly uneven levels of thematic competence would imply a similar scenario with reference to terminological errors, which had instead comparable CFs in both assignments.

CFs should be seen also in the light of the number of ST items which generated translation errors. We can observe that terminological errors have comparable CFs in the two tasks but different NoI-STs, with the one of ASTRO 1 (NoI-ST = 11) being more than double that of ASTRO 2 (NoI-ST = 5). Hence, ASTRO 2 made approximately the same number of terminological errors as ASTRO 1 despite the number of challenging items in the ST being half. This is particularly clear when calculating the mean of errors per ST item, which is almost twice as high in ASTRO 2 (E/StI = 30.2) as compared to ASTRO 1 (E/StI = 14.45). A similar tendency can also be observed with reference to phraseology, with the E/StI of ASTRO 2 (35.00) being two and a half times higher than that of ASTRO 1 (13.50). In this case, the NoI-STs are comparable in both tasks (6 for ASTRO 1 and 7 for ASTRO 2) while the CFs show a remarkable difference, with ASTRO 2 making over three times as many errors than the other cohort (CF = 81 for ASTRO 1 and 245 for ASTRO 2). This supports the hypothesis of a lower level of thematic competence in the second cohort, which largely underperformed ASTRO 1 in terms of the average number of errors per ST item. At the same time, this analysis suggests an imbalance in the number of difficulties in the two STs, which appear to have an equal number of phraseological challenges but a higher number of potential terminological difficulties. Such considerations can be useful for the trainer/ researcher when selecting the STs for future assignments and/or comparing multiple assignments by the same or different cohorts.

ASTRO 2 also scored higher means of errors per TT items with reference to both terminology (E/TtI = 13.73 vs 6.36) and phraseology (E/TtI = 16.33 vs 10.13), which indicates that the students in this cohort tended to make the same translation errors, while those in ASTRO 1 proposed a wider array of different unacceptable solutions.

To gain further insights into the variety of errors made by each cohort with respect to the different ST items, the investigation also looked at the distribution of errors per ST item (Figure 6.2), which shows how many different unacceptable solutions were proposed per each ST item and their corresponding absolute frequencies (AFs).

What clearly emerges from the distribution of terminological and phraseological errors in both assignments is the relatively low number of different target-language solutions for each ST item. With the sole exception of *wiggle*, for which ten different erroneous solutions were proposed by ASTRO 1, the other 28 ST items all have no more than four different unacceptable target-language equivalents. Precisely, only one ST item – i.e.,

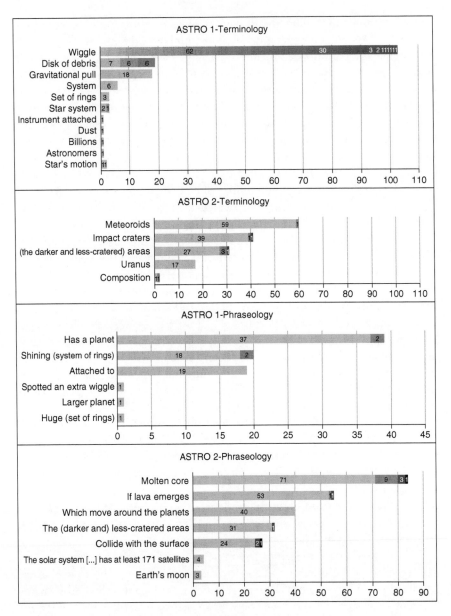

FIGURE 6.2   Distribution of errors per ST item

molten core – has four equivalents, five ST items have three equivalents, seven ST items have two equivalents, and the remaining 15 ST items only have one proposed unacceptable equivalent. Seven of the ST items having only one equivalent also scored very low frequencies, with the sole equivalent being found only once in the RM. At the same time, when multiple unacceptable target-language versions are proposed for the same ST item, one of these generally largely outnumbers the others, as is the case for the terms *wiggle*, *impact craters (the darkest and less-cratered), areas*, and the phrases *molten core, if lava emerges (the darkest and), less-cratered areas, collide with the surface, has a planet*, and *shining (system of rings)*. The students' faulty solutions thus generally tend to cluster around very few – where not single – target-language versions. This finding can have crucial consequences for translation teaching as error predictability, in terms of both the ST items which can prove more challenging and the TT versions which are more likely to be selected, can help the trainer to plan more targeted learning activities and raise the students' awareness about the main types of pitfalls specific LSPs might be fraught with and the main types of errors they might commit. To this end, it is also essential to analyse the most frequent TT items from a qualitative standpoint to determine their nature and their causes, at least tentatively.

As far as terminology is concerned, our analysis focuses on the seven ST items – three for ASTRO 1 and four for ASTRO 2 – having high-frequency equivalents, and examines their corresponding most frequent unacceptable target-language solutions. As shown in Table 6.1, most errors seem to be connected to very limited thematic – or even encyclopaedic – knowledge, which is not counterbalanced by info-mining skills. Specifically, some errors, i.e., *Uranio* (uranium) for *Uranus* and *meteoriti* (meteorites) for *meteoroids*, appear to be blunders due to a (temporary) loss of focus. On the one hand, the difference between the planet and the chemical element can be considered basic encyclopaedic knowledge and, on the other hand, the term meteoroids can be easily mistaken with meteorites, especially given its greater popularity and more frequent use also in general language.

The other equivalents show opposite approaches towards the use of calques. In cases where lexical calques should be adopted – i.e., *disco* instead of *anello* (lit. ring) for *disk of debris* and *da impatto* instead of *meteoritici* (lit. meteoritic) for *impact craters* – these are avoided, while they are retained in cases where the equivalent terms have different lexical structures – i.e., *spinta* instead of *attrazione* (lit. attraction) for *gravitational pull* and *aree* instead of *zone* (lit. zones, regions) for *areas*. These issues could have been easily solved by querying the Italian comparable corpus of astronomy that the students had at their disposal or by simply using the Web as a corpus, e.g., by limiting their searches to popularising magazines and websites. This points to a lack of awareness about their level of thematic competence but also to still underdeveloped info-mining skills.

Lexical calques also account for a considerable number of phraseological errors (see Table 6.2). In most cases, they are used in place of more technical phrases of which the trainees were possibly unaware or which simply caused

TABLE 6.1 Qualitative analysis of terminological errors

	ST item	TT item	AF	Correct solution	Reason(s)
ASTRO 1	...astronomers spotted an extra <u>wiggle</u> in the star's...	oscillazione/i movimento	62 30	perturbazione	Level of technicality (General language vs LSP)
	...may be caused by the <u>gravitational pull</u> of a second, larger planet...	spinta gravitazionale	18	attrazione gravitazionale	Interference > Lexical calque Level of technicality (General language vs LSP)
	... if the planet exists it is probably surrounded by a <u>disk of debris</u> or a huge set of rings	anello di polvere anello di detriti	13 (7+6)	disco	Limited thematic knowledge
ASTRO 2	a constant bombardment by <u>meteoroids</u>	meteoriti	59	meteoroidi	Limited thematic knowledge
	the Earth's moon is covered with <u>impact craters</u>	crateri meteoritici	39	crateri da impatto	Limited thematic knowledge
	these are the darker and less-cratered <u>areas</u> of our satellite	aree	27	zone	Interference > Lexical calque
	moons such as those orbiting Jupiter, Saturn and <u>Uranus.</u>	Uranio	17	Urano	Limited SL or thematic knowledge

TABLE 6.2 Qualitative analysis of phraseological errors

	ST item	TT item	AF	Correct solution	Reason(s)
ASTRO 1	Proxima Centauri [...] has a planet roughly the same size as Earth...	ha/avere un pianeta	37	ospita un pianeta	Interference > Lexical calque Level of technicality (General language vs LSP)
	[They] used SPHERE, an instrument attached to the Very Large Telescope in Chile....	collegato al	19	montato sul	Limited thematic knowledge
	...it is surrounded by a huge disk of dust or even a shining system of rings.	un sistema di anelli brillante	18	un sistema di anelli luminoso	Level of technicality (General language vs LSP) Limited thematic knowledge
ASTRO 2	a rocky planet with a molten core and volcanoes,	nucleo (interno) (allo stato) fuso	71	nucleo fluido	Level of technicality (General language vs LSP) Limited thematic knowledge
	If lava emerges from the interior...	lava emersa/che emerge	53	lava fuoriuscita/che fuoriesce	Interference > Lexical calque
	satellites, also called moons, which move around the planets,	che si muovono intorno/ attorno	40	ruotano intorno	Interference > Lexical calque
	these are the darker and less-cratered areas of our satellite	e meno craterizzate	31	con meno crateri	Interference > Lexical calque
	bombardment by meteoroids that collide with the surface.	si scontrano/rono/si sono scontrati con/contro la sua superficie	24	si schiantano	Level of technicality (General language vs LSP) Limited thematic knowledge

a source-language interference due to the strong morphological resemblance of the English phrase and the Italian most direct literal equivalent, e.g., *avere un pianeta* instead of *ospitare* (lit. to host), *emergere* instead of *fuoriuscire* (lit. to come out), and *muoversi attorno/intorno* instead of *ruotare* (lit. to revolve around). In one case, i.e., *meno craterizzate*, the lexical calque even produces a neologism given the lack of a corresponding Italian adjective, which again suggests a source-language interference.

Two out of the remaining phraseological errors are due to an inadequate level of technicality, with general-language phrases being used in specialised contexts, e.g., *brillante* (lit. shining/bright) instead of *luminoso* (lit. shining/bright), *scontrarsi* (lit. to clash/collide) instead of *schiantarsi* (lit. to crash/collide), and *nucleo fuso* (lit. molten) instead of *nucleo fluido* (lit. fluid). Finally, the use of *collegato al* (lit. connected to) rather than *montato sul* (lit. installed/mounted) reveals a lack of thematic knowledge as the instrument referred to in the text is actually mounted on the telescope rather than just connected to it. Lexical calques thus prove to be at the core of terminological and phraseological errors, as also emerged in previous studies concerning different cohorts and different LSPs (Quinci, 2023; Quinci and Musacchio, 2023), though in these previous analyses they were never avoided when necessary. They appear to be largely caused by source-language interference, which makes the students struggle to distinguish between general language and LSP.

5. Back to the classroom: conclusions, main applications, and cost-benefit ratio

This chapter aimed to show how the computer-assisted revision tool *translationQ* can be implemented in the translation classroom for didactic and research purposes. Specifically, it sought to determine the types of data available and the way they can be analysed to assess the students' thematic and info-mining competences, also from a contrastive perspective.

As explained in section 4.1, the data useful for the purposes of this analysis can mainly be extracted automatically from the revision memory and can be used also in combination with one another to analyse the frequency and nature of specific (types of) translation errors. Our investigation considered the datasets produced by two cohorts of 98 first-year MA translation trainees, who completed two different translation assignments concerning the popularisation of astronomy. Given the objectives of the study, the analysis was limited to two error types, i.e., terminological and phraseological errors.

The quantitative analysis showed that the two source texts selected for the assignments included a comparable number of terminological problems, while phraseological ones were more common in one of them. However, we could compare the two cohorts' performances by considering the average number of errors made per each terminological or phraseological problem in the source text. This showed that the first cohort largely outperformed the second one, thus proving how this tool and type of analysis can serve for measuring the acquisition of thematic competence by trainees from a comparative – or longitudinal – perspective. The distribution of errors was also investigated and revealed that the terminological and phraseological items resulting in translation errors are in fact very few. Errors are not evenly distributed across multiple source-text items, but rather tend to cluster around 1–3 terms and phrases, which account for the majority of errors. Likewise, unacceptable target-language solutions appear little varied, with the same or very similar unacceptable equivalents being proposed by more than half of the students. This makes these types of errors predictable in terms of both the source-language items which can originate them and the unacceptable target-language solutions that are more likely to be selected.

When analysed qualitatively, the most frequent errors appear to be generally connected to source-language interference resulting in the adoption of lexical calques, most of which were possibly chosen because of their morphological closeness with the source-language items. Unacceptable calques also derived from the preference for general over special language and/or the inadequate consideration of the level of specialisation of the target-language readership.

In conclusion, computer-assisted revision can have three main applications in translation and revision didactics. First, the parallel corpus of translation errors in the RM can be used by the trainer to study unacceptable solutions, discuss them with trainees, and develop specific training activities to anticipate the most common types of mistakes. Possible correlations between specific types of errors and domain-specific languages or types of training can also emerge by studying the corpus. Second, *translationQ* can assist in monitoring individual or group performances by comparing different tasks by the same class or different samples. As such, it would also be a tool to test the efficacy of specific training strategies. Third, the data can serve to identify the ST segments proving to be more challenging for trainees so as to predict the ST difficulty, also comparatively, as well as to select the segments to evaluate when assessing translation quality through sampling procedures.

Moreover, *translationQ* can be used by the trainees as revisers. This would help them realise the importance of intratextual terminological consistency as the software automatically detects repeated errors within the same text. They could also reflect upon the different weights of translation errors depending on their nature, the text function, and the purpose of revision. Since they are compelled to assign a score to each error, they are encouraged to reflect upon these aspects and empirically realise that, for instance, language errors are generally less severe than accuracy ones. Finally, the presence of multiple versions to revise could limit their tendency to over-revision by raising their awareness about the existence of different equally viable translations.

Indirectly, this would also widen their linguistic repertoire and help them consolidate their specialised vocabulary through repeated readings of the same source- and target-language LSPs.

From the end-user's perspective, CAR proved a valuable technology with a positive cost-benefit ratio. As happened with translation memories back in the 1990s, the implementation of a database in which previous revision work can be stored and automatically retrieved whenever useful represents a major benefit for the reviser as it minimises the risk of missing or errors while increasing the consistency of error scoring. In this respect, it not only assists the reviser, but also ensures a fair assessment across translators, across revisers, and over time, which appears equally crucial in translator training and the translation market. Still, the return on investment can only be seen in the long run, i.e., as revision memories are populated with revision units and thus ensure an increasing number of matches.

On the part of the translator, *translationQ* requires no previous training or effort as the interface is quite intuitive and translations can be easily entered manually segment by segment or by uploading the target-text file and eventually adjusting any wrong alignments with the source-text segments. Another benefit is the feedback provided to the translator, who receives a text file with tracked changes and comments including the error labels. Conversely, training and practice are needed for the reviser to familiarise themselves with the revision procedure and – most importantly – to develop an effective approach to the selection of the error to minimise the number of irrelevant matches resulting from decontextualised items (e.g., "and", which might apply to all "and" in the text or the segment). Initially, the delayed benefits of using revision memories are made even less visible to the reviser due to the time required by the revision procedure. Differently from translation memories, which automatically grow when new segments are confirmed, revision memories need the manual intervention of the reviser not only for adding the item to be corrected and the corresponding correction, but also for selecting the penalty/bonus and the label to be assigned as well as other customisable options, e.g., the possibility to limit the match to the given segment or apply the penalty also to repeated errors within the same translation, or the semi-automatic propagation of the correction to other translations. This can make revision particularly lengthy and frustrating when working with unpopulated memories. Yet, the benefits of CAR soon become clear when using populated memories and getting matches for most errors in the translation.

Despite the limitations surviving in the current version, e.g., the lack of more refined and diverse filters for the revision memories or an option for enabling/disabling case sensitiveness, as well as the inability to identify fuzzy matches, the cost-benefit ratio of *translationQ* remains highly positive due to the invaluable increase in the quality and consistency of revision as well as the much-reduced burden of frustration and repetitiveness put on the reviser.

As in the case of CAT, the implementation of glossaries, termbases, and artificial intelligence might bring CAR to a new level. Terminological and phraseological checks might become semi-automatic and customised grammar rules or stylistic conventions might be used as a reference for the system to identify potential errors and suggest corrections. The renewed attention that ISO 5060 (ISO, 2024) will bring to quality metrics and error scoring might attract investment in this field and allow the development of increasingly sophisticated systems.

Notes

* Maria Teresa Musacchio wrote sections 1 and 2; Carla Quinci wrote sections 3, 4, and 5.
1 Personal communication.
2 www.markin.co.uk/update/markin_update.php

References

Cronin, M. 2017. *Eco-translation. Translation and Ecology in the Age of the Anthropocene.* Abingdon and New York: Routledge.

EMT Expert Group. 2009. Competences for Professional Translators, Experts in Multilingual and Multimedia Communication.

EMT Expert Group. 2022. EMT Competence Framework 2022 [Online]. Available from: www.ec.europa.eu/info/resources-partners/european-masters-translation-emt/european-masters-translation-emt-explained_en.

EN. 2006. EN 15038 – Translation Services – Service Requirements.

Giacomini, L. 2022. The Contextual Behaviour of Specialised Collocations: Typology and Lexicographic Treatment. *Yearbook of Phraseology.* 13(1), pp. 55–80.

Humbley, J. and Picton, A. 2017. Introduction: Multiple Perspectives on Terminological Variation. In: P. Drouin, A. Francœur, J. Humbley and A. Picton, eds. *Multiple Perspectives on Terminological Variation.* Amsterdam and Philadelphia: John Benjamins, pp. 1–7.

Hurtado Albir, A. (Ed.) 2017. *Researching Translation Competence by PACTE Group.* Amsterdam and Philadelphia: John Benjamins. https://doi.org/10.1075/btl.127.

ISO. 2015. ISO 17100 – Translation Services — Requirements for Translation Services.

ISO. 2019. ISO 1087 – Terminology Work and Terminology Science — Vocabulary.

ISO. 2024. ISO 5060 – Translation Services — Evaluation of Translation Output — General Guidance.

Mossop, B. 2019. *Revising and Editing for Translators.* 4th ed. London and New York: Routledge.

MQM 2023. Multidimensional Quality Metrics. [Accessed 22 September 2023]. Available from: www.themqm.org/error-types-2/1_scorecards/.

Olohan, M. 2016. *Scientific and Technical Translation.* Abingdon: Routledge.

Quinci, C. 2023. Using Technology to Investigate Thematic Competence in Specialised Translation: A Follow-Up. In: G. Palumbo, K. Peruzzo and G. Pontrandolfo, eds. *What's Special about Specialised Translation? Essays in Honour of Federica Scarpa*. Bern: Peter Lang, pp. 217–245.

Quinci, C. and Musacchio, M.T. 2023. Analysing, Revising and Teaching LSP Phraseology: An Integrated Approach. In: G. Henrot Sostero, ed. *Alle radici della frasologia europea*. Bern: Peter Lang, pp. 529–550.

Scarpa, F. 2020. *Research and Professional Practice in Specialised Translation*. London: Palgrave.

Stubbs, M. 2009. The Search for Units of Meaning: Sinclair on Empirical Semantics. *Applied Linguistics*. 30(1), pp. 115–137.

van Egdom, G.-W. 2021. Improving Revision Quality in Translator Training with translationQ. In: M. Koponen, B. Mossop, I. S. Robert and G. Scocchera, eds. *Translation Revision and Post-editing Industry Practices and Cognitive Processes*. London and New York: Routledge, pp. 203–225.

van Egdom, G.-W., Segers, W., Bloemen, H., Kockaert, H.J. and Wylin, B. 2018. Revising and Evaluating with TranslationQ. Bayt Al-Hikma. *Journal for Translation Studies*. 2018(2), pp. 25–56.

Wright, S.E. 2011. Scientific, Technical, and Medical Translation. In: K. Malmkjær and K. Windle, eds. *The Oxford Handbook of Translation Studies*. Oxford: Oxford University Press, pp. 243–261.

Wright, S.E. 1993. The Inappropriateness of The Merely Correct: Stylistic Considerations in Scientific and Technical Writing. In: S.E. Wright and L.D. Jr. Wright eds. *Scientific and Technical Translation*. Amsterdam and Philadelphia: John Benjamins, pp. 69–86.

PART II

Collaborative pedagogies

7

EVALUATING PROJECT-BASED LEARNING IN TRANSLATION CLASSROOMS

A case study

Xijinyan Chen, Qifei Kao, Chenqing Song, Tong Wu, and Lulu Lun

Keywords: translation pedagogy; project-based learning; problem-solving; teamwork; advantages and disadvantages of project-based learning

1. Introduction

The translation and localisation industry has undergone rapid changes since COVID-19, with decreased demands in previously popular areas like travel and leisure and increased needs in healthcare and pharmaceutical markets (CSA Research, 2020). These changes, coupled with the rise of online working models, increased requirements for tech-focused solutions, and diverse forms of cooperation (Luo, 2021), highlight the importance of creative and flexible translation pedagogical approaches to prepare translator trainees for these shifting contexts. In addition to acquiring translation and language-related knowledge and skills, trainees must improve their problem-solving skills and teamwork abilities and adapt to online work to enhance their employability and competitiveness in post-pandemic environments.

Project-Based Learning (PjBL) is a widely recognised pedagogical approach that effectively engages students in real-world projects, fostering the development of critical thinking, problem-solving, and collaboration skills (PBLWorks, 2023). In an academic context, translation courses are particularly suitable for PjBL. This suitability arises from two key factors: first, commercial translation behaviours inherently exhibit project-like characteristics, and second, when teaching translation, instructors often use authentic translation materials to simulate real-world tasks. In many practical translation courses offered at the university level, students do numerous translation exercises by adopting translation strategies from textbooks and receive feedback from

DOI: 10.4324/9781003440970-9

instructors and peers. This methodology of translation training places more emphasis on acquiring individual translation skills than the professional skills required by real-world projects, despite the inherently project-like nature of translation in the industry. Consequently, students entering the professional translation field often need to enhance essential non-translation skills such as project management, time management, multitasking, and teamwork, as highlighted in the European Master's in Translation (EMT) competence framework (EMT Board, 2022). While these novice translators may excel at translating texts, they may encounter difficulties when attempting to complete projects independently or as part of a team.

To bridge this instructional disparity, a research team comprising five Translation Studies scholars from the United States and China conducted a quasi-experimental study on implementing PjBL in translation classrooms during the summer of 2022. The study assessed the impact of using PjBL on students' translation skills and career-related transferable skills and evaluated the efficacy of using PjBL in teaching translation. Specifically, the study sought to answer two key questions: 1) To what extent does integrating PjBL enhance the development of essential non-translation skills needed by the industry? 2) What are the advantages and disadvantages of using the PjBL model in the translation classroom? Our findings suggest that 1) the incorporation of PjBL into translation classrooms proves effective in equipping students with practical exposure to real-world translation projects and essential non-translation skills, including problem-solving skills and teamwork abilities, thereby preparing them comprehensively for future careers. However, 2) while the employment of the PjBL model yields advantages in acquainting students with industry dynamics, it also exhibits certain drawbacks, notably the substantial time commitment required and concerns regarding the sustainability of source texts.

2. Literature review

Project-based learning (PjBL) is a pedagogical approach that promotes experiential learning and has gained global recognition for fostering deep learning, critical thinking, and collaboration. John Dewey and William Heard Kilpatrick were early proponents of PjBL, emphasising the value of engaging students in meaningful tasks that simulate real-world scenarios (Condliffe et al., 2017).

Dewey's notion of personal investment in education and Kilpatrick's belief in the relevance of education to students' lives form the foundation of PBL philosophy. According to Dewey, students develop personal investment by engaging in authentic, meaningful tasks that simulate real-world scenarios. In *The School and Society* (1900), he discusses the value of teaching occupational skills and argues that vocational education serves as a vehicle for preparing students for their future in society. Kilpatrick, heavily influenced by Dewey's philosophy, believes that education should be more relevant to students' lives and that PBL is an effective way to achieve this goal. Kilpatrick's work, *Project Method* (1918), exemplifies PjBL as a means of applying knowledge and skills to real-world problems, as seen in High Tech High schools in San Diego, California, where teachers combine "grade-level content, real-world skills, and student interests" in designing projects that engage students in learning (Pieratt, 2010, p. 60).

In higher education, PjBL succeeds in capstone courses, research projects, and service learning (Klyoster et al., 2018). It has been found to enhance critical thinking skills, teamwork, and workplace readiness in business education (Danford, 2006), foster creativity and lifelong learning in STEM fields (Wengrowicz et al., 2017), and increase motivation and engagement in science education (Krajcik and Blumenfeld, 2006). Clearly, the application of PjBL finds limited use in certain humanities fields, such as literature. The discrepancy may be attributed to the humanities' emphasis on traditional teaching methods and literary analysis skills, which may not align as seamlessly with project-based learning. However, exploring ways to incorporate PjBL into humanities could potentially offer students interdisciplinary opportunities and comprehensive learning experiences.

In addition, challenges such as time constraints, resource limitations, assessment methods, student readiness, community partnerships, and flexibility may arise during PjBL implementation (Imaz, 2021). Concerns about students' workload, self-directed learning, and the potential narrow problem focus also occur in medical education (Dolmans et al., 2016).

Within the broader context of translation education, the utilisation of Project-Based Learning (PjBL) has been extensively explored in various studies, employing both qualitative and quantitative methodologies to assess its advantages and drawbacks. Li et al. (2015) focused on student reception and provided a case study of teaching business translation in the Chinese context. The study concludes that PjBL enhances many necessary skills beyond translation-specific competencies, such as critical thinking, interpersonal communication, collaboration, and research based on student questionnaires. However, this study did not delve into the potential downsides of this teaching method. In contrast, García González and Veiga Díaz (2015) conducted a qualitative case study addressing both the advantages and disadvantages of PjBL, such as time consumption and limited experience in teamwork activities.

In a more recent qualitative study, Herget (2020) demonstrates the benefits of PjBL in a master's translation course that integrates a computer-assisted translation tool, Memsource. The study concludes that this method offers problem-solving and collaborative strategies required in the real world. Mixed methods, as utilised by Moghaddas and Khoshsaligheh (2019), reveal improvements in critical thinking and partial enhancements in teamwork skills among Iranian university students. The authors believe that the lack of significant improvement in teamwork skills may be due to the Iranian context and educational background. Moreover, students may not be empowered with effective collaboration in the short term.

The International Network of Simulated Translation Bureaus (INSTB) emerges as a noteworthy example of PjBL implementation, specifically focused on simulated translation environments. This approach involves collaborative projects from initiation to completion, aligning with the findings of Li et al. (2015). The simulated translation bureau model, exemplified by INSTB, further supports these conclusions by immersing students in real-life conditions, emphasising client interaction, project preparation, translation processes, and final product delivery (INSTB, 2017; Kerremans & Van Egdom, 2018). Within simulated translation bureaus, student teams collaborate comprehensively, navigating translation projects from inception to conclusion. This hands-on, market-oriented experience aims to bolster graduate employability, with all members collectively committed to replicating real-life conditions.

Turning to specific studies within this context, Buysschaert's paper (2017) reviews the current practices surrounding the simulated translation bureaus implemented by INSTB members. The review suggests that authentic experiential learning through simulated translation bureaus is well-received by students, welcomed by teachers, and highly valued by employers. This qualitative assessment adds depth to understanding the positive reception of simulated translation bureaus among key stakeholders. Shifting the focus to another notable contribution, Paradowska's paper (2021) presents an authentic collaborative translation project carried out in the spring of 2019, highlighting the development of service provision competence, organisational skills, interpersonal skills, and information competence, all of which are highly desirable in translators. The evaluation of the project's success is based on various data sources, providing a rich qualitative understanding of the outcomes of authentic collaborative translation projects. In a different vein, Van Egdom's study (2020) designed and tested a survey instrument for perceived entrepreneurial competence and self-efficacy to gauge the effect of entrepreneurial Simulated Translation Bureau activities. This research provides valuable quantitative insights into the impact of simulated translation bureaus on students' entrepreneurial skills and self-efficacy. Transitioning between these studies, it becomes evident that a comprehensive exploration of PjBL within simulated translation environments involves diverse research, blending qualitative and quantitative methodologies to gain a holistic understanding of its impact on students and stakeholders.

While existing studies shed light on the potential benefits and a few challenges of implementing PBL in translation education, there is a need for further investigation using mixed methods to assess its impact on students' translation skills and career-related transferable skills and comprehensively examine both the advantages and disadvantages of the PjBL model. Mixed methods research is essential as the research questions require a more profound, multi-dimensional understanding of the PjBL model, and the benefits, challenges, and impacts need to be assessed from both quantitative and qualitative perspectives to inform policy, practice, and future research. Additionally, this study can contribute to optimising the implementation of PjBL in diverse contexts and among various student populations.

3. Methods

This quasi-experimental study adopted project-based teaching in an online learning environment. The research team recruited college-level participants with diverse backgrounds to complete a translation project of approximately 20,000 words during a two-week online translation workshop in the summer of 2022. The project consists of English-written documents pertaining to school policy, student registration, health, and post-COVID recovery plans; all were created for parents to read. These documents were identified as critical but incomprehensible, partially or entirely, to immigrant parents with limited English proficiency. To ensure the relevance of the materials, the research team collaborated with the Vestal School District in New York State, finalising the selection of documents deemed essential for the families. Furthermore, student participants conducted interviews with school officials and local parents via Zoom, aiming to understand their specific needs and requirements comprehensively.

3.1 Participants

Participants were undergraduate and graduate students from universities in China. Participation in the translation workshop was voluntary, and participants had the right to withdraw from the study at any stage. Those who expressed interest were informed of the benefits of participation, which included opportunities to interact with fellow translation enthusiasts, access complimentary translation skill enhancement sessions, and refine their translation abilities. The objective of the study was not disclosed to the participants. A total of 45 individuals signed up for the workshop and completed all the onboarding steps, which included a pre-workshop translation exercise and a pre-workshop questionnaire. Ultimately, 20 participants successfully completed the workshop, and Table 7.1 provides a comprehensive overview of the sample characteristics. Among the participants, four were male, and 16 were female. Four participants were enrolled in graduate programs specialising in MTI (Master of Translation and Interpretation) at Chinese universities, while the remaining 16 were pursuing undergraduate degrees in diverse

TABLE 7.1 Participants' profile

	Personal and academic-related characteristics	*N (%)*
Gender		
	Male	4 (20)
	Female	16 (80)
Year of college		
	First year	5 (25)
	Second year	7 (35)
	Third year	3 (15)
	Fourth year	1 (5)
	Postgraduate	4 (20)
Major		
	Translation and interpreting, including MTI	15 (75)
	English	2 (10)
	Teaching Chinese as a foreign language	1 (5)
	Product design	1 (5)
	Digital media arts	1 (5)

academic disciplines such as English, Teaching Chinese as a Foreign Language, and Product Design. Individuals who have had overseas living or studying experiences were excluded to maintain similar participant experiences, allowing clearer observation of changes within the two-week period.

3.2 Methods

The study employed a mixed-method approach, incorporating qualitative and quantitative data collection and analysis methods. Quantitative data were collected through two questionnaires (see the English versions through the link[1]) to assess the pre- and post-workshop problem-solving skills and teamwork awareness, and ability of the trainees. Excel was used to calculate and analyse the obtained scores, enabling the evaluation of significant changes between the pre- and post-intervention scores. Qualitative data, on the other hand, were collected through students' reflection journals to explore potential reasons and factors contributing to the observed differences in the pre- and post-workshop quantitative data and to examine the merits and drawbacks associated with the PjBL model. The qualitative analysis involved a manual coding process, where key themes were identified by creating a coding system to organise and categorise the data. Patterns and connections were sought within the data, and interpretations were made to understand the underlying meanings and implications. Representative quotes were selected to support and illustrate the identified themes. To ensure the credibility of the findings, the qualitative data were triangulated with the quantitative data, providing a comprehensive understanding of the research phenomena. Moreover, input from co-authors was sought to validate the interpretations and conclusions drawn from the analysis, thus ensuring the rigour and reliability of the study's findings.

3.3 Procedure

The study was conducted in three phases: the pre-workshop preparation stage, the workshop and data collection stage, and the post-workshop data analysis stage.

During the pre-workshop preparation stage, the research team took the following steps to ensure effective workshop planning. Starting in September 2021, the team held weekly meetings to review the literature on PjBL, select an appropriate framework, and develop the workshop plan. In March 2022, the Institutional Review Board of Wake Forest University approved the project (IRB00024585), and participant recruitment began. Digital flyers were distributed on social media platforms, including student groups on WeChat, to attract potential participants, who then filled out sign-up forms. In April, the team established communication with school officials and parents who agreed to be interviewed. An online information session was conducted in late April, providing details on the workshop's timing, format, and requirements. Around 100 participants attended the session, and their questions and concerns were documented. In May, a pre-workshop translation exercise was administered as a prerequisite, and participants who completed it by the deadline were invited to join the workshop. About a month before the workshop commenced, the 45 invited participants attended orientation sessions in small groups, where the research team, including the workshop instructors, interacted with each participant to understand their backgrounds, self-perceived translation competence, and expectations. Participants who would like to take part in the workshop and the study provided consent and completed a pre-workshop questionnaire focussing on their current understanding of teamwork ability and problem-solving skills.

During the workshop stage, the research team conducted a two-week translation workshop designed and structured to engage participants in a collaborative process for translating real-world projects pre-selected by the instructors. The workshop aimed to provide participants with practical translation experience, enhance their teamwork and time management skills, and offer opportunities for reflection and feedback.

The timeline and each week's contents were as follows:

Week 1 – Translation practice:

> In Week 1, participants were assigned translation works, which they did as pre-lecture tasks in groups assigned by instructors, and joined three online

lectures that each lasted about two hours on Monday, Wednesday, and Friday. They also prepared for interviews with school officials and parents in Week 2.

1. Asynchronous translation practice
   • Participants were randomly assigned to groups of four and assigned translation tasks of approximately 1,500 words before the first and second synchronous sessions.
   • Each group collaborated to divide the task into four sections, with each participant taking on a different role: project manager, translator, editor/proofreader, and simulated "client" for each section.
   • Prior to the first two synchronous sessions, participants had the opportunity to work with various team members. This collaborative phase centred on the translation of authentic project documents. Simultaneously, participants maintained daily reflection journals to record challenging terminology and expressions encountered during the translation process.

2. Synchronous lecture sessions
   • During the lectures, the instructors provided detailed analyses of difficult-to-translate expressions and cultural concepts and facilitated discussions.
   • The sessions also covered critical skills for translators, including time management, teamwork, communication skills, and quality control, some of which were requested by students in their reflections.

3. Interview preparation
   • Participants signed up for interview slots with the school officials and parent interviewees, scheduled for the following Tuesday.

4. Week 2 translation preparation
   • At the end of the week, participants were grouped based on the number of retained participants and their previous collaborating experience.
   • Each group selected a real-world translation project from a list provided by the instructors.

Week 2 – Translation project:

In Week 2, the participants' learning pattern remained similar to Week 1 with one key difference: they were given the freedom to choose their own translation tasks from the projects provided by the instructors. They joined three two hour-long online lectures and conducted group interviews with real clients, i.e., school officials and parents. They also completed an end-of-workshop translation evaluation and a questionnaire.

1. Asynchronous translation project
   • Participants continued collaborating with their team members on their translation projects using the techniques they learned in the previous week.

2. Synchronous lecture sessions
   - Participants received feedback from the instructors during the synchronous sessions held on Monday, Wednesday, and Friday.
   - They also had the opportunity to meet with team members in a virtual breakout room to reflect on their translation.
3. Interviews
   - On Tuesday, participants conducted group interviews with parents and school officials, documenting the process and their reflections in written reports. To encourage collaboration with members from different teams, instructors made minor adjustments to the interview grouping based on the sign-up from Week 1. The interview groups were different from their Week 2 translation project groups.
   - Student participants interviewed a total of seven parents and two school officials from the Vestal School District, with each interview lasting approximately 20 minutes.
   - Following the interviews, participants reviewed and revised their translations based on the insights gained from the interview process.
4. Wrap-up
   - Between the fifth and final synchronous sessions, participants translated a separate document of similar difficulty and length to assess changes in their problem-solving and teamwork skills and awareness.
   - Before the conclusion of the final synchronous session, all participants completed a post-workshop questionnaire.

The post-workshop data analysis stage served as the final phase of the study, following the pre-workshop preparation stage and the two-week workshop stage. During this stage, the researchers conducted a comprehensive analysis of the collected data, which encompassed both quantitative and qualitative components. The quantitative data included an evaluation of students' self-perceived transferable skills, while the qualitative data comprised students' reflection journals. A total of 20 student participants actively participated in all workshop sessions and diligently completed all translation assignments, resulting in the production of approximately 20,000 translated words.

3.4   Quantitative data collection: pre- and post-workshop questionnaires

Participants in this study were required to complete both a pre-workshop questionnaire before the start of the workshop and a post-workshop questionnaire prior to the conclusion of the final live session. The questionnaires incorporated a majority of the questions from a collection of 35 items sourced from the Problem-Solving Inventory (PSI) developed by Heppner and Peterson (1982), as well as the Behaviorally Anchored Rating Scale (BARS) established by Ohland et al. (2012), which is widely utilised for self and peer evaluation of teamwork abilities. These assessment methods have undergone extensive research and validation. For example, previous studies such as Marian et al. (2012) have successfully employed the PSI to evaluate problem-solving skills within a sample of Romanian participants, confirming the efficacy and generalisability of the inventory. Matosas-López and Cuevas-Molano (2022) have examined the validity and reliability of an adapted BARS instrument designed to assess teaching effectiveness in blended learning environments. Their findings supported the impeccable validity and reliability of the BARS when evaluating teaching efficacy in blended learning methodologies.

Both the pre- and post-workshop questionnaires were meticulously structured into three sections. The first section collected demographic information and general insights regarding translation and the workshop. The second section assessed participants' teamwork skills, while the third section evaluated their problem-solving abilities. The pre-workshop questionnaire established baseline measurements for participants' teamwork and problem-solving skills in a quantitative manner. The post-workshop questionnaire closely resembled the pre-workshop version but included scenario-based questions to assess participants' ability to apply their newly acquired skills in real-world situations. Notably, many of the scale rating questions in the pre-workshop questionnaire had corresponding counterparts in the post-workshop questionnaire, facilitating quantitative analysis and allowing for a comparison of participants' self-assessments before and after the workshop. These situational questions gauged participants' practical application of teamwork and problem-solving abilities following the training.

3.5 Qualitative data collection: reflection journals

When participants were divided into groups of four, each assumed specific roles (project manager, translator, editor/proofreader, and client). These groups submitted their translations and reflection journals on Mondays, Wednesdays, and Fridays. The reflection journal presented distinct sets of questions tailored to each role. Project managers reported on coordination difficulties and overall task smoothness, while translators discussed the time taken, translation steps, challenges, and unresolved issues. Editors/proofreaders detailed their review process and commented on translation quality, while simulated clients evaluated their satisfaction and criteria for judgment. Additionally, the group reflected on lecture content, expressed future interests, and assessed group dynamics and improvements. The reflection journal also included the interview reports conducted in Week 2, where students had the chance to interview actual clients – namely, parents and school officials within the school district. In these reports, students documented the interviews and reflected on the insights gained from the experience. These journals not only fostered a routine habit of reflecting on their workshop experiences but also served as valuable references when composing their final end-of-workshop reflections, which constituted the primary source material for the qualitative analysis. The end-of-workshop reflections comprised two components. First, participants reflected on their evolving understanding of translation throughout the two-week workshop and completed prompts in the final class, which included expressing previous beliefs (I used to think...), new insights gained (Now I know/ understand...), and key takeaways. Second, in their final translation exercise, participants summarised their workshop experience, outlined the translation process, identified challenges, discussed how they addressed them or why they failed to do so, and shared any questions or thoughts about the workshop.

4. Results and analysis

The present study aims to provide insights into the effectiveness of PjBL as an instructional approach for fostering problem-solving and teamwork among translator trainees. This section presents the findings and analysis of the collected data, shedding light on the potential benefits and limitations associated with the incorporation of the PjBL model in the translation classroom.

4.1 Quantitative data on problem-solving and teamwork

The research team employed specific questionnaire items to assess the changes in students' problem-solving skills (PS) and teamwork abilities and awareness (TW) before and after the workshop. The responses to Items 39–43 in the pre-workshop questionnaire[2] were analysed as a baseline measure of PS. Correspondingly, the results of Items 13–17 in the post-workshop questionnaire[3] were calculated to gauge the impact of the workshop on PS. Similarly, Items 45–46 and Items 49–59 in the pre-workshop questionnaire and Items 30–52 in the post-workshop questionnaire provided insights into changes in TW. To assess the statistical significance of data differences, a t-test was conducted, as presented in Table 7.2. The results indicate that the average scores for PS and TW in the post-translation phase are significantly higher compared to the pre-translation scores (p for PS = 0.00004; p for TW = 0.019). The calculated t-values also support the rejection of the null hypothesis, indicating a

TABLE 7.2 T-test results

	N	Mean	Variance	P (2-tailed)	T-critical (2-tailed)	Cohen's d
Pre-workshop PS	20	3.61	0.486	<0.001	2.093	1.107
Post-workshop PS	20	4.49	0.145			
Pre-workshop TW	20	4.113	0.195	<0.05	2.093	0.422
Post-workshop TW	20	4.378	0.200			

significant difference between the means of the two groups. These findings provide strong evidence for the effectiveness of the intervention in improving problem-solving and teamwork skills and awareness among the participants.

The results demonstrate a significant improvement in both PS as well as TW among the participants. Specifically, the average scores for PS increased from 3.64 to 4.49, and Cohen's d value (1.107) suggests a large and meaningful effect size, indicating a substantial enhancement in these skills. Similarly, the average score for TW rose from 4.09 to 4.38, while Cohen's d value (0.422) falls into the "moderate effect size" category, highlighting a noticeable and relevant increase of TW awareness.

Notably, the majority of participants demonstrated considerable growth in PS and TW. Among the participants, 85% experienced an increase in their PS scores, ranging from 5.88% to 76.92%, as shown in Figure 7.1.

Additionally, 75% of the participants observed an improvement in their TW scores, ranging from 0.88% to 36.59%, as depicted in Figure 7.2. It is worth noting that a small proportion of participants (15% and 25%, respectively) reported a decrease in their awareness levels. These findings further support the overall positive impact of the intervention while acknowledging individual differences in outcomes.

Overall, the quantitative data analysis provides robust evidence of the effectiveness of the intervention in enhancing PS and TW among the participants.

These findings underscore the overall positive impact of the intervention on improving PS and TW among the majority of the trainees. However, it is crucial to acknowledge the presence of individual variations within a subset of participants. To gain deeper insights into these variations, a comprehensive analysis of the qualitative data will be conducted to explore potential reasons and factors contributing to the observed differences in PS and TW outcomes. By examining the qualitative data, we the research team aim to uncover valuable insights and provide a more nuanced understanding of the individual variations observed among the participants.

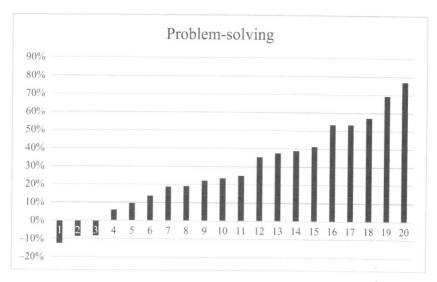

FIGURE 7.1 Changes in PS

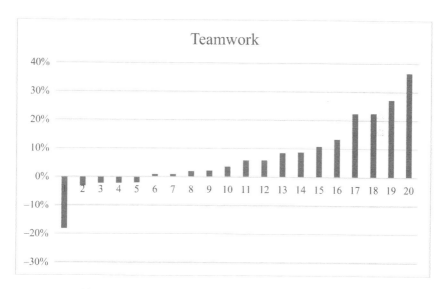

FIGURE 7.2 Changes in TW

4.2 Qualitative data analysis

The research team has taken rigorous steps to analyse qualitative data. The selection of relevant quotes that exemplified the identified themes was accompanied by a thorough scrutiny and validation process conducted by co-authors. This collaborative approach enhanced the overall robustness of the study. Furthermore, the qualitative findings were triangulated with the quantitative data, leading to a cohesive and comprehensive understanding of the impacts of the PjBL model in the translation classroom.

During the analysis of qualitative data, insights derived from students' end-of-workshop reflections provided valuable perspectives regarding the positive changes they experienced in their problem-solving skills throughout the translation process, which aligned with the quantitative results. Here are some quotes from the participants translated from Chinese into English by the research team:

Participant 1:
I've learned many skills and ways to look up words.

Participant 2:
In the past, I only used machine translators and e-dictionaries during translation.
     Now, I can find many glossaries and important information using a variety of online resources, sometimes proving the machine translators and e-dictionaries wrong or at least not comprehensive.

Participant 3:
Now, I know that we need to do lots of research for every translation project.
     My biggest takeaway is that I've learned how to use rich resources from Chinese and foreign websites to produce an accurate, faithful, fluent, and elegant translation.

As illustrated by the quotes, participants acquired word lookup skills, improved translation accuracy, and utilised diverse online resources for cross-checking. Emphasising extensive research, participants expressed the importance of using rich resources for accurate and elegant translations.

The qualitative analysis also sheds light on the significance and improvement of teamwork and communication skills. Students universally acknowledged that translation projects necessitate collaboration and the assumption of multiple roles, underscoring the vital contribution of each team member. Through collaborative experiences, students developed a heightened awareness of teamwork and honed their communication skills. They came to recognise that translation is a collective effort and emphasised the critical importance of coordination, communication, and proofreading. One participant's perspective resonated with this theme:

I used to believe that if multiple translators participate in a project, it increases efficiency. Now I know that translation styles can be very different. There is also a need to keep glossaries consistent. So, it's not "the more translators, the more efficient." In a real project, we need to limit the number of translators.

This valuable insight underscored the significance of embracing different perspectives and the need for efficient coordination among translators, project managers, and proofreaders. Another participant shared a similar sentiment:

I've experienced all the different roles in the project and worked with project managers who had different working styles. I believe that a good project manager can coordinate every step and distribute work well. Translators and proofreaders need to do research carefully and de-verbalize boldly.

These observations highlighted the pivotal role of a skilled project manager who can effectively distribute tasks and oversee every step while emphasising the necessity for translators and proofreaders to engage in thorough research and demonstrate adept de-verbalisation skills.

In addition to addressing the first research question, the advantages and disadvantages of the PjBL model were also reflected and analysed, revealing three primary benefits emphasised by students. First, through the translator-parents and translator-school official interviews, students gained practical knowledge about real-world scenarios, fostering a better understanding of the role of translators in the US community. They learned to see the bigger picture, recognising translation as a multi-player game influenced by cultural differences. This firsthand experience allowed them to delve deeper into clients' real needs, considering variations in English proficiency levels and clients' preferred translation styles. For example, some participants reflected:

Participant 4:
In the past, I assumed that Chinese immigrants in US communities had relatively high English proficiency levels. The truth is, some of them still rely on translation tools. Consequently, some parents may not hold very high standards for translations; they consider readability and comprehensibility to be sufficient.

Participant 5:
I discovered that the teachers we interviewed prefer a paraphrased version of the source text, especially for official documents whose language is already complicated. This insight will help me translate more effectively in the future.

Second, they developed time management skills to handle multiple tasks within a team workflow effectively. Finally, students recognised the irreplaceable role of human translation and the importance of making appropriate adjustments based on clients' needs, as one participant mentioned in the reflection:

> Participant 6:
> Through the interview, I understand that lifestyle, education level, and self-learning ability vary among target readers. Therefore, we should consider the purpose of translation and what we aim to convey to our clients. For instance, parents seek information about their children's performance and interpersonal relations at school. Hence, when translating, we should also take into account the emotions and feelings of the parents, delivering our translation objectively without influencing the clients.

While the qualitative analysis provided valuable insights, it is essential to consider the disadvantages of the PjBL model. Instructors dedicated a significant amount of time and effort, investing up to 12 hours per day in class preparation and conducting quality assurance. This intensive workload may pose challenges in terms of sustainability and resource allocation. Despite the challenges, there are solutions to address these issues. If this model can be replicated and expanded to degree-based translation classes, it could effectively resolve such problems. Collaborating with local school districts or community partners, or even establishing long-term partnerships, could address these issues and easily tackle accompanying ethical and copyright concerns.

Additionally, the 55.6% dropout rate (25 out of 45 participants dropped out) suggested that the PjBL model may only be suitable for some individuals. Some students who dropped out midway provided personal reasons as their withdrawal justification. Unfortunately, exit surveys were not conducted for the study. In the future, it would be beneficial to investigate further whether the reasons for withdrawal are related to the fact that participants are all volunteers with no strings attached or if they are associated with the nature of the experiment itself. Exploring whether the dropout rates differ in other non-PjBL studies could also provide valuable insights.

Furthermore, the assessment of translation quality was not conducted during the two-week workshop due to the limited timeframe for significant improvements. However, some students expressed concerns about the uncertain possibility of improving translation quality within the limited two-week timeframe, emphasising the importance of addressing this aspect in future investigations. It is worth mentioning that the instructors proofread the translations and performed quality assurance before submitting to the actual clients.

Overall, the analysis of both quantitative and qualitative data presents a coherent picture, highlighting the overall positive impact of the PjBL model in the translation classroom. The findings indicate significant improvements in various aspects, including problem-solving skills and awareness, teamwork, time management, communication, and gaining knowledge about real-world translation industry workflows and processes. These outcomes suggest that the PjBL model effectively enhances participants' awareness and abilities in these areas.

Nevertheless, it is crucial to acknowledge that the suitability of the PjBL model may vary among individuals. Although the study did not focus on individual differences, the data suggest that students with lower scores in PS and TW abilities and awareness are more likely to drop out of the workshop. This implies that the PjBL model may be more beneficial for certain students, while others may find it less suitable or effective in their learning journey. Further research could delve into the factors influencing individual differences and explore strategies to better support the diverse needs of learners in the translation classroom.

5. Limitations

Several limitations should be acknowledged. First, the absence of a control group restricts direct comparison between the outcomes of the PjBL model and alternative approaches, limiting our ability to attribute improvements solely to PjBL. Second, the two-week workshop duration may have limited the depth and sustainability of the observed effects. A more extended intervention period could allow for more comprehensive skill development. Additionally, the small sample size of 20 volunteer participants limits generalisability and statistical power, hindering the detection of subtle effects or variations. Future research should include a more extensive and more diverse sample. Lastly, reliance on self-reported measures and qualitative reflections may introduce bias and interpretation subjectivity. Efforts were made to ensure reliability, but social desirability bias should be considered. These limitations underscore the need for careful interpretation and suggest avenues for future research to address them, enhancing our understanding of PjBL in translation pedagogy.

6. Conclusion

This study aimed to address the gap in evaluating PjBL in translation classrooms. Through a quasi-experimental study, the research team evaluated the effectiveness of the PjBL model in developing students' translation and career-related transferable skills. The study focused on two research questions: 1) the impact of PjBL on specific skills, namely problem-solving and teamwork abilities and awareness, among translation trainees; and 2) the advantages and disadvantages of implementing the PjBL model in the translation classroom.

The findings, obtained through a mixed-method approach combining questionnaires and reflection journals, demonstrate that integrating PjBL into translation courses provide students with valuable practical experience in translating real-world projects by equipping them with essential non-translation skills such as problem-solving skills and teamwork abilities. The quantitative analysis reveals a significant improvement in problem-solving and teamwork skills and awareness following the intervention. The average scores increased, indicating an overall enhancement in these skills and awareness. Although most participants experienced growth, a small percentage reported decreased awareness levels. The qualitative analysis of students' reflections further supports these findings, highlighting improvements in problem-solving skills and emphasising the importance of teamwork and communication. Additionally, students identified several benefits of the PjBL model, including gaining real-world knowledge and developing time management skills. These findings suggest that PjBL effectively enhances the development of specific skills, positively influencing problem-solving and teamwork among translation trainees.

Furthermore, the study reveals additional advantages of employing the PjBL model in the translation classroom. Students had the opportunity to engage with authentic translation materials, interact with clients and end-users, and gain a deeper understanding of their needs. By integrating PjBL, students were better prepared for future careers in translation as they acquired practical experience, improved their language proficiency, and developed essential professional skills.

The study also acknowledges drawbacks of the PjBL model, such as the heavy workload for instructors and concerns about sustainability and resource allocation, which could be potentially resolved by replicating the model to degree-based translation classes and establishing long-term collaboration with local communities. The high dropout rate indicates that the PjBL model may be more suitable for certain individuals, or the voluntary nature could be a contributing factor. Additionally, the limited timeframe hindered the assessment of improvements in translation quality, and students expressed concerns about this impact.

This research contributes to translation pedagogy by demonstrating the effectiveness of PjBL in translation classrooms. By incorporating PjBL, educators can provide students with a comprehensive learning experience that bridges the gap between theory and practice. This approach enhances students' translation skills and equips them with the necessary non-translation skills crucial for success in the professional translation industry.

In conclusion, the findings of this study support the effectiveness of PjBL in translation pedagogy, echoing the other PjBL studies (Herget, 2020; Van Egdom, 2020; Paradowska, 2021). Future research could explore the long-term effects of PjBL on students' translation competencies and career trajectories, as well as investigate the applicability of PjBL in different translation contexts and language pairs. It is recommended that translation educators consider integrating PjBL into their teaching methodologies to provide students with practical, real-world translation experiences, and foster the development of essential skills for their future careers. By continually exploring innovative teaching approaches like PjBL, translation pedagogy can evolve to meet the demands of the rapidly changing translation industry and better prepare students for professional success.

Notes

1   https://drive.google.com/drive/folders/19s6KdFLIEWWxk8TioEOjTsnv40IPykb5 ?usp=sharing
2   https://docs.google.com/document/d/1sApLa0BAFf6Cklu2Gj8eev2ocF1hSp-l/edit ?usp=sharing&ouid=108280638319542262164&rtpof=true&sd=true
3   https://docs.google.com/document/d/17QebI5XwehO1sGkx7p_deWHlRAaAcQZ5/ edit?usp=drive_link&ouid=108280638319542262164&rtpof=true&sd=true

References

Buysschaert, J. and van Egdom, G.W. 2017. Professionalising the curriculum and increasing employability through authentic experiential learning: The cases of INSTB. *Current Trends in Translation Teaching and Learning E*. 4, pp. 78–111.

CSA Research. 2020. *COVID-19 effects on freelance linguists – As of August 2020*. [Online]. [Accessed 28 July 2023]. Available from: www.csa-research.com/Featu red-Content/For-LSPs/Industry-Data-and-Resources/Freelancer-2-Survey.

Condliffe, B., Quint J., Visher M.G., Bangser M.R., Drohojowska S., Saco L. and Nelson, E. 2017. *Project-Based Learning: A Literature Review*. Working Paper. Available at: https://eric.ed.gov/?id=ED578933.

Danford, G.L. 2006. Project-based learning and international business education. *Journal of Teaching in International Business*. 18(1), pp. 7–25.

Dewey, J. 1900. *The School and Society*. Chicago: University of Chicago Press.

Dolmans, D.H., Loyens, S.M., Marcq, H. and Gijbels, D. 2016. Deep and surface learning in problem-based learning: a review of the literature. *Advances in Health Sciences Education*. 21, pp. 1087–1112.

EMT Board. 2022. European Master's in Translation: Competence Framework 2022. [Online]. [Accessed January 11, 2024]. Available from: www.commission.europa. eu/system/files/2022-11/emt_competence_fwk_2022_en.pdf.

García González, M. and Veiga Díaz, M.T. 2015. Guided Inquiry and Project-Based Learning in the field of specialised translation: A description of two learning experiences. *Perspectives*. 23(1), pp. 107–123.

Heppner, P.P. and Petersen, C.H. 1982. The development and implications of a personal problem-solving inventory. *Journal of Counselling Psychology*. 29(1), p. 66.

Herget, K. 2020. Project-based learning: A practical approach to implementing Memsource in the classroom. In: *6th International Conference on Higher Education Advances (HEAd'20), 2–5 June 2020, Valencia*. Editorial Universitat Politècnica de València, pp. 717–724.

Imaz, J.I. 2021. "How has your city changed?" Using project-based learning to teach sociology of education. *Education and Urban Society*. 53(9), pp. 1019–1038.

INSTB. 2017. Professionalising the curriculum and increasing employability through experiential learning: The cases of INSTB. *Current Trends in Translation Teaching and Learning E (CTTL E)*. 4, pp. 78–111.

Kerremans, K. and Van Egdom, G. 2018. Professionalisation in translator education through virtual teamwork. In: Mousten, B. et al. (eds.). *Multilingual Writing and Pedagogical Cooperation in Virtual Learning Environments*. Hershey, PA: IGI Global, pp. 291–316. DOI: 10.4018/978-1-5225-4154-7

Kilpatrick, W.H. 1918. The Project method: The use of the purposeful act in the educative process. *Teachers College Record*. 19, pp. 319–335.

Klyoster, A.M., Elkin, V.V. and Melnikova, E.N. 2018. *Project-Based Learning in the System of Higher Education*. Astra Salvensis. Available from: www.ceeol.com/search/article-detail?id=647681

Krajcik, J.S. and Blumenfeld, P.C. 2006. Project-based learning. In: Sawyer, R. Keith. ed. *The Cambridge Handbook of the Learning Sciences*. Cambridge: Cambridge University Press, pp. 317–334.

Li, D., Zhang, C. and He, Y. 2015. Project-based learning in teaching translation: Students' perceptions. *The Interpreter and Translator Trainer*. 9(1), pp. 1–19. DOI: 10.1080/1750399X.2015.1010357

Luo, X. 2021. Translation in the time of COVID-19. *Asia Pacific Translation and Intercultural Studies*. 8(1), pp. 1–3. DOI: 10.1080/23306343.2021.1903183

Marian, M. and Roseanu, G. 2012. Adaptation study of the problem solving Inventory on the Romanian population. *International Journal of Education and Psychology in the Community*. 2(2), p. 89.

Matosas-López, L. and Cuevas-Molano, E. 2022. Assessing teaching effectiveness in blended learning methodologies: Validity and reliability of an instrument with behavioral anchored rating scales. *Behavioral Sciences*. 12(10), p. 394.

Moghaddas, M. and Khoshsaligheh, M. 2019. Implementing project-based learning in a Persian translation class: A mixed-methods study. *The Interpreter and Translator Trainer*. 13(2), pp. 190–209.

Ohland, M.W., Loughry, M.L., Woehr, D.J., Bullard, L.G., Felder, R.M., Finelli, C.J., Layton, R.A., Pomeranz, H.R. and Schmucker, D.G. 2012. The comprehensive assessment of team member effectiveness: Development of a behaviorally anchored rating scale for self-and peer evaluation. *Academy of Management Learning & Education*. 11(4), pp. 609–630.

Paradowska, U. 2021. Benefits and challenges of an Intra-university authentic collaborative translation project. *New Voices in Translation Studies*. 24(1), pp. 23–45.

PBLWorks. 2023. Available from www.pblworks.org/

Pieratt, J.R. 2010. Advancing the ideas of John Dewey: A look at the high tech schools. *Education and Culture*. 26(2), pp. 52–64.

Van Egdom, G.W., Konttinen, K., Vandepitte, S., Fernández-Parra, M., Loock, R. and Bindels, J. 2020. Empowering translators through entrepreneurship in simulated translation bureaus. *HERMES (ÅRHUS)*. 60, pp. 81–95.

Wengrowicz, N., Dori, Y.J. and Dori, D. 2017. Meta-assessment in a project-based systems engineering course. *Assessment & Evaluation in Higher Education*. 42(4), pp. 607–624.

8

NEWCASTLE CALLS

A translation project management simulation enabling professional development and cross disciplinary collaboration

Barbara Guidarelli, D. Carole Moore, and Cristina Peligra

Keywords: cross-disciplinary collaboration; professional competence development; project-based professional simulation; task-based translation workshops; technology-facilitated translation teaching

1. Introduction

A key factor to boost students' learning is motivation (Olson, 1997, as cited in Williams & Williams, 2011, p. 2), and increased motivation improves student performance and competence (González Davies, 2004, p. 2, Uribe de Kellett, p. 135). The Newcastle University's 2020–2022 *Newcastle Calls* Project aimed to increase engagement and motivation among BA and MA students of Italian and their Lecturers by adopting a collaborative, task-based approach to translation teaching and learning. Skype and Zoom were first used in the language classroom to facilitate three BA student-led, interactive video interviews with Italian experts abroad and in the UK, while the free subtitling software Aegisub was employed in subsequent MA or BA student-led, collaborative subtitling workshops to transform the interviews into bilingual documentaries later integrated into formal teaching and assessment and archived as materials for asynchronous, independent online language learning aimed at a wider audience (see section 2.1).

Kiraly has argued for empowering "students by making them proactive agents of their own learning through authentic, collaborative work leading to autonomy and expertise" (2005, p. 1104). Drawing on such a claim, as part of the Project, Lecturers worked collaboratively with their class to create authentic teaching and learning resources. Through technology-facilitated real-life situation simulation, students were empowered to co-shape and take

DOI: 10.4324/9781003440970-10

responsibility for their learning experience and professional development. The Project demonstrated the potential of digital tools in boosting language and translation students' skill base and facilitating flexible learning models (Guidarelli, 2020; Guidarelli et al., 2022c). However, whilst the use of technology in language and translation teaching was important for the success of the Project, piloted just before and during the COVID-19 pandemic, its unique approach of cross-level interdisciplinary collaboration was particularly beneficial to foster peer learning and professional development, enhancing the participants' employability skills. Specifically, as MA translation students' involvement was extracurricular, they worked against given deadlines and were paid by the hour, therefore simulating a real-life professional situation, the Project helped them to prepare for the transition from Academia to the world of work. In addition, it has provided an opportunity for Modern Languages teaching and Film Studies staff to engage in the Project, thereby encouraging collaboration between departments outside of their formal curricula.

This chapter aims to assess the final stages of *Newcastle Calls*, using feedback from participants and the experience of the facilitators to give recommendations for creating similar types of task-based translation and subtitling projects simulating professional conditions. Specifically, it explores and evaluates the organisation, challenges, and results of the student-led subtitling workshops held from 2020 to 2022 to create the bilingual scripts for the final documentaries made from the three foreign language video-interviews, and how BA and MA translation students benefitted from these in terms of professional, project and conflict management skills, arguing in favour of their addition to translator education.

2. *Newcastle Calls* 2020–2022

2.1 Project structure

The *Newcastle Calls* 2020–2022 Project was divided in two phases. First, in January 2020, Newcastle University's BA Italian language students at Intermediate level, their Lecturer and an MA Translation Lecturer used Skype to interview Italian researchers at the Italian Antarctica base Mario Zucchelli (ENEA, 2020). Two further interviews were conducted via Zoom: in March 2020 students interviewed a professional Italian theatre actor in Italy when the country was in lockdown; and in February 2021 they spoke to an Italian chef living and working in the North East of England. With the permission of students and guest speakers, the interviews were recorded.

In the second phase the interviews were edited into three formal documentaries and used both as teaching and assessment material, and as self-learning and research material made available to a wider audience by providing bilingual (Italian/English) subtitles. In particular, the subtitled documentaries lay the foundation for a digital database of teaching and learning material for independent language learners with level-graded online listening, reading, and translation tasks based on the interviews (Guidarelli et al., 2022c, p. 79), using Newcastle University's VLE platform Canvas (see section 4).

The process of subtitling the recorded interviews is the main focus of this chapter. Based on the information presented at the 2022 APTIS conference (Guidarelli et al., 2022b), the following sections explore the Project's theoretical background (section 2.2.) and rationale (section 2.3), examine how subtitling software was used in a simulated professional situation and to foster independent learning and professional development (sections 3.1 and 3.2) and assesses the benefits and challenges reported by student feedback (section 3.3) to make recommendations for translation teachers (section 3.4).

2.2 Background

The 2020 COVID-19 lockdown required students and Lecturers to adapt to new styles of teaching and learning very quickly. In the post-pandemic world policy makers and HE institutions have reflected on lessons learned and the potential benefits brought by the recent digital shift (Snelling, 2021). It must be acknowledged that the pandemic "accelerated trends that were already apparent in higher education" (QAA, 2020, p. 11). Successful practice and research have highlighted the advantages of using technology in language teaching and learning (Romaña Correa, 2015; Lenkaitis, 2019; Rodríguez Oitavén 2022) before, during, and after the pandemic. Integrating digital tools in classroom activities stimulate student interest, motivation, engagement, and attention levels (Bavendik, 2022; Li, 2022). Especially in students at beginner's and intermediate language proficiency levels, the use of machine translation-generated parallel text promotes close reading and deep engagement (Bavendik, 2022), while video-conferencing tools such as Skype encourage social engagement and language fluency (Romaña Correa, 2015). Furthermore, pandemic-induced synchronous language learning has enabled more student-centred learning in stressful times and fostered formative assessment (Li, 2022). Technology has also supported autonomous learning and critical thinking (Bandevik, 2022). Asynchronous online teaching allows for both multimodal interaction and for the creation of differentiated "learning pathways" accommodating a diverse range of language proficiencies (Rodríguez Oitavén, 2022).

Technology has become an integral and constantly advancing aspect of the translation profession and research has shown the need to integrate and develop digital competencies as part of university level translation training (Bowker, 2002; Doherty, 2016; Kenny, 2020; Ping, 2022). It is crucial to explore technology's potential to foster independent learning in the translation teaching context, as digital tools have the potential to simulate real-life learning and professional situations. Kiraly (1995, 2005) has long argued in favour of more authentic teaching methods in the translation classroom, also clearly pointing out that translation graduates risk lacking the practical skills and autonomy they need to be successful in the world of work as translation education is often too theoretical. The use of technology can help ensure students' competencies after graduation meet employers' expectations (Kiraly, 2005). Several scholars have successfully applied Kiraly's socio-constructive approach to translation teaching: "independent learning monitored by a competent teacher leads to the skills, competences and abilities required to meet professional challenges" (Mitchell-Schuitevoerder, 2011), receiving positive feedback (Ping, 2022). Studies demonstrate that this task- or project-based approach to translation teaching boosts students' professional competence (Mitchell-Schuitevoerder, 2011; Ping, 2022; Uribe de Kellett, 2022). When aimed at simulating a real-life task and a work environment, specifically, its benefits for students are twofold. First, they understand what is required in a professional situation, what tools are available in such contexts and what challenges may arise. Second, they are empowered to tackle those challenges autonomously, developing essential problem-solving and evaluation skills, and applying translation theory to their practice (Mitchell-Schuitevoerder, 2011).

The benefits of project-based, professional simulation also include the possibility to connect translation exercises with other content modules' material, for example when specific terminology needs to be applied (ibid.). Yet the potential technology has to encourage interdisciplinary and external collaboration in such cases and how translation education can be tailored to promote socio-cultural awareness and employability skills (Pérez-Nieto & Llop Naya, 2022) still needs to be investigated further. By taking as examples excellent initiatives such as Newcastle University's *Real Translation Project* (RTP), whereby final-year students engaged in the community by providing translation of real documents (Uribe de Kellett, 2022), and exploring how they can be taken further by using digital tools and cross-disciplinary involvement, scholars can reflect on translation programme's potential to create socially aware, "all-rounded future professionals of translation" whose problem-solving skills can lead to creative solutions to enable change (Neves, 2022).

2.3   *Rationale and innovation*

In the wake of the above-mentioned studies, the *Newcastle Calls* Project was developed at Newcastle University, basing its rationale on the need to innovate teaching tools and methods in the Italian language classroom (Guidarelli, 2020). Italian is currently taught at Newcastle University as an optional Beginners and Intermediate level course as part of the BA in

Modern Languages and is offered as a working language in the Professional Translation for European Languages MA.

Introducing videoconferencing tools in the Italian language classroom offered less traditional and more engaging non-artificial interaction in the language, by applying David Marsh's (1994/2002) Content and Language Integrated Learning (CLIL) methodology to facilitate the synthesis of language and content teaching. Videoconferencing tools helped achieve Marsh's aims by providing "authentic, meaningful and significant communication with others" (ibid., p. 72).

During the Project's subtitling workshops, translation students not only had to deal with technical translation aspects, but also immerse themselves in Italy's contemporary cultural issues, to apply professional standards and to conduct appropriate online research to complete their assigned task. The workshops were student-led and used collaborative working techniques online. However, these workshops were not part of any formal curricula and as such not assessed, but the students were paid for their work. Inspired by studies exploring "project-based learning" in the translation classroom (Kiraldy, 2005; Mitchell-Schuitevoerder, 2011), translation students were confronted with a simulated professional situation, helping them gain professional skills. The workshops were organised to mimic a professional assignment, which they had to complete as a team under minimal Lecturer supervision, to specific standards and against a tight deadline. The workshop participants were responsible for preparation and delivery of assigned tasks, namely script transcription, subtitling, script input onto Aegisub, and update of shared material. Their Lecturers acted as facilitators but did provide advice and guidance if requested to do so by the students or if the students had misunderstood an expression. The students took turns to act as Project Managers, realising quickly that they had to develop excellent communication and conflict management skills to agree on each clip.

Within this framework, the application of technology was twofold. First, using Zoom helped facilitate remote working modes and interaction, thus encouraging inclusiveness, as students not living on campus were able to take advantage of paid work opportunities which would otherwise have been less accessible. Second, both students and Lecturers benefitted from learning to use Aegisub, thereby boosting their digital competence, which is "essential in today's translation market" (Nitzke et al., 2019, p. 297).

It is thanks to the subtitling workshops that the *Newcastle Calls* Project became a truly interdisciplinary team venture, in an innovative and collaborative setting. Knowledge was shared within Newcastle University's School of Modern Languages, as the Project organisers needed subtitling training which was provided by an expert colleague. From the very beginning Lecturers and students of Italian at Newcastle operated as a cross-level, cross-disciplinary team. In practice, three Lecturers with different expertise (language and culture, Translation Studies) and students at different stages (BA and MA) and with different backgrounds (native and non-native English/ Italian speakers, some with different language majors) collaborated to make three bilingual documentaries. Both BA and MA students of Translations Studies with a knowledge of Italian were invited to attend the subtitling workshops. However, numbers were limited due to the timing of the sessions, which had to be planned carefully. As this was an extracurricular activity, official permission was obtained for the workshops to take place outside of the formal teaching period, during the summer vacation, when MA students were involved in writing final Translation Projects.

Finally, assistance in creating the final documentary films came from the Film Studies department, facilitating cross-school collaboration within the Faculty of Humanities and Social Sciences (HaSS). Specifically, a Film: Theory and Practice MA student was enlisted to edit the three final documentaries. This student also worked to a set deadline for each documentary and was paid an hourly fee, as in a real-life professional context. Due to time restraints only the Translation Lecturers, as Project Managers, interacted with the Film Studies student, who prepared the initial film for the students to subtitle and then completed the final film editing.

While the involvement of the Lecturers organising the Project was on a voluntary basis, financial assistance was requested (Nutela Small Grants and HaSS Teaching Development Fund) to pay all the students involved in subtitling and editing the documentaries. While students were all enthusiastic to take part in the Project to gain subtitling skills and add to their CV, the organisers strongly believed the ability to remunerate the Project's participants encouraged professionalism, as it created the context of a real-life subtitling/ translation assignment and differentiated the workshops from more generic translation activities (see section 3.3).

The positive impact of the collaborative, student-focused approach of *Newcastle Calls* is not only demonstrated by its success (see sections 3.2 and 3.3), but also by the fact that it inspired another task-based language-and-content-integrated translation Project within the School of Modern Languages at Newcastle University: i.e., the *Law of identity of origin* Project – *Grandmothers of Plaza de Mayo* Project organised by Maria Zubelzu de Brown and Dr Philippa Page, in which students of Spanish analysed and translated genuine documents and short films which were later included in a documentary (Guidarelli et al., 2022a).

2.4   Feedback and evaluation

In line with similar case studies on the application of technology-enhanced or project-based learning in translation education, student feedback (Li, 2022; Pérez Nieto, 2022), class discussion (Bavendiek, 2022) and reflective exercises (Li, 2022; Pietrzak, 2019) proved to be effective evaluation methods to continuously review the Project's structure and quality. At the end of each of the three subtitling workshops, the facilitators allowed some time for discussion to gather thoughts and suggestions, encouraging self-reflection, which is a key skill to enhance students' learning experience (ibid.). In addition, participants were asked to fill in feedback forms to check their experience of the preparation, organisation, and delivery of the sessions. Forms were analysed individually and comparatively across the three years. Finally, the organisers met to examine the feedback and discuss their own insight and experience. In this way, the organisers were able to develop the Project to its full potential by evaluating what worked well and what needed to be improved.

The way the Project changed shape and grew also encouraged the facilitators to work to enhance the feedback and evaluation processes. Student response and the need to gather more detailed information for management and research purposes favoured the transition from a one-page, paper feedback form asking more general questions in the pilot, to a longer, more in-depth (15 open-ended questions) online feedback form in Year 3. Specifically, while the first version of the feedback form looked at students' reasons for participating in the Project, their experience of, and feedback on the subtitling workshops and how these helped them in terms of professional development (Guidarelli et al., 2022c), the final version of the feedback form also included an appraisal of the preparation process and the participants' views on how the Project related to their other academic work, with the aim of considering how such an experience could best be integrated within the broader BA and MA study programmes.

3. The subtitling workshops

3.1 Pilot and unforeseen challenges

The first subtitling workshop (2020) acted as a pilot (Guidarelli et al., 2022c) and enabled the organisers to check if any adjustments were needed in the following two workshops. The first documentary ready to be subtitled was the interview with an Italian actor. Factoring in possible Zoom fatigue and the fact that the three MA students were also working on their final Translation Projects, the planned sessions consisted of a half day training on the software Aegisub, led by one of the Project facilitators, and a full day student-led subtitling workshop, in which the two translation Lecturers acted as consultants.

The short duration of the sessions at the pilot stage meant that students had less exposure to translation technology and more preparation was required on their part. The students were only briefly introduced to the new software and the software's features were given priority over subtitling theory. Due to time restraints, students were asked to arrive at the subtitling workshop with a draft translation of the interview to discuss as a team of Italian and English native speakers. However, while they managed the tight deadline very well as they were used to bringing a draft translation to discuss in class, they had difficulties in taking into account the full context of the task. Initially they did not fully grasp the difference between the subtitling requirements and translating a written text, with the result that the team ran out of time and were unable to finish the translation, creating additional workload for the facilitators.

Students struggled to visualise and cater for the intended audience and approach correctly the translation of speech (ibid., p. 76). They had to learn that they could not focus too much on what "sounded better" in the target language, as that might not work in subtitling, due to the space constraints and the need to respect the idiosyncrasies of the actor's style of speaking. They also had to deal with the speaker's hesitation or repetition in the subtitles in a different way than they would have done for a written translation, and, most importantly, they all had to agree on a final solution (ibid.).

Notwithstanding the challenges, both students and Lecturers learned from the pilot, which was evaluated by taking into account the student feedback questionnaire and Lecturer discussions post student feedback. In spite of the limitations, the half-day online training session proved successful, as students felt they were ready to start using the software right away, leading to the decision to repeat it in the following years and record it to allow the students extra individual practice time (see section 3.2). Additionally, experiential learning also proved very effective as students internalised their mistakes and developed professionally, by reflecting on their practice, both in the questionnaire and in final discussions with their Lecturers on the day. In particular, the learning curve included a broader awareness of the need to analyse the translation context in more depth, which is a key first step in their transition from students to professionals.

3.2   Second and third year

After the pilot stage, it was decided to extend the translation workshops to three one-day sessions in both Year 2 and Year 3 of the Project. To avoid Zoom fatigue, the sessions were held on non-consecutive days, and frequent breaks were included. The interview with the Italian chef was used to create the second documentary in 2021. The organisers acted on the feedback collected after the pilot to improve working methods for this session. Based on the pilot's software training session's positive reception, this was repeated online via Zoom and recorded with everyone's permission, so that the students could refer to the information as required. The session was adjusted to last an hour to leave the students time to practise using the software independently rather than as a group, encouraging autonomous troubleshooting before attending the subtitling workshops.

This time three BA translation students of languages other than Italian, but who were studying Intermediate Italian agreed to participate, as MA participants were unable to take part due to connectivity issues. The students were advised to watch the video of the Italian chef's responses to questions prior to the training session to familiarise themselves with the speaker's tone and expression. After the experience of the pilot, students were not asked to prepare a draft translation but just to consider possible translations and strategies. They inserted their target text directly onto the software, rather than copying and pasting unedited drafts. This not only saved facilitators and students both preparation and post-editing time, but also allowed participants to more easily grasp the translation situation with which they were working. Despite a few initial technical glitches, the 2021 subtitling Project proved successful.

For the Project in 2022, the translation team for the Antarctica video only consisted of two MA students, one Italian and one English native speaker, due to the availability of students during the period they were working on their final Translation Projects. The English native speaker was actually an MA student of French-English translation, but with an Intermediate Level of Italian. However, it was found that, in this smaller MA team, participants had the right amount of time for research, discussion and completion, allowing them to finish the Project within the set time framework, post-editing included. The interview with the researchers in Antarctica inevitably had more technical vocabulary (e.g., "chlorofluorocarbons", "wind chill factor", "perpendicular state of the magnetic flux"), making it more suitable for an experienced MA student team, as it required more thorough research than the other two recordings. They were even able to check certain points with the researchers in Antarctica via e-mail.

When asked about their preparation in the Project's feedback form, both participants in the final year of the Project confirmed the training session recording had been "useful", particularly to gain an understanding of the software's features. The recorded training session had been integrated with a brief "introduction section" where the facilitators explained the aims and challenges of the Project in great detail, showing the pilot's final product and reviewing previous participant feedback. In particular, the differences between such a task and other projects in the students' course were stressed, and the target audience was carefully discussed. However, in their feedback students explained that they were not able to watch the full Antarctica interview prior to the sessions, as they were working on their final MA Translation Projects.

3.3   *Student feedback*

Looking at the feedback collected from 2020 to 2022, it can be said that all students involved felt that they greatly benefitted from the subtitling workshops. In Year 3 the more technical translation task was perceived as "challenging but very enjoyable", and students stated they gained new skills. In the words of one student:

> I enjoyed [the translation task], it was new, different, and exciting compared to all other translation tasks I've done. I'd never before dealt with subtitles, so it was interesting to see its aims (i.e., clarity and comprehension, even in low-register and basic English, adjusting time codes and line lengths to the optimum).

Interestingly, with the justifiable exception of a few issues (connectivity issues, Zoom fatigue, students feeling faint after vaccinations), overall feedback remained rather consistent across the cohorts. Comparatively analysing the three sets of feedback, it is possible to make three key points:

1. The reasons for participating in such a Project remained constant throughout the cohorts, i.e., boosting one's CV by gaining real-life translation and project management experience. Students expressed an interest in gaining subtitling experience. One student said: "I am interested in working in a similar field and the subtitling/translation experience will be very beneficial for my CV" (2022 cohort).
2. For the above-mentioned reason, students would be in favour of repeating similar experiences and/or integrating such a Project into their course curriculum.

   Expanding these first two points, it can be stated that the students' feedback signals that their programme did not include practical subtitling skills, thus agreeing with Kiraly's (2005) claims of a mismatch between translation education and practice. Although it cannot be denied that this is constantly being reviewed, as digital translation skills become more important to Newcastle University's School of Modern Languages as the years and cohorts go by, at the time of participating (i.e., the end of their one-year master's degree, from 2020 to 2022), the students described their link to the professional world as: " [having] little professional translation experience" (2020), "my bare CV" (2022). By analysing students' response to the workshops, however, it is possible to see that the Project positively impacted on their confidence, both in terms of work experience and of technical knowledge. One student wrote: "It has added work experience as well as knowing how to use another piece of software to my CV" (2022 cohort).

Therefore, while these findings fully underpin the current inclusion of subtitling as part of an assessed collaborative translation task within Newcastle University's Modern Languages Translation and Interpreting BA Honours programme, for the reasons mentioned it becomes crucial to advocate the addition of more such project-based tasks within MA translation practical programmes. The authors strongly believe a Project like *Newcastle Calls* has the potential to bridge the gap between the academic and the professional world, as it applies theory to a job-like setting, giving students something to demonstrate the skills they have learned and the ability to follow instructions and meet deadlines.

3. The collaborative aspect of the Project was the most appreciated, even being referred to as "the key to its success" (2022 cohort), although it entailed some complications. One student named it as the "most challenging" aspect of the Project, in fact, as they needed to handle disagreement: "The most challenging aspect of the Project for me was I think disagreeing with others on what was idiomatic English [...]. I believe we managed to find solutions through compromise" (2022).

It is important to stress that one of the innovative aspects of this Project was that, by participating, translation students not only gained insight into technology, subtitling theory and practice, specialised terminology and cultural issues, but they also learned to work as a team and to deal with project and conflict management, realising the key role these professional skills play in translation practice. The fact that the Lecturers present during the subtitling workshops only acted as facilitators, while students worked in full autonomy on the target text, meant that students had to agree on the final version submitted, which was not always straightforward. Thanks to the Project, they gained conflict resolution skills, which will be extremely valuable in their professional life; they practised justifying their chosen strategies by giving evidence in support of their suggestions and learning to compromise, which was particularly appreciated.

One aspect which still needs further research is how being remunerated for the translation benefitted the students in terms of self-confidence and employability. Indeed, they were able to list the activities undertaken in their CV as paid work. It would be interesting to study this further by looking at both students' and employers' perception of such a Project.

3.4 Recommendations

Based on an evaluation of the *Newcastle Calls* Project, it is possible to formulate some recommendations to educators planning to incorporate in their course professional simulations based on project-based tasks and subtitling workshops. These teaching guidelines relate to the ideal number of participants, research, preparation, and delivery.

First, the ideal would be to limit the student participants to groups of two or three, with one source language native speaker and one target language native speaker working together to complete the translation in order to ensure accuracy of expression. A third student, preferably a target language native speaker, would work as Project Coordinator in order to arbitrate in any disagreement over terminology. This would enable students to actively comprehend the role of informants within the translation process. Educators should stress the importance of research and checking meanings and any jargon with experts.

Indeed, *Newcastle Calls* participants appreciated having specific vocabulary explained and terminology doubts clarified by experts. In the words of one student:

> [The most challenging part of the Project was] vocabulary, because it was very specific and sometimes not very clear. Having native speakers for both languages, support from our teachers and the possibility to ask the speakers for clarification meant we were able to tackle the issue.
>
> *(2022 cohort)*

Participating in such a Project could also help students practise a language they are not majoring in. Depending on the level of difficulty of the speech, it is suggested cohorts at different study levels could be considered, providing they are conversant with translation strategies and willing to work collaboratively.

FIGURE 8.1 Training session materials[1]

Second, the use of online training and preparation material is to be encouraged. In addition to having received positive feedback on the matter, online resources can help foster an inclusive teaching and learning environment, allowing students to learn at their own pace, and Lecturers to cater for individual learning styles (Fleming, 2006). Specifically, in the case of *Newcastle Calls*, in the recording of the training session, images and screenshots from the interviews and screenshots from the software were shown to explain context and procedures and to act as visual aids (e.g., coloured arrows and highlighting). Titles and lists were added to guide independent practice (see Figure 8.1).

4. Concluding thoughts and the future of *Newcastle Calls*

In this chapter, Newcastle University's 2020–2022 cross-disciplinary *Newcastle Calls* Project Management Simulation has been presented and evaluated through an analysis of student and organiser feedback.

Although both the initial online interviews in the foreign language and the final collaborative, online subtitling workshops of the *Newcastle Calls* Project provided the Lecturers and students involved with a variety of hurdles, they also created a learning curve where requirements had to be identified (e.g., the need for subtitling training and practice) and solutions found, demonstrating the Project's potential to boost students' skills and facilitate innovative learning modes. The analysis of the outcomes of the subtitling workshops raises awareness of the need to use professional simulations in MA Translation courses.

It can be said that the results from this Project evaluation support the recent inclusion of subtitling as part of assessed collaborative translation tasks at BA level at Newcastle, but also the addition of subtitling skills training for MA translation students in October 2024. It must be stressed that the MA students participating in *Newcastle Calls* were enthusiastic about the Project, partly because it was an extracurricular activity and partly because they received payment, in accordance with University guidance procedures. Furthermore, the collaborative nature of the Project, which enabled the sharing of knowledge between Lecturers and students and between different departments made a positive difference. Indeed, as facilitators, we firmly believe that the collaborative nature of the Project was the key to its success. In practice, as a valuable task within the BA and/or MA translation programmes, selected videos could be introduced to be subtitled by students working in small groups with one native speaker of the foreign language and one target language speaker. This would highlight the role of informants in translation practice.

Finally, one of the goals of the *Newcastle Calls* Project was also the preparation of a digital database of self-study materials for independent learners, based on the interviews (Guidarelli et al., 2022c, p. 79). The documentaries with the translated subtitles can help lower-level language students' comprehension and enable them to self-evaluate their language skills. To further add to this database, the interviewees from the three documentaries were asked to provide shorter follow-up videos to update the digital archive explaining post-Covid changes. As presented in Guidarelli & Peligra (2023), all videos are digital testaments of a specific moment in time (2020–2022).

Students and Lecturers could work collaboratively on a terminology database on contemporary key topics, such as the climate crisis, or COVID-19, which would include neologisms and new meanings attributed to words in a specific context, keeping research and teaching in Translation Studies abreast of the times. To give an example, in his follow-up video, the Italian actor discussed life in Italy after the pandemic and included terms like *evitare assembramenti* (to avoid large crowds), *mascherina* (face mask), *essere positivi* (to be COVID-19 positive) or *smart working* (flexible working), terms which have recently been gaining new usage and meanings and could therefore pose a challenge to translation students by requiring thorough research and consultation of parallel texts. In this way, through videorecording and subtitling technology, students and Lecturers are provided with updated, relevant material to tackle how translation theory and practice can develop quickly.

Acknowledgements

The *Newcastle Calls* Project was first presented on Newcastle University's LTDS online database of teaching practice.

We thank: NUTELA Small Grants Fund and HaSS Teaching Development Fund; the XXXV Italian Antarctica Expedition, Antonio Giuseppe Peligra and Gerardo Falivene; Newcastle University Intermediate Italian (UG) students, the Professional Translation for European Languages MA students acting as translators; Bradley Sampson for editing the documentaries; Dr Pauline Henry-Tierney, Lecturer in French and Translation Studies at Newcastle University, for acting as subtitling consultant.

Note

1 Authors' work. Software screenshot. Copyright © 2012–present, Aegisub Project.

References

Bavendiek, U. 2022. Using machine translation as a parallel text to access literature for modern language learning. In Salin, S. and Hampton, C. (eds.) *Innovative language teaching and learning at university: Facilitating transition from and to higher education.* Research-Publishing.net, pp. 57–67. https://doi.org/10.14705/rpnet.2022.56.1373

Bowker, L. 2002. *Computer-Aided Translation Technology. A Practical Introduction.* Ottawa: University of Ottawa Press.

Doherty, S. 2016. The impact of translation technologies on the process and product of translation. *International Journal of Communication* 10, pp. 947–969.

ENEA. 2020. *Italia in Antartide.* [Online]. [Accessed 23 June 2023]. Available from www.italiantartide.it/stazione-mario-zucchelli/

Fleming, N.D. 2006. *V.A.R.K Visual, Aural/Auditory, Read/Write, Kinesthetic.* New Zealand: Bonwell Green Mountain Falls.

González Davies, M. 2004. *Multiple Voices in the Translation Classroom.* Amsterdam: John Benjamins.

Guidarelli, B. 2020. *Newcastle Calls collaborative teaching project.* [Online]. [Accessed June 23 2023]. Available from www.microsites.ncl.ac.uk/casestudies/2020/08/31/the-newcastle-calls-collaborative-teaching-project/

Guidarelli, B., Moore, D.C., Peligra, C., and Zubelzu de Brown, M. 2022a. *Adopting CLIL and technology in collaborative projects as a bridge between language learning and research content: The Newcastle Calls Project and La Semana de l'Activismo.* SML TLC Conference, 1 July 2022, Newcastle University.

Guidarelli, B., Moore, D.C., and Peligra, C. 2022b. *Managing collaborative and individual projects through technology: Newcastle Calls project's final stages as a guide to independent learning.* APTIS Conference 2022, 18–19 November 2022, University of Leeds.

Guidarelli, B., Moore, D.C., and Peligra, C. 2022c. Using remote communication tools to facilitate student engagement, language learning and cross-disciplinary professional development before, during and after the pandemic: The *Newcastle Calls* project 2020 as a case study. In Salin, S. and Hampton, C. (eds.) *Innovative language teaching and learning at university: Facilitating transition from and to higher education.* Research-Publishing.net, pp. 69–80. [Online]. Available from www.research-publishing.net/manuscript?10.14705/rpnet.2022.56.1374

Guidarelli, B. and Peligra, C. 2023. *Beyond the Newcastle Calls project: Exploring memory within language teaching in the Digital Age.* Where Are We Now? The Location of Languages and Cultures, MLaC Conference 2023, 19–21 April 2023, Durham University.

Kenny, D. 2020. Technology and Translator Training. In O'Hagan, M. (ed.) *The Routledge Handbook of Translation Technology.* Abingdon: Routledge, pp. 498–515.

Kiraly, D. 1995. *Pathways to Translation: Pedagogy and Process.* Kent: Kent State University Press.

Kiraly, D. 2005. Project-based learning: A case for situated translation. *Meta* 50(4), pp. 1098–1111.

Lenkaitis, C.A. 2019. Technology as a mediating tool: Videoconferencing, L2 learning, and learner autonomy. *Computer Assisted Language Learning* 33(5–6), pp. 483–509.

Li, M. 2022. Student-centred learning and formative assessment: A possible answer to online language and literature teaching and learning. In Salin, S. and Hampton, C. (eds.) *Innovative language teaching and learning at university: Facilitating transition from and to higher education.* Research-Publishing.net, pp. 93–102. [Online]. https://doi.org/10.14705/ rpnet.2022.56.1376

Marsh, D. 1994. *Bilingual Education & Content and Language Integrated Learning* Paris: International Association for Cross-cultural Communication, Language Teaching in the Member States of the European Union (Lingua), University of Sorbonne.

Marsh, D. 2002. *Content and Language Integrated Learning. CLIL/EMILE The European Dimension: Actions, Trends and Foresight Potential*. Brussels: European Commission.

Mitchell-Schuitevoerder, R.E.H. 2011. *Translation and Technology in a Project-Based Learning Environment*. Session 3 – Training translators. Tralogy I. Métiers et technologies de la traduction: quelles convergences pour l'avenir?, 3 March 2011, Inist-Cnrs Paris.

Neves, J. 2022. Project-based learning for the development of social transformative competence in socially engaged translators. *The Interpreter and Translator Trainer* 4, pp. 465–483.

Nitzke, J., Tardel, A., and Hansen-Schirra, S. 2019. Training the modern translator– the acquisition of digital competencies through blended learning. *The Interpreter and the Translator Trainer* 13(3), pp. 292–306.

Pérez-Nieto, N. and Llop Naya, A. 2022. Task-based projects for transition from university to placements abroad: Development of academic, sociocultural, and employability skills for students of Spanish as a foreign language. In Salin, S. and Hampton, C. (eds.) *Innovative language teaching and learning at university: Facilitating transition from and to higher education*. Research-Publishing. net, pp. 121–132. [Online]. https://doi.org/10.14705/rpnet.2022.56.1379

Pietrzak, P. 2019. The potential of reflective translator training. *inTRAlinea Special Issue: New Insights into Translator Training*. [Online]. Available from www.intrali nea.org/specials/article/the_potential_of_reflective_translator_training

Ping, Y. 2022. Student perceptions of translation technology in a scientific and technical translation course. In Abels, K. et al. *Re-Thinking Translator Education*. Berlin: Frank & Timme, pp. 269–282.

QAA. 2020. *How UK Higher Education Providers Managed the Shift to Digital Delivery During the COVID-19 Pandemic*, The Quality Assurance Agency for Higher Education. [Online]. [Accessed June 2023]. Available from www.qaa. ac.uk/docs/qaa/guidance/how-uk-higher-education-providers-managed-the-shift-to-digital-delivery-during-the-covid-19-pandemic.pdf

Rodríguez Oitavén, C. 2022. From face-to-face to online in foreign language teaching: an outstanding experience. In Salin, S. and Hampton, C. (eds.) *Innovative language teaching and learning at university: Facilitating transition from and to higher education*. Research-Publishing.net, pp. 113–120. [Online]. Available from www.research-publishing.net/manuscript?10.14705/rpnet.2022.56.1378

Romaña Correa, Y. 2015. Skype conference calls: A way to promote speaking skills in the teaching and learning of English. *PROFILE, Issues in Teachers' Professional Development* 17(1), pp. 143–156.

Snelling, C. 2021. *Lessons from the pandemic: Making the most of technologies in teaching*, Universities UK. [Online]. [Accessed June 2023]. Available from www. universitiesuk.ac.uk/what-we-do/policy-and-research/publications/lessons-pande mic-making-most

Uribe de Kellett, A. 2022. Real-world translating: Learning through engagement. In Salin, S. and Hampton, C. (eds.) *Innovative language teaching and learning at university: Facilitating transition from and to higher education*. Research-Publishing. net, pp. 133–142. [Online]. https://doi.org/10.14705/rpnet.2022.56.1380

Williams, K. and Williams, C. 2011. Five key ingredients for improving motivation. *Research in Higher Education Journal* 11, pp. 121–123.

9

COACHING IN TRANSLATOR EDUCATION

Exploring the potential benefits of group coaching in simulated translation bureaus and beyond

JC Penet

Keywords: experiential learning; group coaching; emotion management; empathy development; well-being

1. Introduction

Since the turn of the century, the rapid automation of the language industry has led to a proliferation of new job titles, roles, and tasks for professional translators (Massey et al., 2023; see also Bond, 2018). Looking at the relentless reshaping of what it means to work as a translator in this "emerging new translation industry" he calls "Translation 4.0", Schmitt (2019, p.193) convincingly argues that "[t]he future will be for translators who have the competences defined in the EMT (European Master's of Translation) and who adapt to the changing translation ecosystem". Consequently, as translator educators we must re-evaluate the skills and competences trainee translators hone on our programmes in order to ensure that they are in a position to adapt to this fast-changing industry, in which the role of translators is becoming increasingly multifarious and ill-defined (see Massey et al., 2022; see also Risku and Schlager, 2021). This involves, among other things, helping them tolerate ambiguity (Hubscher-Davidson, 2018b) by developing their "adaptive expertise", which Angelone (2022, p.64) defines as the ability to perform "[...] in contexts where tasks are more ambiguous and when they call for novelty in problem-solving".

Simulated translation bureaus (STBs), which require students to work collaboratively in fictitious translation agencies in order to successfully deliver complex, life-like translation projects, are a good way to do so (see Buysschaert et al., 2017). This is because they "act as a mock workplace [...] but in a

DOI: 10.4324/9781003440970-11

safe educational environment" (Penet and Fernandez-Parra, 2023, p.333). As such, STBs can generate strong emotions, such as stress, among students, which are not unlike the ones experienced by professional translators (ibid; see also Courtney and Phelan, 2019). Even though emotions like stress can be experienced both positively and negatively, during STBs students often find that they negatively impact their engagement with, and performance on, this form of experiential learning (Penet and Fernandez-Parra, 2023).

It is important, therefore, to support our students' well-being during STBs by helping them to recognise and manage the potential impact of emotions such as stress on their ability to perform (ibid). As a "process of enquiry, learning and action" (Starr, 2021, p.8) that aims to "[...] unloc[k] a person's potential to maximise their performance" (Whitmore, 1992, p.8), coaching seems a particularly apt way to do so. Indeed, coaching makes use of structured conversations to give coachees "the time and space to focus on their circumstances, explore the issue they may be experiencing, and generate their own solution" (Tang, 2015, p.564). As such, coaching could help students recognise and reflect on the role of their emotions – and those of others – on their performance during collaborative work such as STBs, and help them generate their own solutions to manage these better.

What could be the benefits, then, of offering group coaching to students during STBs? Could group coaching be an effective way to help trainee translators recognise and manage the potential impact of emotions during STBs? Beyond the immediacy of STBs, could there be other, potentially longer-terms benefits of embedding group coaching into translator training? These are the questions we will seek to answer in this chapter in light of the data collected via psychometric surveys (TEIQue) and a focus group for an exploratory action research project that took place across two UK universities (Newcastle University and Swansea University) during the academic year 2022–2023.

2. Literature review

Studies into the role of emotions in translation have evidenced that a translator's emotional attitude towards either the task or their ability to perform can affect the quality of the work they produce (see Bolaños-Medina, 2016). Recently, Koskinen (2020, p.30) also argued that translation is "affective labour" in that it requires "the creation and manipulation of emotions, the production and distribution of feelings, and the management of affinity or distance". Indeed, while the texts translators translate can be seen as a first source of "affective labour" (ibid), the complex production networks contemporary translators must engage with, which provide "constellations of mutual dependence where translators, project managers, revisers, terminologists and IT people and other parties are in constant [...]

contact", should be seen as a "second layer of affective labour" (ibid, p.39). Further, the – sometime imposed – use of (new) translation technologies can generate a form of "technostress"[1] among (trainee) translators, which in turn can "reduc[e] performance and har[m] individual well-being" (ibid, p.146). From all this, Koskinen concludes that (ibid):

> If we consider affective labour to be related to the management of affects and emotions of oneself and others, and if we accept the view of translating and interpreting as forms of interpersonal, situated and embodied human communication, with the resulting affective and emotional complexities involved and also bodily felt, we also need to acknowledge the role of affective labour in successful professional performance.
>
> *(p. 32)*

If managed poorly, such "emotional complexities" can result in negative emotions which, in turn, can lead to diminished well-being and decreased job satisfaction, thus making the translation profession less sustainable (Hubscher-Davidson, 2020). In fact, Hubscher-Davidson's (2018a) empirical study into professional translators' emotion traits and behavioural dispositions shows a clear correlation between the way individual translators perceive, regulate and express their emotions and their ability to thrive in the profession. The impact emotions have on (trainee) translators' well-being and their ability to flourish in the language industry has therefore led to calls to further embed EI literacy into translator training programmes (Hubscher-Davidson, 2018a; Hubscher-Davidson and Lehr, 2021; Perdikaki and Georgiou, 2022; Penet & Fernandez-Parra, 2023).

To do so, it is useful to adopt Trait EI theory's conception of EI as a "disposition", a personality trait that can be evaluated by personality-like, self-report questionnaires (Nelis et al., 2009, p.36). In his Trait EI model, for instance, Petrides describes EI as a "[...] distinct (because it can be isolated in personality space), compound (because it is partially determined by several personality dimensions) construct that lies at the lower levels of personality hierarchies" (Petrides et al., 2007, p. 283). Such a conception of EI as a disposition could be seen to suggest that, like other personality traits, it is relatively stable over time. However, based on the recent work of scholars in this field, we can argue that personality traits are more dynamic than previously thought (Allemand and Flückiger, 2022). Similarly, EI traits are also somewhat malleable, as attested by recent empirical studies showing that "short and well-designed interventions" can influence individuals' emotional abilities in an enduring way (ibid, p.33; see also Hodzic et al., 2018; Kotsou et al., 2019).

According to Mikolajczak (2009, p.27), interventions that target what she describes as the three levels of EI – Knowledge, Abilities, and

Dispositions – could prove particularly effective in influencing individuals' emotional dispositions. The first level of EI, Knowledge, focuses on an individual's "knowledge about emotions and how to deal with emotional situations" (ibid). The second level, Abilities, refers to their ability to implement a certain strategy when facing "emotion-laden situations" (ibid). Finally, as the last level of EI, Dispositions, which is their "propensity to behave in a certain way in emotional situations", are "captured by all emotion-related traits" (ibid). In Mikolajczak's model, "[...] the three levels of EI-related individual differences are therefore 'loosely connected'; knowledge does not necessarily – *but can* – translate into abilities which, in turn, do not always – *but can* – translate into dispositions" (Penet and Fernandez-Parra, 2023, p.335). Consequently, interventions that target EI Knowledge and Abilities could lead to improvement in the EI Disposition level, as attested by recent studies (see Campo et al., 2016).

Drawing on Trait EI theory, as part of soft skills training, in order to develop our students' ability to recognise and manage the potential impact of emotions on their work could have positive pedagogical implications. Not only have past studies shown that trait EI can help respond better to stress and increase general well-being (Dave et al., 2021), it has also been evidenced that high EI "[...] contributes to increased motivation, planning, and decision making, which positively influence academic performance" (Fernando et al., 2011, p.152). Interestingly for us in the context of STBs, trait EI has also been found to "correlate positively with translators' ambiguity tolerance and to play an important role in other areas that are key to translation professionals' working lives, such as team effectiveness and collaborative practices" (Hubscher-Davidson and Lehr, 2021, p.36).

Embedding Trait EI theory through interventions therefore seems an appropriate way to better support trainee translators engaging with authentic experiential learning[2] on STBs. Indeed, the initial phase of this action research project suggested that when trainee translators are asked to engage with authentic, project-based learning by working in an STB, they often experience feelings very similar to those experienced by professional translators, and that these that can hinder their willingness to engage with, or ability to perform on, STBs (Penet and Fernandez-Parra, 2023). From this first phase, which explored whether Trait EI theory can help support students on STBs, we concluded that (ibid):

> [...] targeted [well-being] workshops and talking openly about the important role emotions play throughout an STB can help students manage their emotions in general, and their cohort's less adaptive [or] functional trait EI facets [for the purposes of an STB] in particular, more successfully in their STBs (Abilities).

(p. 349)

Interestingly, on several occasions the qualitative data from this initial project pointed in the direction of coaching as a potentially powerful way to both help students manage their emotions during STBs, and to further develop their empathy (ibid, p. 348). This was in line with something already highlighted by Hubscher-Davidson and Lehr (2021, p. 51), namely that interventions that adopt a coaching approach can be a particularly effective way to "help translators to better understand their emotions and work through issues". This may be because, as a "[…] human development process that involves structured, focused interaction and the use of appropriate strategies, tools and techniques to promote desirable and sustainable change for the benefit of the coachee" (Bachkirova et al., 2010, p.1), coaching has been shown to help improve self-confidence, relationships, communication skills, interpersonal skills, and work performance among coachees (ICF, 2009). It has also been shown to help with motivation, assertiveness and fear of failure (Dryden, 2018, p. 34).

A commonly used coaching tool to help people "better understand their emotions and work through issues" is effective questioning (Hubscher-Davidson and Lehr, 2021, p.51), that is the use of simple, open questions that promote reflection, constructively challenge the coachee's assumptions and enable creativity (Clutterbuck, 2021). Effective questioning in coaching can also encourage perspective taking – either directly or indirectly – among coachees, that is to say their ability to view a situation from another person's perspective. This, in turn, has been shown to foster empathy (Cooke et al., 2018). According to Koskinen (2020, p.167), empathy, which she defines as the "ability to identify, understand and resonate the emotions of others", is a core competence to develop among (trainee) translators in the age of machine translation. Indeed, empathy, she argues, is what "differentiates between human and machine translators" and what will, therefore, "keep humans in intercultural communication for the foreseeable future" (ibid). Using coaching to help students recognise and manage their emotions STBs could therefore have both a short-term positive impact (e.g., help with students' self-confidence, interpersonal skills, motivation, or assertiveness) as well as a longer-term one (e.g., further develop their empathy levels).

3.   Research question and methodology

Given the potential benefits of coaching to support trainee translators' development in general, and during STBs in particular, and given the fact that this remains a largely unexplored area of research in translator education, the author of the present chapter led a research project in collaboration with Dr Fernandez-Parra (Swansea University) as co-investigator during the academic year 2022–2023 to explore this further. Building on the findings of the initial phase of our action research project (Penet and Fernandez-Parra, 2023), the second phase of the project used a mixed-method sequential approach that gathered both quantitative and qualitative data[3] to explore the following research question: how effective are targeted, group coaching interventions in helping students manage their emotions both for the purposes of the STB and beyond? As coaching encourages perspective taking, which in turn has been shown to foster empathy, our project also explored whether the group coaching sessions could be seen to help develop empathy among trainee translators.

3.1 Setting and participants

The study took place across two UK universities, Newcastle University (NU) and Swansea University (SU), where students on translation programmes take part in STBs as part of their studies. At both universities, STBs followed the same timeline in 2022–23 (see Figure 9.1):

- Phase 1 (October to December 2022): Students were introduced to Translation Project Management (TPM) and the technological (CAT/AVT) tools needed to deliver their STB projects successfully;
- Phase 2 (mid-January to mid-April 2023): Students worked collectively in their assigned STBs to deliver the projects;
- Phase 3 (May to June 2023): Students were asked to reflect critically on their learning journey on STBs.

All students participating in STBs in 2022–2023 were invited to join our action research project on a voluntary basis. All 18 eligible NU students on

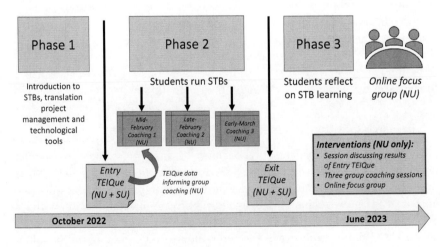

FIGURE 9.1 STB timeline and research project interventions

TABLE 9.1 Gender, age, and ethnic background of participants

	NU (n = 18)	SU (n = 22)
Gender		
Female	14	15
Male	4	7
Age		
18–22 years old	16	17
23–25 years old	2	–
26–30 years old	–	4
41–50 years old	–	1
Ethnic background		
Other	3	18
White UK/Irish	15	4

the final-year undergraduate programme initially joined the study. At SU, 22 eligible students across the BA and MA programmes initially joined. As shown by Table 9.1, most NU and SU participants were 18–22 years of age and identified as female. We can note the ethnically more diverse student cohort at SU.

3.2   Research design and data collection

As shown in Figure 9.1, at both institutions students joining the study were asked to complete a psychometric survey at the end of Phase 1 ("Entry TEIQue") and at the beginning of Phase 3 ("Exit TEIQue") of the STB timeline. In order to be in a position to cross-reference the results of the Exit TEIQue with those of the Entry TEIQue while maintaining anonymity, participants were asked to create a personal identifier known only to them by combining the first two letters of their mother's – or father's – first name and the last three digits of their mobile phone, and to enter it at the beginning of each TEIQue.

Trait Emotional Intelligence Questionnaire (TEIQue) was chosen for this study as it allows for a comprehensive measurement of trait EI (Petrides, 2010). Taking 30 minutes to complete, this self-report questionnaire evaluates a person's general emotional functioning by generating a Global Trait EI score. It also provides more detailed scores across four factors (Well-being, Self-Control, Emotionality, and Sociability) subdivided into 15 facets of EI (such as Self-Esteem, Stress-Management, Assertiveness, or Empathy). Past empirical studies have demonstrated that TEIQue has "superior psychometric properties and greater validity" than other self report measures of EI (Andrei et al., 2016, p.263). Academic researchers can access TEIQue free of charge at: https://psychometriclab.com.

At NU, averaged group-level scores from the Entry TEIQue were used to identify, for this cohort, three facets of EI that could be seen as less adaptive or functional for the purposes of an STB. This informed the development of three group coaching sessions designed to support students with these facets of EI during Phase 2. NU's Entry TEIQue scores were also used as the basis of an initial intervention at the end of Phase 1 during which averaged scores were shared with students. This was a first opportunity for NU students to start reflecting on some of the potential implications of their cohort's EI profile for their collective STB work in Phase 2. The objective was to start enhancing students' emotion-related Knowledge and Abilities (Mikolajczak, 2009, p. 27). Finally, NU participants were asked to take the Exit TEIQue at the beginning of Phase 3. Our objective was to measure empirically the potential impact of the group coaching sessions on NU students' global trait EI, the three EI facets targeted by the group coaching sessions as well as the EI facet Empathy, defined in Trait EI theory as seeing the world from someone else's point of view (Petrides, 2009).

At SU, participants were also asked to complete the Entry TEIQue and the Exit TEIQue but the students taking part in STBs were not offered group coaching sessions during Stage 2. In other words, SU acted as a control group allowing the two investigators to test the potential effectiveness of group coaching on the experimental group's perceived EI abilities and dispositions.

Further, in order to gain a more in-depth understanding of the perceived impact of group coaching on NU students' perception of their ability to recognise and manage emotions during STBs and beyond, NU participants were invited to take part in a one-hour focus group (FG) during Phase 3. Taking place over Zoom, the FG was structured around a series of open-ended questions (see section 5.2). These were designed to encourage participants to discuss their perceptions of the influence of emotions and of group coaching on STBs. The FG played a dual role in this research project. First, it allowed the researcher to add valuable qualitative data to the existing qualitative data through qualitative content analysis (Saldanha and O'Brien, 2014, p.190). Second, by giving participants the opportunity to reflect on the role of emotions (their own and those of others) in STBs, it acted *de facto* as a final intervention for this cohort (see Figure 9.1).

4. Design of the group coaching interventions

At NU, the averaged group-level scores from the Entry TEIQue allowed the two project researchers to identify three facets of EI potentially requiring development for the purposes of the STBs. This was achieved by singling out the three facets with the lowest scores and with a Cronbach score greater than .70,[4] namely Assertiveness (3.9, $\alpha = 0.86$), Stress Management (4.19, $\alpha = 0.85$) and Self-Motivation (4.27, $\alpha = 0.75$). A fellow academic with expertise in the field, Séverine Hubscher-Davidson, was then invited to develop and deliver three online group coaching interventions addressing those three facets of EI for NU students.[5] All three sessions were delivered online via Zoom.

Building on guiding principles provided in Hubscher-Davidson and Lehr (2021), Session 1 (mid-February 2023) focused on the management of emotions and aimed to raise awareness of the importance of emotional competencies and psychological well-being for translation work. Students were provided with some theoretical guidance, illustrative examples, and practical advice for managing emotions such as stress, and leveraging their psychological resources. They were also coached with the silent coaching exercise (Thomson, 2009), a self-directed and experiential coaching tool with acknowledged emotional learning and self-regulation benefits. Silent coaching is thought to "[…] stimulate translators' self-awareness and sense of personal responsibility during an intervention, thus fostering ongoing self-directed learning and personal growth" (Hubscher-Davidson and Lehr, 2021, p. 53).

Session 2 (late February 2023) focused on Stress Management in more depth. After completing a self-evaluation questionnaire to identify strengths and areas of development in relation to how they feel about – and behave – in stressful situations, students completed some reflection activities around their results which aimed to raise awareness of the impact of these situations on their work-related behaviours. Students were then asked to reflect on potential steps to take to improve their stress-management, and information was provided on stress facts, triggers, symptoms, and the physical as well as cognitive effects of stress. They were coached with the ABCDEF coaching exercise (Ellis, 1991), a tool which enables the identification and challenging of psychological blocks and negative automatic thoughts in order to generate more adaptive responses. The aim was to identify stressful thought patterns and gain new perspectives and strategies.

Session 3 (early March 2023) tackled the traits of Assertiveness and Self-Motivation more specifically. To start with, students were introduced to the wider topic of positive emotions and current understandings of well-being, highlighting the recent emphasis on positive psychological perspectives in relation to emotions (e.g., MacIntyre et al., 2019). Subsequently, reflection activities around identifying core values and character strengths were completed. These aimed to encourage self-belief and to provide a sense of rootedness from which discussions around what it means to be assertive and motivated could be facilitated. Once these traits were explained and illustrated with practical scenarios, a structured reflection completed the session whereby students managed an emotion-eliciting work situation applying key points/ideas learned during coaching.

Dedicated time for interaction was also included during the sessions, due to its potential influence on the effectiveness of the coaching (e.g., Hubscher-Davidson and Lehr, 2021). In addition, as students' engagement with, and reactions to, the coaching was difficult to monitor in an online setting, topics and examples used were chosen carefully and did not include sensitive material. Finally, we should note that Empathy was not addressed directly in the coaching sessions. This is because perspective-taking interventions are highly sensitive to group dynamics and can risk, in some contexts, aggravating tensions (Weisz and Zaki, 2017, p.213). As such, it was felt that raising students' awareness of other aspects of EI would be sufficient for the purposes of this study, and still impact empathy indirectly. For instance, a student who becomes more knowledgeable about stress symptoms and their consequences would, in theory, be better able to appreciate how things seem to a fellow student exhibiting stress behaviour.

5. Findings and discussion

5.1   Quantitative data: TEIQue Entry and Exit scores

Our action research project set out to use TEIQue to evaluate the effectiveness of group coaching interventions on students' ability to manage their emotions and develop their empathy during STBs. To that end, NU participants' Exit TEIQue scores were compared to their Entry TEIQue Scores to identify potential variations for the EI facets targeted by the coaching interventions (namely, Assertiveness, Stress-Management and Self-Motivation and, indirectly, Empathy). As TEIQue is a self-report questionnaire, it was hoped this would give us an indication of whether the group coaching sessions had a positive impact on NU students' perceived abilities and dispositions for these facets of EI. Further, the variations in NU students' Entry and Exit scores were compared to SU students' (where no coaching interventions took place) with the aim of ascertaining whether coaching, or the mere fact of participating in an STB during Phase 2, could be seen as the main factor behind the observed score changes. Finally, as one of our broader objectives with this study was to see whether group-coaching during STBs could lead to "desirable and sustainable change" (Bachkirova et al., 2010, p.1) among students by helping develop their general emotional functioning, we also compared Entry and Exit TEIQue scores for Global Trait EI.

Unfortunately, only 26 of the 40 students who had initially agreed to participate in our research project completed the Exit TEIQue at the end of Phase 2 (NU = 10 out of 18; SU = 16 out of 22).[6] Further, the anonymised personal identification system put in place to track students' individual scores seems to have caused some confusion among SU students. Indeed, 13 of the 16 SU students who completed the Exit TEIQue used a different identifier to the one they had used in the entry TEIQue. The same problem arose with one of the NU respondents. For all these students, the absence of matching identifiers made it impossible for the author of this paper to compare individual scores. This data therefore had to be discarded, which resulted in a very small sample of tracked respondents for the SU cohort (SU: n = 3; NU: n = 9). This is one of the most important limitations of this exploratory study; the sample size does not allow us to draw any definitive conclusions at this stage. However, as pointed out by Saldanha and O'Brien (2014, p. 195), small samples remain useful for "generating hypotheses" that can then be probed further. Accordingly, the findings from the quantitative data presented in Table 9.2 were used to generate some initial hypotheses concerning the potential effectiveness of the group coaching interventions in helping NU students manage their emotions and develop their empathy during STBs. The validity of these hypotheses was then probed through triangulation with the qualitative data from the FG (ibid, p. 201).

The data was analysed using the statistical analysis software IBM SPSS Statistics. For each dataset, the lead investigator avoided to "pre-test" for normal distribution of the data with tests such as Shapiro-Wilk, as "[…] such tests are no longer seen as acceptable practice in statistics" (Mellinger and Hanson, 2017, p.93). It was decided, instead, to follow Walker's (2020, p.257) recommendation to "[…] make a decision on the approximation of normality by informal inspection of the data or using data visualisations" with the use of QQ plots. For all NU datasets, the data points followed the 45-degree upward line, thus showing they could be considered normally distributed.

As can be seen from Table 9.2, the NU Exit TEIQue means for the three facets targeted by the group coaching sessions and for Global Trait EI are all lower than the NU Entry TEIQue means; indeed, we observe a drop for Assertiveness (–0.91), Stress Management (–0.32), Self-Motivation (–0.20), and Global Trait EI (–0.11). However, we can also observe an increase in the Empathy Exit means (+0.35). We should note that, with the exception of Assertiveness, the SD for the Exit means are very similar to the SD for the Entry means. Concerning the SU Exit TEIQue means, they are all higher than the Entry means apart from Empathy (–0.59) and Self-Motivation (–0.26), although we should note the high SD for the latter (σ = 1.24). With the important caveat of the very small sample size for SU, we can hypothesise that the sheer fact of participating in an STB allowed SU students to develop slightly more adaptive Assertiveness (+0.18) and Stress Management (+0.53). Concerning NU students, one might be tempted to conclude from the quantitative data that the group coaching sessions had a negative effect on their Assertiveness, Stress management, Self-motivation and Global Trait EI. As explained earlier, however, the limited sample size means that the data is insufficient to corroborate such an interpretation with any degree of certainty. Instead, the observed means variations merely allow us to hypothesise that the group coaching sessions may not have been as effective in helping NU students manage the targeted facets for the purposes of the STBs as we would have liked.

TABLE 9.2 Global Trait EI, Assertiveness, Stress Management, Self-Motivation, and Empathy TEIQue Entry/Exit scores for NU (n = 9) and SU (n = 3) tracked respondents

	NU Entry TEIQue		NU Exit TEIQue		Comparison	
	Mean	SD	Mean	SD	p	g [95% CI]
Global Trait EI	4.81	0.63	4.70	0.69	0.250	−0.16 [−1.08, 0.77]
Assertiveness	4.23	1.18	3.32	0.74	0.197	−0.88 [−1.85, 0.09]
Stress Management	4.37	0.88	4.05	0.89	0.054	−0.34 [−1.28, 0.59]
Self-Motivation	4.48	0.77	4.28	0.79	0.172	−0.24 [−1.17, 0.68]
Empathy	5.25	0.89	5.60	0.92	0.178	0.37 [−0.56, 1.30]

	SU Entry TEIQue		SU Exit TEIQue		Comparison	
	Mean	SD	Mean	SD	p	g [95% CI]
Global Trait EI	4.93	0.42	4.86	0.49	0.365	−0.12 [−1.72, 1.48]
Assertiveness	4.26	0.17	4.44	0.40	1	0.47 [−1.15, 2.09]
Stress Management	4.50	0.90	5.03	0.83	0.292	0.49 [−1.14, 2.11]
Self-Motivation	4.93	0.84	4.67	1.24	0.383	−0.20 [−1.80, 1.41]
Empathy	5.74	0.28	5.15	0.72	0.309	−0.86 [−2.53, 0.81]

Further, in order to check the statistical significance of these observed means variations, two-way paired *t*-tests were run in SPSS (yielding a *p*-value). As a *p*-value (*p*) is normally considered to be statistically significant if $p \leq 0.05$, one must conclude that none of the observed means variations in Table 9.2 are statistically significant, although *p* for NU Stress-Management is very close to statistical significance (0.054). The perceived arbitrariness of $p \leq \alpha$ is the reason why Walker (2020, p.265) argues that "[...] the precise *p*-value should not be over-interpreted" and that *g* (Cohen's *d* standardised effect size with Hedges' correction) should be used as well "to supplement the statistical judgement [...] with a substantive judgement on the size of the difference". In Table 9.2, the *g* scores for NU students are supportive of a trend showing large-to-very large reduction in Assertiveness (–0.88), a small-to-medium reduction in Stress Management (–0.34) and Self-Motivation (–0.24) and a small-to-medium increase in Empathy (0.37). For SU students, the *g* scores are supportive of a trend showing large-to-very large reduction in Empathy (–0.86), a small-to-medium reduction in Self-Motivation (–0.20) and a small-to-medium increase in Assertiveness (0.47) and Stress Management (0.49). Interpreted on its own, the data thus seem to suggest that, unlike what had been anticipated, the group coaching sessions were not effective in in helping NU students manage the targeted EI facets for the purposes of the STBs. Similarly, and still unlike what had been anticipated, holding group coaching sessions during STBs seems to have had little to no effect on students' Global Trait EI. Interestingly, however, the data also point to the fact that attending group coaching sessions during STBs may have helped NU students not just maintain but also develop their Empathy, that is their ability to see the world from someone else's point of view (Petrides, 2009).

Based on these findings from the quantitative data, it can be hypothesised that holding group coaching sessions discussing the role of emotions during STBs allowed NU students to develop their Knowledge – although not necessarily their Abilities or Dispositions (Mikolajczak, 2009, p.27) – of the targeted EI facets and, in the process, to become more aware of their own emotional functioning and that of others during the STBs. This increased knowledge of emotions and emotional functioning may have led to the lower self-reported Exit TEIQue scores for the EI facets classed under the "Self-control" and "Sociability" factors in Petrides' EI model, namely Stress Management and Assertiveness. Conversely, NU students' increased knowledge of emotions may also have led to enhanced abilities and dispositions for Empathy, which is an "Emotionality" factor (see Petrides, 2009). As our project adopted a mixed method approach, the qualitative data that follows allowed us to probe this further through triangulation (Saldanha and O'Brien, 2014, p.201).

5.2   *Qualitative data: focus group*

Taking place over Zoom at the beginning of Phase 3, the one-hour focus group (FG) aimed to gather qualitative data on the perceived impact of group coaching on NU students' perceptions of the potential benefits of the group coaching sessions for the purposes of the STBs and beyond. Six students volunteered to attend the FG; four were female (P1, P4, P5, and P6) and two male (P2 and P3). All had completed both the Entry and the Exit TEIQue and taken part in the group coaching sessions.

The FG was structured around six questions that encouraged open discussion among participants. In the first question (Q1), FG participants were asked to type in the chat two to three emotion words they felt best described their experiences of Phase 2. Participants' answers confirmed that, as identified by the Entry TEIQue, stress was a common emotion for NU students during STBs. Indeed, "stress" was named by all six participants. It was closely followed by words or expressions indicating the respondents' fears of not being up to the task and/or of letting their course mates down. Even though a certain amount of pressure can be helpful in that it may help students find the motivation to get the job done, too much (self-inflicted) pressure may add to students' existing stress. Stress then becomes maladaptive for the purposes of an STB by, for instance, making students question their ability to perform during the STBs: "So it's pressure on yourself to do what you're expected to do [...]. And it was, for me at least, it was more pressure on me by me [rather] than the group putting pressure on me" (P3). The FG thus confirmed the pre-identified need to support students with Stress Management during Phase 2.

Q2 then asked participants how useful they found seeing and discussing their cohort's Trait EI profile – in particular, the three EI facets identified as potentially less functional for the purposes of an STB – during the initial intervention at the end of Phase 1. Rather encouragingly, most participants found this initial intervention useful in that it helped raise their awareness of the role of emotions during collaborative work: "[Y]ou saw how mainly just, like, how your emotions dictate your work" (P4); "I don't think it was necessarily something we'd have talked about as a group on our own without that being brought up" (P6). One FG respondent (P5) also mentioned the fact that this initial session made them discuss their own emotional functioning with others during their initial meeting as an STB, which they felt helped avoid miscommunication during Phase 2. However, we should note that another respondent didn't find this initial intervention very helpful, mostly because they believed that, with hindsight, this information didn't make any difference to their perceived ability to manage their emotions on the STB (P2).

Concerning the three group coaching sessions, most participants said they found them effective in making them think about the emotion-management issues they were facing in a concrete way during Phase 2, which they might not have done otherwise (Q3). We should note, here, that half the participants agreed that they found the practical coaching exercises more "useful" than the theoretical guidance during group coaching. In particular, the silent coaching exercise, which takes the students through a series of 20 questions that helps them structure their own thinking around a concrete issue unique to them, was singled out several times as something they found particularly effective. This exercise is used by coaches to help coachees enhance self-regulation (Thomson, 2009). From all this we can conclude that the FG participants expected concrete help with their own Abilities and Dispositions from the coaching sessions, rather than their Knowledge (Mikolajczak, 2009, 27).

This may explain why some participants felt the group coaching sessions didn't directly help them manage their less adaptive emotions – stress in particular – during Phase 2 (Q4):

> I would attend the coaching sessions and think... I don't need to be too stressed... I can do this. But realistically when it comes back to focusing on the work and look at the deadline, I'll still feel the exact same and put the pressure on.
>
> *(P4)*

There seemed to be palpable frustration among some FG participants that the sessions didn't offer the magic bullet they had hoped for to help them manage their emotions during Phase 2. This could betray a misunderstanding of the purpose of coaching, which is about helping individuals "[...] maximise their own performance [by] helping them to learn rather than teaching them" (Whitmore, 1992, p. 8). Even though the group coaching sessions helped students learn about emotions and emotional functioning (Knowledge), they may not have been enough to support a meaningful transition from Knowledge to Abilities during Phase 2 (Mikolajczak, 2009, p. 27).

The timing of the sessions was also mentioned by most participants as something needing to be looked into (Q5). When some felt the sessions were scheduled too early (P1, P2), others felt they came too late (P3). As summarised by P3, "Unfortunately, when I was stressed about the [STB] was not when we were doing the sessions". Similarly, some FG participants also made the interesting point that they didn't always have the headspace to attend the sessions (Q5). In the words of P2, "I was feeling overwhelmed at the time [...] I didn't want to think too deeply about my life and my stressful situation [...] I didn't want to sit for an hour and hear about how stressful everything is". P2 added this feeling was shared by many of their fellow group members who, according to other FG participants, may have had "preconceived ideas on coaching" (P1) and therefore "closed themselves off even more" to the idea of attending the session (P5). Most other FG participants nodded in agreement. Again, this touches upon an important aspect of coaching, which is the pre-requisite willingness for individuals to engage with the process. There are many reasons why individuals may – consciously or sub-consciously – be reluctant to engage with coaching (e.g., fear of the coaching process, misconceptions about coaching etc.) and yet coaching has been shown to be less effective on reluctant coachees (see Gysbers et al., 2014). This is because "[c]oaching is intended to increase self-awareness in support of growth and change and [...] necessitates some reflection on one's action, purpose and relationships with others" (Joyce, 2013, p. 85). As acknowledged by P5: "You get what you put into it". Interestingly, though, an FG participant explained that, even though they didn't find the sessions directly useful for the STBs, they did find them helpful for other areas of their life:

> Whenever the emotion sessions were on, I just happened to be stressed by other things in my life. So I ended up using the activities to help me reflect on other things that I was more stressed about at the time, and they were really useful in helping me cope with those.
>
> *(P3)*

In their answers to the final question (Q6), all respondents agreed that the group coaching sessions had made them much more aware of the role of other people's emotions and of their own during STB work (Knowledge), which in turn developed their ability to recognise and accept the role of emotions not just for their own performance, but also that of others (Empathy):

> It's made me a lot more aware of [...] how people respond to different things in new, stressful situations. And at least in my group, I noticed which people buried their stress until we had a meeting in which people [...] came forward and said "Look, I'm struggling with this" [...] It's made me a lot more aware of... you need to really be aware of people's mentalities and just because you're coping fine doesn't mean they are [...] [A]nd make sure you can notice signs... [...] [A]nd not just noticing them but acting upon them.
>
> *(P3)*

Other participants echoed this by highlighting how talking openly about emotions during the coaching sessions made them more conscious of everyone else's emotions during Phase 2, which in turn made it "a lot easier to be kind of patient" (P2). Emotion-related Knowledge thus seems to have enhanced participants' Abilities for Empathy which, based on the quantitative data for that trait EI facet displayed in Table 9.2, also seems to have enhanced their Dispositions (Mikolajczak, 2009, p.27): "I think I will have that empathy for other people [...] that I might not have had in the past to that extent" (P4).

6. Conclusion

The findings from our action research project thus suggest that there is no evidence from this study that the group coaching interventions were a particularly effective way to help students manage the targeted EI facets (Stress Management, Self-Motivation, and Assertiveness) during STBs. However, the data from our action research project also seems to suggest that group coaching could be an effective way to develop students' knowledge of emotions and emotional functioning, which in turn seems to have a positive impact on their Abilities and Dispositions concerning Empathy. Indeed, in light of the FG the fact that NU students' self-perceived dispositions for the three targeted EI facets decreased in the Exit TEIQue (see Table 9.2) could be read as reflecting the fact that they started becoming more aware of their own – potentially limited – abilities concerning their emotional functioning in general, and the targeted EI facets in particular, as they became more familiar with the importance and complexity of emotions through the group coaching sessions. To put it simply, the more they started to find out about these EI facets, the more conscious they became of their own potential limitations. This, in turn, seems to have made them more understanding of fellow group members' potential emotion-related limitations. This seems to be corroborated by the findings from the control group, where the Exit TEIQue scores reported higher self-perceived abilities and dispositions for the same EI facets, but a lower one for Empathy.

The data from the control group, however, points to the most serious limitation for our study. The sample sizes in our exploratory study mean that our findings should be taken with caution, and that a re-run with larger sample sizes will be needed to confirm them empirically. Such a re-run should also take other factors, such as the ethnic background of participants, into consideration as we know that completing the TEIQue in a language that is not your mother tongue may have an impact on the scores (see Gökçen et al., 2014).

This notwithstanding, our exploratory study suggests that group coaching interventions during STBs can be an effective way not only to encourage reflexivity and self-awareness among trainee translators, but also to develop their empathy. Both reflexivity and empathy are core elements of the "critical pedagogy" Koskinen (2020, p. 165) champions in translator education because it "allows us to discuss elements such as personal growth or liberation as fundamental goals of education". Planning coaching interventions during experiential learning could thus help us translator educators promote Education for Sustainable Development (ESD) on our programmes for the benefit of both (trainee) translators and wider society, as the "emphasis on competencies related to empathy [   ] contributes not only to the success of individuals, but also to the collective survival and prosperity of the global community" (UNESCO, 2020, p. 14).

Acknowledgements

This research project was funded by Newcastle University (HASS FEDF, 2022). The author and lead investigator is also grateful for Dr Fernandez-Parra's (Swansea University) and Dr Hubscher-Davidson (The Open University) contributions to this project.

Notes

1 Technostress, here, is understood as the "inability to adapt or cope with new computer technologies in a healthy manner" (see Brod, 1984).
2 As shown by Massey (2019),

> authentic experiential learning in translator education is generally predicated on the assumption that only through deliberate practice [...] and reflection-in-action [...] can the adaptive expertise necessary to the professional activity of translation and language mediation evolve. It is therefore compatible with social-constructivist approaches to competence development that assume meaning is collaboratively constructed in social learning environments, appropriately scaffolded by teachers to facilitate growing learner autonomy and the development of learners' self-regulatory capacities.

3 For reasons explained under "Findings and Discussion", the quantitative data was insufficient on its own to draw any definitive conclusions. However, the qualitative data collected as part of our mixed-method approach complemented it in a way that still allowed us to answer our research question. This is because, as pointed out by Saldanha and O'Brien (2014, p. 201), "[i]ntegrating both quantitative and qualitative data is generally seen as a way of combining the best of both paradigms and overcoming their weaknesses".
4 Cronbach's Alpha is a measure of internal consistency. A value of 0.70 or over is seen as indicative of an adequate level of internal consistency.
5 The author is grateful for Séverine Hubscher-Davidson's input into the drafting of this section of the chapter.
6 We should note, though, that this still represents a response rate of 65%, which remains significantly higher than the 44% average response rate for online surveys in educational research (Wu et al., 2022).

References

Allemand, M. and Flückiger, C. 2022. Personality change through digital-coaching interventions. *Current Directions in Psychological Science* 31(1), pp. 41–48.

Andrei, F., Siegling, A.B. et al. 2016. The incremental validity of the Trait Emotional Intelligence Questionnaire (TEIQue): A systematic review and meta-analysis. *Journal of Personality Assessment* 98(3), pp. 261–276.

Angelone, E. 2022. Weaving adaptive expertise into translator training. In: Massey, G., Huertas-Barros, E. and Katan, D. (eds.) *The Human Translator in the 2020s*. Abingdon: Routledge, pp. 60–73.

Bachkirova, T., Cox., E. and Clutterbuck, D. 2010. *The Complete Handbook of Coaching*. London: Sage.

Bolaños-Medina, A. 2016. Translation psychology within the framework of translation studies: New research perspectives. In De León, C.M. and González-Ruiz, V. (eds.) *From the Lab to the Classroom and Back Again: Perspectives on Translation and Interpreting Training*. Frankfurt-am-Main: Peter Lang, pp. 59–99.

Bond, E. 2018. The Stunning Variety of Job Title in the Language Industry Slator News. Retrieved from: www.slator.com/the-stunning-variety-of-job-titles-in-the-language-industry/

Brod, C. 1984. *Technostress: The Human Cost of the Computer Revolution*. Reading: Addison-Wesley.

Buysschaert J., Fernandez-Parra, M. and van Egdom, G.-W. 2017. Professionalising the curriculum and increasing employability through authentic experiential learning: The cases of INSTB. *Current Trends in Translation Teaching and Learning-E (CTTL-E)* 4, pp. 78–111.

Campo, M., Laborde, S. and Mosley, E. 2016. Emotional intelligence training in team sports. *Journal of Individual Differences* 37(3), pp. 152–158.

Clutterbuck, D. 2021. Questions in coaching. In Passmore, J. (ed.) *The Coaches' Handbook*. London: Routledge, pp. 92–103.

Cooke, A.N., Bazzini, D. G., Curtin, L.A. et al. 2018. Empathic understanding: Benefits of perspective-taking and facial mimicry instructions are mediated by self-other overlap. *Motivation and Emotion* 42, pp. 446–457.

Courtney, J. and Phelan, M. (2019). Translators' experiences of occupational stress and job satisfaction. *The International Journal of Translation and Interpreting Research* 11(1), pp. 100–113.

Dave, H.P., Keefer, K., Snetsinger, S.W., Holden, R.R. and Parker, J.D.A. 2021. Stability and change in trait emotional intelligence in emerging adulthood: A four-year population-based study. *Journal of Personality Assessment* 103(1), pp. 57–66.

Dryden, W. 2018. *Cognitive-Emotive-Behavioural Coaching*. London: Routledge.

Ellis, A. 1991. The revised ABC's of rational-emotive therapy (RET). *Journal of Rational-Emotive and Cognitive-Behavior Therapy* 9(3), pp. 139–172.

Fernando, M., Pietro, M. D., Alemeida, L. S., Ferrándiz, C. et al. 2011. Trait emotional intelligence and academic performance: Controlling for the effects of IQ, personality, and self-concept. *Journal of Psychoeducational Assessment* 29(2), pp. 150–159.

Gökçen, E., Furnham, A. et al. 2014. A cross-cultural investigation of trait emotional intelligence in Hong Kong and the UK. *Personality and Individual Differences*, 65, pp. 30–35.

Gysbers, N. C. et al. 2014. *Career Counselling: Holism, Diversity and Strengths*. 4th ed. Hoboken: Wiley.

Hodzic, S., Scharfen, J. and Ripoll, P. et al. 2018. How efficient are emotional intelligence trainings: A meta-analysis. *Emotion Review* 10(2), pp.138–148.

Hubscher-Davidson, S. 2018a. *Translation and Emotion. A Psychological Perspective*. Abingdon: Routledge.

Hubscher-Davidson, S. 2018b. Do translation professional need to tolerate ambiguity to be successful? A study of the link between tolerance of ambiguity, emotional intelligence and job satisfaction. In Jääskeläinen, R. and Lacruz, I. (eds.) *Innovation and Expansion in Translation Process Research*. Amsterdam: John Benjamins, pp. 77–103.

Hubscher-Davidson, S. 2020. The psychology of sustainability and psychological capital: New lenses to examine well-being in the translation profession. *European Journal of Sustainable Development Research* 4(4), p. em0127.

Hubscher-Davidson, S. and Lehr, C. 2021. *Improving the Emotional Intelligence of Translators. A Roadmap for an Experimental Training Intervention.* London: Palgrave Macmillan.

ICF International Coach Federation. 2009. ICF Global Coaching Client Study: Executive Summary. International Coaching Federation. Retrieved from: www.res earchportal.coachingfederation.org/Document/Pdf/abstract_190

Joyce, M. 2013. Why some leaders and managers are reluctant to be coached. In Forman, D. et al. (eds.) *Creating a Coaching Culture for Managers in Your Organisation.* London: Routledge, pp. 83–107.

Koskinen, K. 2020. *Translation and Affect: Essays on Sticky Affects and Translational Affective Labour.* Amsterdam: Benjamins.

Kotsou, I., Mikolajczak, M., Heeren, A. et al. 2019. Improving emotional intelligence: A systematic review of existing work and future challenges. *Emotion Review* 11(2), pp. 151–165.

MacIntyre, P.D., Gregersen, T. and Mercer, S. 2019. Setting an agenda for positive psychology in SLA: Theory, practice, and research. *The Modern Language Journal* 103(1), pp. 262–274.

Massey, G. 2019. Learning to Learn, Teach and Develop. Co-emergent Perspectives on Translator and Language-mediator Education. inTRAlinea. Special Issue: New Insights into Translator Training. Retrieved from: www.intralinea.org/specials/article/2429

Massey, G., Huertas-Barros, E. and Vine, J. 2022. *The Human Translator in the 2020s.* London: Routledge.

Massey, G., Piotrowska, M. and Marczak, M. 2023. Meeting evolution with innovation: an introduction to (re-)profiling T&I education. *The Interpreter and Translator Trainer* 17(3), pp. 325–331.

Mellinger, C. and Hanson, T. 2017. *Quantitative Research Methods in Translation and Interpreting Studies.* London: Routledge.

Mikolajczak, M. 2009. Going beyond the ability-trait debate: The three-level model of emotional intelligence. *E-Journal of Applied Psychology* 5(2), pp.25–31.

Nelis, D., Quoidback, J. et al. 2009. Increasing emotional intelligence: (how) is it possible? *Personality and Individual Differences* 47(1), pp.36–41.

Penet, J.C. and Fernandez-Parra, M. 2023. Dealing with students' emotions: Exploring trait EI theory in translator education. *The Interpreter and Translator Trainer* 17(3), pp. 332–352.

Perdikaki, K. and Georgiou, N. 2022. Permission to emote: Developing coping techniques for emotional resilience in subtitling. In: Hubscher-Davidson, S. and Lehr, C. (eds.) *The Psychology of Translation.* London: Routledge, pp. 58–80.

Petrides, K.V. 2009. Psychometric properties of the Trait Emotional Intelligence Questionnaire (TEIQue). In Parker, J., Saklofske, D. and Stough, C. (eds.) *Assessing Emotional Intelligence.* Boston: Springer, pp. 85–102.

Petrides, K.V. 2010. Trait emotional intelligence theory. *Industrial and Organizational Psychology* 3(2), pp. 136–139.

Petrides, K.V., Pita, R. and Kokkinaki, F. 2007. The location of trait emotional intelligence in personality factor space. *The British Journal of Psychology* 98(2), pp. 273–289.

Risku, H. and D. Schlager. 2021. Epistemologies of translation expertise. In Halverson, S. L. and García, Á. M. (eds.) *Contesting Epistemologies in Cognitive Translation and Interpreting Studies*. New York: Routledge, pp. 11–31.

Saldanha, G. and O'Brien, S. 2014. *Research Methodologies in Translation Studies*. Abingdon: Routledge.

Schmitt, P. 2019. Translation 4.0. Evolution, revolution, innovation or disruption? *Lebende Sprachen* 64(2), pp.193–229.

Starr, J. 2021. *The Coaching Manual*. 5th ed. Harlow: Pearson.

Tang, A. 2015. Coaching emotion: The use of coaching as a management technique to support the emotional labour of new teachers. *International Journal of Arts & Sciences*, 8(8), pp. 563–572.

Thomson, B. 2009. *Don't Just Do Something, Sit There: An Introduction to Non-Directive Coaching*. 1st ed. Oxford: Chandos Publishing.

UNESCO. 2020. *Education for Sustainable Development: A Roadmap*. Paris: UNESCO.

Walker, C. 2020. *An Eye-Tracking Study of Equivalent Effect in Translation*. London: Palgrave MacMillan.

Weisz, E. and Zaki, J. 2017. Empathy building interventions: A review of existing work and suggestions for future directions. In Seppala, E. et al. (eds.) *The Oxford Handbook of Compassion Science*. Oxford: Oxford University Press, pp. 205–217.

Whitmore, J. 1992. *Coaching for Performance*. London: Nicholas Brealey.

Wu, M.-J., Zhao, K. and Fils-Aime, F. 2022. Response rates of online surveys in published research: A meta-analysis. *Computers in Human Behavior Reports* 7, p. 100206.

10

NEW PROSPECTS FOR INTERNATIONAL TELECOLLABORATION IN TRANSLATOR TRAINING

A case study on Leeds-Monash collaboration

Martin Ward and Shani Tobias

Keywords: translator training; international telecollaboration; professional skills; translator competences; intercultural environments

1. Introduction

Translator training, as with other academic and vocational disciplines, has been greatly transformed at the start of the 2020s, notably by the COVID-19 pandemic and significant advances in AI, amongst others. Whilst the negative impacts of the pandemic and other crises on student learning are well known, the focus has also turned to the "new normal", characterised by changes initially forced upon academia to sustain education and training in a context constrained by social-distancing and reduced mobility. The expedited move to online and hybrid forms of delivery and engagement precipitated by a new awareness of the opportunities to develop innovative pedagogies, has also opened up new avenues of remote engagement and collaboration between translator trainers and trainees.

It is well known that collaboration between various stakeholders is vital in the process of professional translator training to support high standards and relevance in the delivery of training, but also to frame the training for trainees to best reflect the professional environment in which they are going to work. Examples of collaboration between academic institutions and industry in the training of translators abound; however what is not so prominent is collaboration between institutions in different countries in the training of professional trainers, although some evidence has been disseminated on related projects (see Marczak, 2023, p. 121 as an example). Pedagogic approaches establishing collaborative work between students at

DOI: 10.4324/9781003440970-12

different HE institutions, not limited to translator training, has often been referred to as "telecollaboration". For clarity, in this chapter we use the term "international telecollaboration" to refer to all kinds of international pedagogical collaborations, under which banner fall virtual exchange (VE) experiences, COIL (collaborative online international learning), and others. Literature on this form of collaboration in education in various forms across disciplines has come to proliferate in recent years.

Telecollaboration has been defined by O'Dowd (2018, p. 5) as:

> the engagement of groups of learners in extended periods of online intercultural interaction and collaboration with partners from other cultural contexts or geographical locations as an integrated part of their educational programmes and under the guidance of educators and/ or expert facilitators.

This definition clearly highlights the key principles of "online" and "other cultural contexts or geographical locations" but does not insist explicitly on collaboration with an institution in a different country. In this connection, the related concept of COIL is more explicit, but according to SUNY (The State University of New York), arguably the most vocal proponent of COIL, a "COIL" activity should be a minimum of four (Guth and Rubin, 2015) or five weeks in length (SUNY, n.d.). Krajka and Marczak (2017, p. 376), however, recognise that telecollaborative projects "may vary in terms of project duration (short-term, mid-term, long-term)", without defining these terms.

Professional translator training in many countries, for example Australia and the UK, tends to take place through specialised MA-level postgraduate degree programmes. Employing international telecollaboration in translator training can potentially further the development of students' skills and furnish them with experiences reflective of likely future undertakings, by simulating real world scenarios for translation work. Students may benefit not only from developing their translation competencies as individuals, but also their ability to work jointly on specific translation projects with other trainee professionals in different contexts, countries, and time zones, with each bringing their various expertise to the project. Such activities also reflect the reality of modes of collaboration likely to be required in their future careers as translators or other professional roles within the language services industry, such as project managers, localisation experts, terminologists, editors, etc., who frequently work as part of a team in large-scale translation or localisation projects.

Further, networks facilitating exchange and collaboration between students in specific fields as well as academics are important in this regard, and some innovative networks have been established in recent years. One example is the East Asian Translation Pedagogy Advance (EATPA) network, founded in late 2020 by one of the authors, seeking to bring together academics around the world teaching the translation of East Asian languages at HE institutions. Due to the fact that these practitioners are broadly geographically removed from each other, frequent in-person networking and collaboration are not feasible, so instead the online space has provided a unique opportunity for sharing best practice, discussing topics pertinent to translation pedagogy, and developing collaborations. Of the collaborations to have been developed out of the EATPA network to date, one which has been gaining traction is an international telecollaborative activity embedded into their teaching practice by the present authors, practitioners in Japanese to English specialised translation pedagogy on opposite sides of the world.

However, to what extent has telecollaboration been employed in translator training to date, and what signs are there that its broader use may contribute to the enhanced effectiveness of translator training and enriched learning experiences which can better prepare students for future collaborative working in translation-related careers? In this chapter we first examine the relevant existing literature around telecollaboration in translator training, and then proceed to introduce a case study of collaboration in Japanese to English specialised translation between the University of Leeds in the UK and Monash University in Australia. The authors hope that this model and the present chapter may go some way to demonstrate the unexplored potential for such collaborations and beneficial outcomes for students.

2. Literature review

The body of literature surrounding the implementation of telecollaboration, virtual exchange, COIL, and all relatable activities under a variety of terms across disciplines is vast and increasing all the time. Here we shall refer to all of these activities under the umbrella of "telecollaboration". Much attention has been paid to the use of telecollaboration in the field of language learning (e.g., Chen and Du, 2022; Nishio et al., 2020). There exists some literature on the use of telecollaboration in translator education, although much of the literature on collaboration in translator training exhibits a focus on in-person education rather than telecollaboration per se. Here we outline the literature most relevant to this chapter.

The basis for collaboration in translator training generally has already been established by Kiraly (2000, p. 60), who noted that, "Learning is best accomplished through meaningful interaction with peers [...]" and there is "tremendous benefit to be gained through group interaction" (2000, p. 37). Over a decade later, Huertas Barros (2011, p. 43) noted in her study on collaborative learning, "teamwork has become more and more important for present-day translators, which justifies the need to implement this methodological solution in education as well as studying its use in translator training." The benefits of collaborative work itself in translator training are also clearly articulated through Huertas Barros' study's survey results, where key benefits perceived by students were generating a diversity of ideas, interaction with others, preparation for future careers, acquisition of new abilities, and myriad others (2011, p. 52). Babych et al. (2012, p. 1) also affirm that, "students aiming for a career in translation will gain from early exposure to [collaborative activity]", and then state explicitly,

> we reject the conception of university translator training as an individual exercise in transforming text from one language to another, with ephemeral, disposable outputs. In contrast, we construe translation as a collaboration between aspiring specialists in the source-language culture and subject domain, terminologists, translators and revisers.
>
> *(p. 3)*

It should be noted, however, that Babych et al.'s study mainly deals with one specific technological platform and does not examine in depth the trainees' experience of telecollaboration itself.

Al-Jarf (2017) examined collaboration in translator training focusing their analysis on the use of a discussion forum and its impact on developing the quality of students' translations. Thelen (2016) also discussed collaboration and cooperation in translator training, but not in an international context. Thelen's study considers the varying definitions of cooperation and collaboration in translator training, concluding that collaborative translation "would certainly enrich the training and contribute to the preparation of students for post-graduation employment" (2016, p. 266).

Marczak (2016) notes with regards to their study that students admitted telecollaboration furthers the development of soft skills (2016, p. 250), and also that "students unanimously approved of telecollaboration as an approach with which to facilitate translator education" (2016, p. 249), although unfortunately no quotes from students are provided to give more detailed insights than this. In terms of ascertaining and disseminating the student experience of COIL, Guth and Rubin (2015, p. 42) note that, "Too often research into COIL projects has been based on feedback from only one group of students, limiting the validity of such results." Even Krajka and Marczak (2017), while presenting some data on the experience of students at two unnamed institutions of a telecollaborative project only provide quantitative responses to surveys and as a result the student voice is not particularly audible.

It is clear then, that whilst research into telecollaboration is abundant, there is a notable paucity of student feedback available for scrutiny on the efficacy and explicit benefits of telecollaboration, and this is particularly so in the case of translator training. There is also adequate basis to conclude that the impact and benefits of telecollaboration in translator training have been under researched, as has the implementation of collaborative translation projects between intra-university partners (Paradowska, 2021, p. 23), and the practice of *international* telecollaboration has been underemployed in translator training. However, Olvera-Lobo, who developed collaborations between students at one institution, stated (2009, p. 165) that, "Given that professional translation work is highly influenced by new communication opportunities, teleworking must occupy its rightful place in translator training at tertiary level." How beneficial, then, for international cross-border collaborations to be developed in the context of translator training against the backdrop of a globalised translation industry.

In summary, the validity of collaboration between students and stakeholders in translator training has already been established, but international collaborative activities between translation trainees are still few in number and the visibility of the impact of these activities on the trainees' experience and development is low. Thus, a case study into an instance of international telecollaboration between translation trainees which opens a window on the student voice will be most beneficial to facilitate and encourage the development of further collaborations.

3. Introduction to the present study

Conscious of the unexplored potential for international telecollaboration in translator training and the potential significant benefits for translation trainees, the authors of this chapter introduced a collaborative translation task into their Japanese to English translation teaching in 2021, bringing together MA students from the University of Leeds in the UK and Monash University in Australia. As in the case of Krajka and Marczak (2017) the task was designed through negotiation between the authors to ensure a good fit for both cohorts of students in terms of relevance, difficulty, and timing. The Leeds students were taking Japanese to English translation as one of their selected specialised translation modules as part of a number of translating, interpreting, or audio-visual translation MAs at the Centre for Translation Studies. The Monash students were taking Japanese to English translation classes as part of the core translation modules in their Master of Interpreting and Translation Studies.

The first iteration of the collaboration was book-ended with synchronous joint classes on Zoom one week apart (morning in the UK and evening in Australia) but before that the participants were given a document outlining the task which they were to review in advance. The collaborative activity involved translating a popular science text on space debris[1] from Japanese into English in mixed groups of Monash-Leeds students for a defined audience and preparing a presentation (Kelly, 2005, p. 100) to deliver in the second Zoom session. Presentations incorporated source text analysis, translation challenges, ensuring consistency, and the collaborative process. The first Zoom session began with introductions and an overview of the task, and then participants were sent to pre-set breakout rooms to meet their team, or syndicate (Kelly, 2005) members, determine roles and divide up the task, and decide together when they would have their minimum one required online team meeting and which platforms they would use to collaborate remotely. The task was formative and scaffolded to students as a valuable, collaborative opportunity reflective of potential future working scenarios, but was not formally assessed at either institution.

In response to participant feedback the activity was gradually adjusted at each roughly semestral iteration with regards to presentation topics assigned, source text selected etc, and in particular extended so that the collaborative classes were conducted two weeks apart instead of one. The number of students fluctuated with varying cohort sizes, but each time student feedback was solicited to further develop the activity. Since student responses were overwhelmingly positive regarding their experience of the task, the authors decided to conduct formal research into the impact and value of the activity to gather empirical data for analysis, discussion, and dissemination.

This international telecollaborative activity for MA-level students is not intended as a form of "virtual mobility" and is by no means an add-on or a second-best substitute for some other kind of activity. Rather it was designed as an integral, formative experience reflective of professional realities, modelling cross-border scenarios and helping make trainees aware of varying national contexts for translation work. The authors see this activity as an essential experience for emerging Japanese to English translators, and firmly believed it would strengthen a variety of specialised and transferrable skills.

4. Research question and methodology

The case study presented in this chapter set out to answer the following research question: How can the application of international telecollaboration in a specialised translation class contribute to the development of key skills required of professional translators? By setting the research aim in this way, it was anticipated that empirical evidence could be gathered which would unhide the student voice regarding their experience of international telecollaboration to indicate the extent to which such activities may be beneficial for trainee translators. This in turn would help to validate the present pedagogic methodology as a model for other practitioners to consider.

To gain an in-depth understanding of the perceptions of the student participants, the authors conducted two rounds of interviews with students taking part in the October 2022 iteration of the activity described above. The first (pre-activity interviews) were conducted in the fortnight leading up to the activity, and the second (post-activity interviews) were conducted within a few weeks following the final synchronous session. In order to ensure that students felt able to express their views freely, all interviews were conducted by a research assistant who was not involved in teaching or assessing any of the students. Participants were recruited via email and provided with an explanatory statement about the research. Informed consent was obtained verbally at the beginning of each interview. Ethical clearance for the study was obtained at both institutions.[2]

There were 11 students in total participating in the activity as part of their Japanese-English translation class for the relevant semester (six from Monash and five from Leeds). A total of seven of these students took part in both the pre- and post-activity interviews (two students from Leeds and five from Monash). It should be noted that for the October 2022 activity that was the subject of this case study, the Leeds students had only just started their master's degree in the two weeks before the telecollaboration and were thus largely new to translation, whereas the Monash students were significantly more experienced (four students had nearly completed two semesters, while the fifth had nearly completed one semester). Only three students had experienced international telecollaboration during their university studies prior to this activity, meaning that the group comprised of students with a mixture of some or no previous experience.

The interviews were semi-structured and conducted in English, one-on-one via Zoom, each lasting approximately 15 minutes. The pre-activity interview questions were designed to identify students' expectations prior to the activity so that these could be compared with their views post-activity to better understand the ways in which their perceptions on the relevant skillsets and the value of international telecollaboration in enhancing these skillsets may have changed or may have been reinforced by their actual experience. Topics covered included perceptions of the factors and skills required to make a collaborative translation project successful, what they hoped to gain through the activity, how it may help develop their translation skills, how it may help them prepare for their future career, their perceptions on the importance of intercultural competence in the context of international telecollaboration, and anticipated challenges of the activity. The post-activity interview topics explored their experience of the activity to elicit opinions on topics including: the challenges of international telecollaboration and their strategies to overcome these, the process of collaborating on a translation, working with people from different cultures or backgrounds, working across time zones, working with online tools and platforms, project management and scheduling tasks, and feedback on how the activity might be improved in future.

In addition to the interviews, which obtained data from seven of the 11 participants in the telecollaboration, a short online survey was also implemented at the end of the final synchronous session on 26 October 2022. All 11 students who participated in the activity completed the survey, which deployed a five-point Likert scale to explore their overall experience and challenges, as well as the extent to which students believed that the activity had helped them develop their skills in translation, intercultural competence, career preparedness, presentation, international collaboration, and project management.

The interviews were recorded via Zoom and transcribed using Zoom's automatic transcription feature. The research assistant checked the transcripts for accuracy and corrected them where errors were found. The transcripts were then analysed by the current authors using qualitative content analysis noted by Saldanha and O'Brien (2014, pp. 189–192), a process of inductive coding whereby sections of the transcript relevant to the research question were highlighted, and key themes and sub-themes were generated from these to code the responses.

5. Findings and discussion

5.1 Pre-activity interviews

With regard to the anticipated benefits of this particular international telecollaboration, several participants mentioned that they hoped to build soft skills, such as teamwork and communication skills, in the context of a cross-border translation project, in preparation for working internationally in their future careers. Since the activity would involve collaborating with peers whom they would be meeting for the first time, participants saw this as exemplifying what happens in a variety of professional settings and a number commented that they hoped the experience would help them learn how to work with a diverse group of people, navigating different expectations and opinions in an online environment. As one participant stated,

> because I want to be a translator in the future, I think it will be really useful to have some experience of working in a group, especially a group that's maybe not the easiest group environment to work in. Because in the real working world, there probably will be situations like that.
>
> *(Amy)*

Several participants discussed the relevance of time management and learning how to manage time zone differences, as well as learning from overseas students from different cultural or educational backgrounds.

Participants believed that the skills needed to make collaborative translation successful were predominantly communication and organisational skills (such as scheduling and task allocation), as well as people skills, to effectively build trust with new colleagues. Specifically, regarding their translation skills, several participants stated that they hoped to learn about other perspectives on translation, and anticipated that revising and editing each other's translations would help them be self-reflexive about their own translation at the same time as developing their revision skills:

> rather than just kind of practicing my own translations on an individual level, it will be helpful in reviewing other people's translations. And then sort of reflexively being able to evaluate my own, based on the differences there.
>
> *(Meg)*

It was also hoped that they would gain experience in negotiating differences of interpretation and approach in translation.

When questioned on their general sentiments about working collaboratively, participants displayed a tendency towards concern or hesitancy, at the same time acknowledging some positive experiences of group work in university settings. The negative comments related to the loss of control (and the challenge of negotiating differences of opinion about the translation approach), the concern that the motivation of group members may vary, and the need to work with colleagues who have different workflows and methods to themselves. On the positive side, participants commented that it can also be beneficial to have others review one's work and offer a different perspective, and that in a safe environment when group members are supportive, collaboration can be very stimulating.

When asked about the nature of intercultural competence and their views on its importance in international telecollaboration, participants exhibited quite a nuanced understanding of potential cultural differences and their implications for the activity, such as differences in communication and politeness norms, and the norms around giving/receiving feedback. They viewed intercultural competence as the ability to listen, be empathetic and non-judgemental, and put oneself in the other person's shoes. They thought that it was important to broaden their own perspectives and be open to adjusting their own communication approach to accommodate cultural differences, such as clarifying expectations, and fostering a friendly environment to build trust.

Six out of seven participants viewed the time zone difference as likely to be a challenge during the activity, and some mentioned that if there was a knowledge gap among the groups of students, this may cause issues. Participants noted possible strategies to deal with the challenges such as setting clear expectations about processes and schedules, having a team leader to keep everyone on track, and making sure that there was open communication among group members.

5.2 Post-activity data

Overall, students commented on the value of peer learning, particularly the Leeds students who were able to learn from peers who were further along in their MA programme and thus more experienced in translation and also in project management (since the Monash students were taking a module on translation project management at the time). A common theme mentioned by the participants was adaptability: "the biggest take away from it is simply being flexible on my feet and trying to work around [issues] to produce something fruitful and collaborative together" (Daisy). This included attempting to work effectively with different types of translators, even if they were less experienced, and building communication and teamwork skills so as to provide mutual support and encouragement. These comments about benefits of peer learning were also reflected in more positive feelings about collaboration compared to the concern expressed at the pre-activity interviews, one participant noting: "This was a lot more professional. People were really passionate about the subject, and they all wanted to do a really good job, and I was inspired by them" (Hannah). The interview comments were supported by the post-activity survey in which all eleven respondents agreed or strongly agreed that the activity was a positive experience overall, and seven of the 11 agreed or strongly agreed that it had helped prepare them for their future careers, with the remaining four neither agreeing nor disagreeing with this statement.

The main challenges identified by participants centred around the time zone differences and the gaps in knowledge between the Monash and Leeds cohorts. With regard to the Leeds students' relative lack of knowledge of translation theory (which was understandable given that they had only just commenced their course), both sides were uncertain how to proceed. One Leeds participant expressed their sentiments as follows: "the Australian students were in semester two and it was challenging to catch up with them in matters of knowledge and I just didn't want to feel useless to them" (Hannah). In contrast, one Monash participant stated:

> I didn't want to overwhelm them with, you know, a lot of information, but the same time I didn't know how to go forward with it. So that kind of dilemma there, um, caused a lot of anxiety. But, I guess, you know, that's also a part of a learning experience as well... There's a lot of things that might happen that you might not expect.
>
> *(Daisy)*

The significance of these challenges was reflected in the survey, in which seven out of 11 agreed or strongly agreed that the activity was more challenging than they had anticipated (four were neutral and one disagreed). At the same time, the fact that students regarded these challenges as learning opportunities is also indicated by the survey results in which ten out of 11 respondents agreed or strongly agreed that where challenges arose, they were able to work with their group members to resolve these effectively.

With regard to the time difference, interview participants recognised that this required them to be patient in receiving feedback on their translation or responses to questions, and it was necessary to compromise regarding their availability for meetings as well as consider what tasks could be done asynchronously. In the survey as well, all 11 students surveyed agreed or strongly agreed that the international telecollaboration had helped them develop strategies for working internationally across time zones.

The interview participants commented particularly about the challenges and learning experiences derived from telecollaboration with colleagues with different backgrounds whom they had never met before. As well as the differences in knowledge and experience, they noted the diversity of translation workflows adopted by their peers, differences in speed at completing tasks, motivation levels, and the stress involved in ensuring that everyone remained on track to meet the deadlines. This was particularly the case for those students who nominated themselves as project managers. They reflected in the interviews on what they might have done better, and the need for effective communication from the outset was noted several times:

> I think the way that we conceptualized [translation] was very different. And again, we should have talked more about that to start with in terms of going, "okay how do you translate?" instead of going, "alright let's translate it!"
>
> *(Jo)*

Instead of making assumptions about translation approaches and the appropriate process, "it made me realize that you need to verbally communicate those sort of things especially across a cultural divide" (Jo).

A couple of the Monash participants commented on the usefulness of being able to apply concepts and skills of project management they were being taught in their university module to this activity, adopting strategies such as utilising a group contract, meeting agendas, taking minutes, and setting clear deadlines, task allocations and sharing resources. In the survey, all 11 respondents agreed or strongly agreed that the activity had helped them develop skills in project management/teamwork such as effective time management, organisation, communication, and sharing of roles.

Through the activity, students were made aware of different translation pedagogies employed at the two universities, which they found insightful, and they also benefitted from sharing resources with their peers overseas. Furthermore, they were able to gain various insights through intercultural exchange: "in my group everyone was from different countries ... It was really interesting to ... see how each one of us would interpret the Japanese text, culturally" (Hannah). In other words, the activity helped them identify that a translator's interpretation and style of translating is strongly influenced by both their educational and cultural background. This was reflected in the survey as well, in which nine out of 11 agreed or strongly agreed that the activity helped develop their intercultural competence.

The task of producing a translation collaboratively and then reflecting on and presenting about the process to the class was regarded favourably by the participants. Several commented that it was very beneficial to compare their translations and give and receive feedback both via written comments as well as in real time:

the whole process of it was enlightening, I think. Because we came to the realization that all three of the people, in my group at least, we all had different ways of translating. We all have different types of writing styles, and trying to combine them all, and ... come to an agreement was something that we needed to negotiate, I suppose.

(Laurie)

Some students reflected that they had not previously considered the need to justify their own translation decisions, and so it was useful for their learning to see how other students did this through their comments on the draft translation. In the survey, nine out of 11 respondents agreed or strongly agreed that the activity had developed their competence in collaborative translation, and the same number agreed or strongly agreed that it broadened their perspectives on different translation approaches and strategies through learning from other students. Ten agreed or strongly agreed that it helped them learn how to work together to solve translation issues, including how to negotiate differences of opinion, and how to give useful and constructive feedback when revising.

For this activity, students were not instructed to use particular online tools or software for their translation project, even though some students had already received training in online CAT tools. Instead, it was left up to the students to decide amongst themselves what platform would best facilitate collaboration, and the groups decided that the Google applications would be easiest for everyone to use. Most used a shared Google Drive where they uploaded all their documents, and some also used WhatsApp group chat and Zoom for meetings. Since most students were already proficient users of these platforms, in the survey, only five out of 11 agreed/strongly agreed that the activity helped develop their competence in the various digital tools needed for collaborative translation. However, students who were less familiar with the latter technologies did comment that the activity helped improve their tech literacy. Since it was not the main objective of the activity to develop advanced skills in this area, the authors considered that it would be more valuable for their learning if students took the initiative themselves in determining the optimal means of online collaboration, including the platforms.

When asked for their suggestions about how to improve the activity for future iterations, the most common point made was that the learning experience would be enhanced if students from both institutions were at similar stages of their degree. Alternatively, if one group of students was new to translation, participants suggested that they could be provided with some introductory materials on translation approaches so that the more experienced students would not need to explain as much. Important feedback was provided regarding the use of Zoom for the joint classes, namely that they should be completely on Zoom for both groups instead of the Leeds students all joining Zoom from their classroom while the Monash students were joining individually from home, since this caused some noise issues and audio feedback. Allowing more time in the first class for students to get to know each other in their project groups was also suggested, as was allocating a Japanese first language speaker to each group where possible, so students could better understand source text nuances.

In response to this feedback and the comments made by students in the interviews and survey, a number of changes were implemented in the March 2023 iteration. Given the different semesters and degree structures, as well as the need to align the academic calendars, it is seldom possible in an international telecollaborative setting to match the cohort levels exactly. While there would be some benefits if this were possible, there are equally a range of useful learning opportunities when the levels of experience differ, as indicated by some of the interview comments. Therefore, before the March 2023 iteration the authors decided to manage expectations by explicitly discussing the benefits of working with peers having diverse backgrounds and levels of experience, particularly pointing out that this mirrors the nature of real-life teams in the workplace and would therefore be useful preparation for students' future roles. Second, in order to emphasise some of the soft skills that would be necessary in the activity, the authors decided to scaffold the students' knowledge about telecollaboration skills by directing them to university resources on groupwork and online collaboration prior to the task. Finally, the authors implemented the students' recommendations to hold the joint classes on Zoom only, and to allow greater time for initial group discussions during the first class. All of these changes were well-received by students in the short post-activity feedback survey.

5.3 Discussion

The above findings strongly support the view that implementing an international telecollaborative activity in a specialised translation course is beneficial in advancing students' translator competences (Kiraly, 2006), particularly regarding the professional skills necessary to interact with project stakeholders in an online environment.

As Krajka and Marczak (2017, p. 375) note, telecollaboration can allow students to apply theory to practice, and this was also highlighted by the interviewees in the present study, both in relation to the translation task itself (such as using theory to inform their analysis of the brief and approach to translation and revision), as well as applying academic discourse about project management to a practical simulation of a collaborative translation project.

Our findings also mirror those of Marczak (2016, pp. 246–247) in suggesting that a telecollaborative activity enables students to develop certain soft skills, defined as "universal, transferrable skills which increase a person's employability", which include "communication skills; teamwork skills; interpersonal skills; cultural awareness; flexibility, strategic planning and self-organisation skills; creativity; (analytical/critical) thinking skills; and leadership skills". Results in Marczak's survey of translation students showed that the majority believed that they had developed key soft skills (particularly in teamwork (94%), communication (78%), leadership (61%) and negotiation (56%)) (2016, pp. 248–249). While the latter study related to a cohort of students studying the same course at a single university, it is likely that such soft skills would be further enhanced when the telecollaboration is international, involving students studying at different institutions, as in the present study. As our participants reflected, when interacting across time zones with colleagues who have different educational and cultural backgrounds, the need for excellent communication, interpersonal, intercultural, and leadership skills is accentuated.

In order for students to take full advantage of the international telecollaborative experience to build these soft skills, the importance of scaffolding has been highlighted. The participants in our study commented on various challenges (such as working with students at different stages in their degree, managing differences in time zones and individual workflows), which should cause educators to consider how such challenges may be turned into learning opportunities, in particular the need to provide students with tools that can assist them to work through issues when they arise. This point is also emphasised by Marczak, who calls for educators to explain the importance of soft skills in the workplace (2016, p. 250) and adequately prepare students for the telecollaborative project. This may involve devoting face-to-face time with the cohorts to discuss the likely issues and allow students to consider in advance how these might be managed, also reflecting on examples of how situations were effectively dealt with in the past (Krajka and Marczak, 2017, p. 381). As Penet and Fernandez-Parra (2023) discuss in their exploration of Trait Emotional Intelligence theory in translator education, collaborative translation projects can generate strong emotions, not only in professional settings but also among student participants in simulated activities. Consequently, preparing students through a pre-activity intervention to build their awareness of their own and team members' personality traits and how they might respond in challenging situations may assist them to develop important coping strategies that they can apply during the task (Krajka and Marczak, 2017, p. 349). The logistics of online communication also pose unique challenges as mentioned by Krajka and Marczak (2017, pp. 378–379), but the 2020s have seen a rapid acceleration of online interaction in educational settings as well as the professional world more broadly, and students in the post-Covid era are learning quickly about the importance of adaptability and flexibility in online multicultural environments. As the interviews in the present study show, some students even value the opportunity afforded by international telecollaboration to take them outside their comfort zone.

The findings of the present study indicate that embedding international telecollaboration within the translation curriculum enriches the students' learning experience regarding the core skills of translation and revision, through peer-to-peer learning and collaboration. Students are able to gain insights into diverse perspectives, translation approaches and pedagogies when interacting with their peers from an overseas institution, more so than in the familiar context of their regular translation classroom. This encourages them to find creative solutions to translation problems and fosters students' ability to reflect on their own choices, negotiate and problem-solve with translator colleagues, and offer constructive feedback, all of which are essential skills for students to demonstrate as part of the learning objectives of a specialised translation course. Importantly, although students may express initial anxiety regarding the possibilities of collaborative group work in an online international setting, when telecollaboration is implemented effectively it can increase students' motivation and cause them to feel more confident about undertaking similar activities in their professional roles.

6. Conclusions and implications

While telecollaboration and COIL have been widely used across disciplines, this study highlights the unexplored potential for international telecollaboration in translator training and the many benefits for trainees in an increasingly closely networked and interlinked world. As previously noted by Krajka and Marczak (2017, p. 380), translator training programmes should employ telecollaboration as a matter of course, but here we would go further to insist on the value of international telecollaboration, involving synchronous interaction between trainees, in professional translator training, given the additional skills sharpening and vital broadened experience it brings to the trainees. In an age where institutions are constantly seeking to update their translator training programmes to keep up with technological and other advances, re-examining broader pedagogical approaches and introducing international telecollaboration is indispensable as it can provide trainees with crucial real-world opportunities and challenges to navigate which will set them in good stead for their future careers. International telecollaboration is extremely versatile and lends itself to almost all areas of translator training.

Acknowledgements

This study was supported by Monash University (Monash Abroad COIL Grant, 2023). The authors are also grateful for the research assistance provided by Monash University PhD candidate, Eliza Nicoll.

Notes

1 「宇宙はゴミだらけ」――NASAもお手上げの「宇宙ゴミ」回収に挑む、日本人起業家の奮闘 Accessible from https://news.yahoo.co.jp/articles/56794008048b3 8d6603f38f645470fa2282a87e9 last accessed 14 September 2021.
2 Monash University Project ID: 34928; University of Leeds: FAHC 21-135.

References

Al-Jarf, R. 2017. Exploring online collaborative translator training in an online discussion forum. *Journal of Applied Linguistics and Language Research (JALLR)*. 4(4), pp. 147–160.

Babych, B., Hartley, A., Kageura, K., Thomas, M. and Utiyama, M. 2012. MNH-TT: A collaborative platform for translator training. In *Proceedings of Translating and the Computer*, 34.

Chen, C. and Du, X. 2022. Teaching and learning Chinese as a foreign language through intercultural online collaborative projects. *The Asia-Pacific Education Researcher*. 31(2), pp. 123–135.

Guth, S and Rubin, J. 2015. How to get started with COIL. In: Moore, A.S. and Simon, S. eds. *Globally networked teaching in the humanities: Theories and practices*. London: Routledge, pp. 28–45.

Huertas Barros, E. 2011. Collaborative learning in the translation classroom: preliminary survey results. *The Journal of Specialised Translation*. 16(3), pp. 42–60.

Kelly, D. 2005. *A handbook for translator trainers*. New York: Routledge.

Kiraly, D.C. 2000. *A social constructivist approach to translator education: Empowerment from theory to practice*. Manchester: St. Jerome Pub.

Kiraly, D.C. 2006. Beyond social constructivism: Complexity Theory and translator education. *Translation and Interpreting Studies*. 6(1), pp. 68–86.

Krajka, J. and Marczak, M. 2017. Telecollaboration projects in translator education–design, implementation and evaluation. In: Smyrnova-Trybulska, E. ed. *Effective development of teachers' skills in the area of ICT and e-learning.* Cieszyn: University of Silesia, Faculty of Ethnology and Sciences of Education (E-learning, Vol. 9), pp. 365–388.

Marczak, M. 2016. Students' perspective on Web 2.0-enhanced telecollaboration as added value in translator education. In: Jager, S., Kurek, M. and O'Rourke, B. eds. *New directions in telecollaborative research and practice: Selected papers from the second conference on telecollaboration in higher education, 21–23 April 2016, Dublin.* Dublin: Research-publishing.net, pp. 245–252.

Marczak, M. 2023. *Telecollaboration in translator education: Implementing telecollaborative learning modes in translation courses.* New York: Routledge.

Nishio, T., Fujikake, C. and Osawa, M. 2020. Language learning motivation in collaborative online international learning: An activity theory analysis. *Journal of Virtual Exchange.* 3, pp. 27–47.

O'Dowd, R. 2018. From telecollaboration to virtual exchange and the role of UNICollaboration: An overview of where we stand today. *Journal of Virtual Exchange.* 1(1), pp. 1–23.

Olvera-Lobo, M.D. 2009. Teleworking and collaborative work environments in translation training. *Babel.* 55(2), pp. 165–180.

Paradowska, U. 2021. Benefits and challenges of an Intra-university authentic collaborative translation project. *New Voices in Translation Studies.* 24(1), pp. 23–45.

Penet. J.C. and Fernandez-Parra, M. 2023. Dealing with students' emotions: exploring trait EI theory in translator education. *The Interpreter and Translator Trainer.* 17(3), pp. 332–352.

Saldanha, G. and O'Brien, S. 2014. *Research methodologies in translation studies.* London: Routledge.

SUNY. n.d. WHAT IS COIL? [Online]. [Accessed 30 June 2023]. Available from: www.online.suny.edu/introtocoil/suny-coil-what-is/

Thelen, M. 2016. Collaborative translation in translator training. *Konińskie Studia Językowe.* 4(3), pp. 253–269.

PART III

Trainee translators' voices on new modes of training

11

HOW COVID-19 RESHAPED PERCEPTIONS OF TRANSLATOR TRAINING

Voices from the classroom

José Ramón Calvo-Ferrer

Keywords: COVID-19 pandemic; online learning; student perceptions; translation studies; teaching methodologies

1. Introduction

This study explores the profound impact of the COVID-19 pandemic on translator training, with a particular focus on the transition from traditional face-to-face instruction to online learning environments. It investigates how this shift has influenced students' perceptions of teaching methodologies and their preferences for learning modes within translation studies. By analysing students' experiences and attitudes at the University of Alicante, Spain, the study aims to shed light on the evolving landscape of translator training in a post-pandemic world. Following this overview, it delves into the global impact of COVID-19, its implications for education and translation studies, and outlines the methodological approach adopted in this research.

1.1 The global impact of COVID-19

The COVID-19 pandemic has had a profound impact on global health. The rapid spread of the virus and the subsequent health crisis urged governments to take drastic measures, including widespread lockdowns and social distancing protocols. These measures, along with the fear of infection and the abrupt changes they brought about, led to a range of health impacts, with mental health being the most extensively studied (Chiesa et al., 2021). Li et al. (2021) investigated the prevalence of depression and anxiety among adolescents during the pandemic, finding significant mental health impacts. Segre et al.

DOI: 10.4324/9781003440970-14

(2021) found most children and adolescents experienced anxiety symptoms, whereas Melo and Soares (2020) highlighted a dramatic increase in negative thoughts, sleep disturbances, and suicidal ideation during the lockdown. A study by Taquet et al. (2022) found that eating disorders among people under 30 were significantly higher in 2020 compared to previous years, with a higher proportion of patients feeling suicidal. A recent literature review by Bera et al. (2022) found that the perceived well-being of teenagers declined during the COVID-19 pandemic, with adolescents being significantly more affected by the lockdown than those in the general population.

1.2 Disruption in education and learning

Not only did the pandemic affect the health of young people, but it also brought about a disruption of their learning environments and educational experiences, as schools and universities worldwide had to transition from face-to-face instruction to online modes of learning. This sudden shift presented a range of challenges, from ensuring access to digital resources to adapting traditional classroom activities for virtual platforms. The transition to online learning also necessitated a re-evaluation of teaching pedagogies, together with the curation of online and offline student experiences (Bryson & Andres, 2020). Fostering active student engagement, a challenging task in traditional classroom settings, became even more critical in online learning environments (Daniel, 2020), and was adversely affected as a consequence of insufficient student interaction, connectivity issues, and poor content delivery, among others (Méndez Santos, 2023). Student engagement was indeed sought after through the use of various active learning techniques, synchronous and asynchronous teaching methods, and educational technologies (Ahshan, 2021). However, the effectiveness of these strategies largely depended on the students' access to digital resources and their ability to adapt to the new learning environment (Salas-Pilco et al., 2022).

1.3 Implications for translation studies

Given the nature of translation studies, which often hinge on collaborative feedback and real-time discussions, the shift to online learning during the pandemic might have had a significant impact on students' experiences. Face-to-face interaction was replaced by virtual interfaces, while group discussions transitioned to digital formats. This sudden and unnegotiated adaptation to a virtual environment, combined with the broader societal impacts of the pandemic, might have reshaped students' perceptions of their discipline, the value of in-person interactions, and the potential of digital tools in their field of study. While some students expressed a longing for the social and interactive aspects of traditional classroom environments, others found value in the flexibility and accessibility of online learning (Tsang et al., 2021;

Unger & Meiran, 2020; Zheng et al., 2021). Taking all these factors into consideration, this study aims to explore how the pandemic-induced shift to online learning has influenced students' perceptions and experiences in translation training, and how these changes may shape the future of this field.

1.4 The present study

This study is exploratory in nature, aiming to illustrate the shifts in students' attitudes and perceptions in translation training owing to the pandemic, which is hypothesised to have led to significant changes towards their field of study. These changes might range from their preferences in learning modalities to their perceptions of how translation should be taught in a digitally connected world. This investigation aims to offer insights for educators, institutions, and translation trainees in the post-pandemic educational context.

Based on the literature on the review, the following questions were examined:

Q1. How has the pandemic influenced students' perceptions of teaching in translation?
Q2. What is the preferred mode of instruction (face-to-face vs online vs blended) among students in the field of translation?
Q3. How have the academic experiences during the pandemic influenced students' preferences regarding tuition methods?
Q4. How have the academic experiences during the pandemic shaped students' views on the best methodologies for teaching translation?

To address these questions, the underlying hypotheses of the study were as follows:

H1. The pandemic has significantly influenced students' perceptions of translation teaching.
H2. Most students express a preference for face-to-face instruction over online methods.
H3. Pandemic-induced tuition has had a significant impact on students' preferences for tuition methods.
H4. Pandemic-induced tuition has had a significant impact on students' views on the optimal methodology for teaching translation.

2. Materials and method

2.1 Sample

The participants for this study were students of the degree in Translation and Interpreting at the University of Alicante ($N = 92$). Of these, 9.6% ($n = 9$) started their studies in 2018–2019, before the pandemic, 59.6% ($n = 56$) in

2019–2020, the year the first lockdown took place, and 30.9% (n = 29) in 2020–2021, a year that began with online tuition due to the pandemic.

2.2 Materials

A questionnaire was developed to explore how the pandemic has affected students' perspectives on the teaching and learning of translation. The questionnaire was designed using an expert judgment approach, in which students from the Translation and Interpreting degree at the University of Alicante (N = 23) shared their insights on the shift to online learning during the pandemic. The discussion, held in class, focused on how the pandemic influenced their perception of their education and whether it prompted any changes in their views on how translation should be taught. Their opinions were processed and formulated to create the questionnaire, which was then shared with the students. After addressing minor errors and making slight adjustments based on their feedback, demographic questions and others related to their preferred tuition methodology were added. The questionnaire, which used a 7-point Likert scale ranging from "completely disagree" to "completely agree", was then distributed to students from other modules from the degree in Translation and Interpreting of the University of Alicante.

2.3 Data analysis

Different analyses were performed to answer the research questions. First, a descriptive statistics analysis was conducted to process the responses to the questionnaire items, as shown in Table 11.1. To assess the reliability of the questionnaire, an internal consistency analysis using Cronbach's alpha was performed, which resulted in a scale score reliability of 0.731 for the sample. According to Nunnally (1967), this score indicates a satisfactory degree of internal consistency for exploratory research. The third step involved a principal component analysis, as Table 11.2 shows, which was used to explore how the different items in the questionnaire clustered together and allowed for the creation of several variables. Once the potential variables had been identified, a regression analysis was performed. The key assumptions of the linear regression model, including normality, linearity, homoscedasticity, and the absence of multicollinearity and autocorrelation were checked and confirmed. All analyses were performed using the SPSS 22.0 statistical software, with a p-value of 0.05.

3. Results

3.1 Students' perceptions of translation teaching

The first hypothesis (H1) about the influence of the pandemic on the students' perceptions of translation teaching, was tested by the results of the

TABLE 11.1 Descriptive statistics

	M	SD
PIT made me have a more favourable opinion of face-to-face teaching.	5.49	1.593
PIT made me realise that teaching of subjects in translation has to focus on practical issues and that their theoretical load needs to be reduced.	5.41	1.454
Face-to-face tuition is necessary for the teaching of translation.	5.12	1.636
I missed attending classes in person during the pandemic.	4.95	2.114
PIT required more effort from me to follow the lectures and carry out the necessary activities.	4.92	1.882
PIT made me improve my knowledge of new technologies applied to translation (glossaries, translators, office automation, etc.).	4.53	1.830
PIT made me realise that translation is a solitary activity.	4.51	1.941
PIT made me improve my autonomy to solve problems related to translation.	4.48	1.600
PIT made me prefer teaching methodologies different from the traditional one.	4.35	1.647
PIT has changed my opinion on how the teaching of translation should be developed.	4.26	1.657
PIT made me have a more favourable opinion of online teaching.	3.90	2.000
PIT made me realise that I would like to continue taking classes remotely.	3.53	2.008
PIT made me realise that physically attending class is not so important.	3.52	2.141
PIT made me become a better translator and interpreter.	3.47	1.433
PIT made teachers put more effort into tuition.	3.35	1.794
PIT made it easier for students to participate in class.	3.11	2.003
PIT made me like translation more than before.	2.80	1.528
I would like to return to the teaching model during the pandemic.	2.78	1.827
PIT made me realise that the teacher is less important than I thought.	2.65	1.600
PIT improved the way translation was being taught up to that point.	2.59	1.469

Note: N = 97. PIT = Pandemic-induced tuition.

study – participant feedback revealed a marked shift in how students viewed the teaching and learning of translation post-pandemic. As the responses to the questionnaire suggest, the highest mean scores were associated with the preference for face-to-face teaching. Specifically, the statement "Pandemic-induced tuition made me have a more favourable opinion of face-to-face teaching" received the highest mean score of 5.49 (SD = 1.593). This was closely followed by "Face-to-face tuition is necessary for the teaching of translation" (M = 5.12, SD = 1.636) and "I missed attending classes in person during the pandemic" (M = 4.95, SD = 2.114). As a consequence of the pandemic, many students recognised the solitary nature of translation (M = 4.51, SD = 1.941), but they also reported that it had improved their

TABLE 11.2 Rotated component matrix

	1	2	3	4	5
Factor 1. Perceptions of online tuition and its impact on learning					
PIT made me realise that physically attending class is not so important.	0.835				
PIT made me realise that I would like to continue taking classes remotely.	0.825				
PIT made me prefer teaching methodologies different from the traditional one.	0.795				
PIT made me become a better translator.	0.764				
PIT made me have a more favourable opinion of online teaching.	0.751				
I would like to return to the teaching model during the pandemic.	0.744				
PIT made me have a more favourable opinion of face-to-face teaching.	-0.696				
I missed attending classes in person during the pandemic.	-0.677				
PIT made me improve my autonomy to solve problems related to translation.	0.658				
PIT improved the way translation was being taught up to that point.	0.625				
PIT made it easier for students to participate in class.	0.507				
Face-to-face tuition is necessary for the teaching of translation.	-0.498				
Factor 2. Effort and challenges associated with online learning					
PIT made teachers put more effort into tuition.		0.570			
PIT made me improve my knowledge of new technologies applied to translation (glossaries, translators, office automation, etc.).		0.555			
PIT required more effort from me to follow the lectures and carry out the necessary activities.		0.415			
Factor 3. Teacher's role and course content					
PIT made me realise that the teacher is less important than I thought.			0.547		
PIT made me realise that teaching of subjects in translation has to focus on practical issues and that their theoretical load needs to be reduced.			0.483		
Factor 4. Nature of translation and its teaching					
PIT made me realise that translation is a solitary activity.				0.535	
PIT has changed my opinion on how the teaching of translation should be developed.				-0.519	
Factor 5. Interest in translation					
PIT made me like translation more than before.					0.554

Note: PIT = Pandemic-induced tuition. Extraction Method: Principal Component Analysis. Rotation converged in 5 iterations.

ability to solve translation-related problems independently. Additionally, many students felt that online instruction required more effort to keep up with lectures and participate in required activities ($M = 4.92, SD = 1.882$). Also, the pandemic-induced shift to online learning led some students to realise the importance of focusing on the practical aspects of translation ($M = 5.41, SD = 1.454$).

3.2 Preferences on teaching methodologies

To test the second hypothesis (H2), which posited that most students express a preference for face-to-face instruction over online methods, their answers to the questions, "Now that the pandemic is over, I can say that the best translation teaching methodology is ...", and "Regardless of the above, I prefer ..." were analysed. The results showed that 50.0% of respondents thought that face-to-face tuition was the best approach for translator training, while 46.7% favoured blended learning, which combines traditional face-to-face and online teaching. Only 3.3% thought online learning was the best approach. When asked about their personal preferences, regardless of what they thought was most effective, the results aligned with views on effectiveness to a certain extent – 63.0% preferred face-to-face tuition, 33.7% liked blended learning, and 3.3% chose online learning.

3.3 Relations between the variables explored

A factor analysis was conducted to address research questions Q3 and Q4, exploring the data's underlying structure to identify how pandemic-induced tuition influenced students' preferences and views on teaching methodologies. The rotation process converged in five iterations, demonstrating the stability of the factor solution. The Kaiser-Meyer-Olkin (KMO) measure of sampling adequacy was 0.826, indicating that the factor analysis was appropriate for the given data. Bartlett's test of sphericity yielded a significance level (p) of 0.00, confirming the presence of significant correlations between the variables and the suitability of the resulting factor model.

The first factor ($M = 3.94, SD = 0.803$) clustered together the students' opinions on the importance of physical class attendance, their preference for continuing remote classes, and their inclination towards non-traditional teaching methodologies due to the pandemic. The loadings for these items, ranging from 0.498 to 0.835, highlight a strong association. The second factor ($M = 4.27, SD = 1.184$), with loadings ranging from 0.415 to 0.570, reflect the perceived effort put in by teachers, the enhancement of students' technological knowledge, and the challenges faced by students during online sessions. The third factor ($M = 4.03, SD = 1.220$) focuses on the perceived role of the teacher in online tuition and the emphasis on practical aspects of translation and interpreting.

With loadings of 0.547 and 0.483, this factor underscores the diminished importance of the teacher in the online setting and the need for a more practical focus in the curriculum. The fourth factor ($M = 4.39$, $SD = 1.324$) delves into the change in students' opinions due to online tuition and their realisation about the solitary nature of translation. The items in this factor, with loadings ranging from 0.519 to 0.535, suggest that online tuition has significantly influenced students' perspectives on translation as an individual activity and has reshaped their views on teaching methodologies. Lastly, the fifth factor ($M = 2.80$, $SD = 1.528$), associated with the personal impact of online tuition on students' passion for translation, bears a strong loading of 0.554.

To understand the relationships between the variables explored a correlation analysis was conducted. Regarding the academic year students began their studies in Translation and Interpreting, i.e., in which course their programmes shifted to virtual tuition, a statistically significant negative correlation ($r = -0.239$, $p = 0.022$) was observed with the factor "Nature of translation and its teaching", suggesting that students having started their programme in face-to-face perceived translation as a more solitary activity as a consequence of the pandemic. Conversely, students' perceptions of the optimal teaching methodology were significantly correlated with the factors "Perceptions of online tuition and its impact on learning" ($r = 0.567$, $p < 0.001$), "Teacher's role and course content" ($r = 0.334$, $p = 0.001$), "Nature of translation and its teaching" ($r = 0.237$, $p = 0.023$), and "Interest in translation" ($r = 0.339$, $p = 0.001$). This suggests that students who view online tuition positively are more inclined to consider it the best teaching approach. Such students also tend to downplay the teacher's role, perceive translation as a solitary endeavour, and exhibit a heightened interest in translation. Very similarly, students' preferences between face-to-face, virtual, and blended learning correlated with the factors "Perceptions of online tuition and its impact on learning" ($r = 0.577$, $p < 0.001$), "Teacher's role and course content" ($r = 0.264$, $p = 0.011$), and "Interest in translation" ($r = 0.249$, $p = 0.017$).

3.4 Effect of the variables explored on participants' opinions on preferred teaching methodology

A regression analysis was conducted to answer the third research question while testing the third hypothesis, which predicted that the shift to online tuition during the pandemic would have a significant impact on students' preferred educational approach for translation training. The analysis, which included the five dimensions identified in the factor analysis performed, was statistically significant ($F (5, 86) = 9.244$, $p < 0.001$). The overall model accounted for 35.0% of the variance in students' opinions on their preferred teaching methodology, as indicated by an R^2 value of 0.350. However, only the first factor "Perceptions of online tuition and its impact on learning", appeared to have a significant impact on students' beliefs ($\beta = 0.600$, $p < 0.001$).

TABLE 11.3 Effect of identified variables on participants' preferred teaching approach

Model	Unstandardized Coefficients		Standardized Coefficients	t	Sig.
	B	Std. Error	Beta		
1 (Constant)	−0.079	0.282		−0.279	0.781
Perceptions of online tuition and its impact on learning	0.415	0.075	0.600	5.560	0.000
Effort and challenges associated with online learning	−0.060	0.044	−0.128	−1.372	0.174
Teacher's role and course content	0.011	0.048	0.025	0.240	0.811
Nature of translation and its teaching	0.010	0.043	0.024	0.233	0.816
Interest in translation	0.004	0.035	0.010	0.105	0.917

Note: n = 92; R^2 = 0.350; adjusted R^2 = 0.312; F (5,86) = 9.244, p = 0.000. Dependent variable: Regardless of the above, I prefer.

To investigate the extent to which the items that comprised such factor could predict the students' opinions regarding their preferred teaching approach, a second regression analysis was then performed. The resulting model was also statistically significant (F (20,71) = 9.411, p < 0.001), accounting for 72.6% of the variance in students' opinions on their preferred teaching methodology, as indicated by an R^2 value of 0.726. Several items emerged as significant predictors of students' inclination towards non-traditional, non-face-to-face instruction. Specifically, students' desire to revert to the pandemic-era teaching model was a strong predictor (β = 0.373, p < 0.001). Conversely, agreeing with the notion that pandemic-induced instruction increased their appreciation for face-to-face teaching was a negative predictor (β = −0.288, p = 0.009), whereas, wishing to continue with remote classes was positive one (β = 0.368, p = 0.005). Finally, the belief that pandemic-induced translation honed their translation skills was inversely related to their preference for non-face-to-face tuition (β = −0.291, p = 0.014).

3.5 Effect of the variables explored on participants' opinions on best teaching methodology

Another regression analysis was conducted to answer the fourth research question, whose corresponding hypothesis predicted that the shift to online tuition during the pandemic would have a significant impact on students' opinions on the best teaching methodology for translation. The analysis was statistically significant (F (5, 86) = 9.211, p < 0.001), as Table 11.4 shows.

TABLE 11.4 Effect of identified variables on participants' opinions on best teaching approach

Model	Unstandardized Coefficients		Standardized Coefficients	t	Sig.
	B	Std. Error	Beta		
1 (Constant)	−0.097	0.286		−0.339	0.735
Perceptions of online tuition and its impact on learning	0.332	0.076	0.473	4.377	0.000
Effort and challenges associated with online learning	−0.015	0.044	−0.031	−0.328	0.744
Teacher's role and course content	0.057	0.049	0.123	1.173	0.244
Nature of translation and its teaching	0.007	0.043	0.016	0.159	0.874
Interest in translation	0.044	0.036	0.121	1.241	0.218

Note: $n = 92$; $R^2 = 0.349$; adjusted $R^2 = 0.311$; $F (5,86) = 9.211$, $p = 0.000$. Dependent variable: Now that the pandemic is over, I can say that the best translation teaching methodology is.

The overall model accounted for 34.9% of the variance in students' beliefs about the best teaching methodology, as indicated by an R^2 value of 0.349. However, only the first factor "Perceptions of online tuition and its impact on learning", appeared to have a significant impact on students' beliefs ($\beta = 0.473$, $p < 0.001$), suggesting its importance in shaping students' opinions.

Considering these results, a further analysis was carried out, incorporating the questionnaire items that comprised the first factor as independent variables. This was done to determine how well they could predict students' views on the most effective teaching methodology for translator training. The resulting model was also statistically significant ($F (20,71) = 3.579$, $p < 0.001$), explaining 50.2% of the variance, as reflected by an R^2 value of 0.502. However, only the item "Pandemic-induced tuition made me prefer teaching methodologies different from the traditional one" emerged as significant ($\beta = 0.313$, $p = 0.043$), which suggests that students' agreement with this statement aligns with their belief that alternative methodologies, shaped by the pandemic's influence on tuition, may offer more effective approaches to translator training than traditional ones.

4. Discussion

The COVID-19 pandemic has had a major impact on education. Our study aimed to explore the consequences of the transition from face-to-face instruction to online modes of learning in translator training. The study analysed the perceptions of students regarding how pandemic-induced instruction affected students' opinions on how translation should be taught. Students reported face-to-face instruction as their preferred teaching approach, which highlights the intrinsic value students place on in-person interactions (Vygosky, 1978) in a discipline as nuanced as translation. However, while students expressed a longing for traditional classroom experiences, they also acknowledged the benefits of blended learning (Garrison & Kanuka, 2004), as almost half of the participants identified blended learning as the best approach for translator training. The pandemic also made students realise the importance of focusing on practical issues in translation. This suggests that, while the medium of instruction shifted, the core of translation, i.e., its practical application, remained essential for students.

The second research question, which was meant to establish whether students would prefer face-to-face instruction over online or blended learning models, was supported by the results of the study. The data showed that a significant percentage of respondents preferred face-to-face tuition over blended or virtual teaching, which is in line with previous studies suggesting that face-to-face instruction, when combined with online teaching, can offer the most robust learning experience (Means et al., 2009). However, when asked about the most effective method for translation training, blended learning and face-to-face tuition were almost equally popular, mirroring previous research comparing the effectiveness of both approaches (Kocoglu et al., 2011). These findings may be attributed to the interactive nature of translation studies – face-to-face interactions allow students to ask questions, receive immediate feedback, and build relationships with their instructors and peers. These aspects are critical in a field that requires not only linguistic proficiency, but also cultural understanding, context interpretation, and real-time problem-solving (Risku, 2002). However, the acceptance of blended learning may indicate that students see the benefits of online sessions, such as flexibility, accessibility, and the use of digital tools that can aid in translation, if combined with in-person interactions. These findings have significant implications for translation education. As Yang (2021) suggests, institutions may want to consider offering more blended learning opportunities, which can provide students with the personal touch of face-to-face sessions and the convenience of online classes.

The increased effort required by students to keep up with online lectures and activities may reflect the challenges inherent in finding alternative teaching methods that replicate the real-time discussions, immediate feedback, and collaborative atmosphere of a physical classroom. This observation points to the need for innovative approaches in online pedagogy that more closely mimic the interactive dynamics of traditional settings. Furthermore, the tendency of students to focus more on practical aspects of translation during online learning suggests that such formats may provide valuable pedagogical insights, emphasizing practical over theoretical approaches. Despite a clear preference for face-to-face interaction, this trend highlights an opportunity for curriculum innovation in translator training. By integrating more hands-on, real-world, experiential learning opportunities, programs can better equip students with both foundational knowledge and the practical skills required for the evolving demands of the translation profession in the digital age. The findings also suggest that, while students may be aware of the benefits of blended learning, they still prefer the personal interaction and engagement that comes with face-to-face teaching. This aligns with the notion that face-to-face teaching allows students to ask questions, get feedback, and build relationships with their teachers and classmates, emphasizing the importance of interpersonal interactions in learning environments. Overall, even though the pandemic introduced many to online and blended learning, traditional face-to-face teaching remains popular in translator training. However, the growing preference for blended learning indicates that combining online and traditional teaching methods is becoming more accepted and could represent a shift in educational preferences in the post-pandemic era.

The third and fourth research questions aimed to explore the factors influencing students' perceptions of translation teaching during the pandemic and to determine how these factors affected their opinions on the best and preferred teaching methodologies. The factor analysis conducted revealed five distinct factors that explain students' experiences and perceptions during the pandemic. These factors ranged from perceptions of online tuition and its impact on learning to ideas about the nature of translation. In line with previous research (Sun et al., 2008), the analysis revealed that students' experiences with online tuition during the pandemic significantly influenced their opinions and preferences on translation teaching methodologies. Furthermore, students who had a positive view of pandemic-induced tuition were more inclined to consider blended learning as the best teaching approach.

This study does not come without limitations. First, it must be noted that the sample consisted only of students of the degree in Translation and Interpreting at the University of Alicante, which may limit the generalisability of the results to other populations. While the University of Alicante followed the same procedures as most universities to implement virtual tuition during the pandemic, its quality and consistency might have varied, potentially affecting students' experiences and perceptions. Second, the study was conducted following the COVID-19 pandemic. This period brought about significant emotional and psychological challenges which might have influenced students' responses, making them more aware of the immediate challenges rather than of long-term observations. Fourth, the study relies on self-reported data, which introduces the potential for biases – students' memories and perceptions might be influenced by other experiences, which could affect the accuracy of their responses. Fifth, the factor analysis is based on the researcher's interpretation, which might introduce subjectivity and might not capture students' actual experiences and perceptions accurately. Finally, the study did not account for individual differences in technological access and proficiency. It must be noted that students with limited access to stable internet or appropriate devices might have had different online learning experiences than those better-equipped.

However, these limitations present opportunities for further research. Future studies could involve students from various global institutions that might have shifted to online instruction by different means and with different resources. The impact of the COVID-19 pandemic on mental health may also have implications for the long-term effects of online learning. Future research should examine these effects beyond immediate perceptions. To counter the biases of self-reported data, combining quantitative methods with qualitative tools like interviews could offer a more detailed view of student experiences and strengthen findings. Finally, understanding the online learning experiences of students with different technological resources and its effects on how it has shaped their perceptions provides interesting avenues for research.

5. Conclusion

The findings of this study underscore the value of face-to-face instruction in translation studies, highlighting the immediacy, interaction, and collaborative atmosphere of traditional classroom settings. While online tuition introduced students to the solitary nature of translation, it also highlighted the challenges of virtual learning, from technological difficulties to the increased effort required to follow lessons. The study also provides insights into how the pandemic has influenced students' perceptions. The shift to online learning not only changed their views on teaching methodologies, but also made them reflect on the very nature of translation as an activity – their emphasis on practical aspects over theoretical ones suggests that the online format might have inadvertently pushed students towards a more hands-on approach to translation. All in all, this study emphasises the importance of preserving traditional teaching methods while being open to the potential benefits of online teaching such as flexibility and accessibility.

References

Ahshan R. (2021). A Framework of Implementing Strategies for Active Student Engagement in Remote/Online Teaching and Learning during the COVID-19 Pandemic. *Education Sciences*, 11(9), 483. https://doi.org/10.3390/educsci11090483

Bera, L., Souchon, M., Ladsous, A., Colin, V., & Lopez-Castroman, J. (2022). Emotional and behavioral impact of the COVID-19 epidemic in adolescents. *Current Psychiatry Reports, 24*(1), 37–46. https://doi.org/10.1007/s11920-022-01313-8

Bryson, J.R., & Andres, L. (2020). COVID-19 and rapid adoption and improvisation of online teaching: Curating resources for extensive versus intensive online learning experiences. *Journal of Geography in Higher Education*, 44(4), 608–623. https://doi.org/10.1080/03098265.2020.1807478

Carvalho Aguiar Melo, M., & de Sousa Soares, D. (2020). Impact of social distancing on mental health during the COVID-19 pandemic: An urgent discussion. *International Journal of Social Psychiatry*, 66(6), 625–626. https://doi.org/10.1177/0020764020927047

Chiesa, V., Antony, G., Wismar, M., & Rechel, B. (2021). COVID-19 pandemic: Health impact of staying at home, social distancing and "lockdown" measures – A systematic review of systematic reviews. *Journal of Public Health (United Kingdom)*, 43(3), E462–E481. https://doi.org/10.1093/pubmed/fdab102

Daniel, S.J. (2020). Education and the COVID-19 pandemic. *Prospects*, 49(1), 91–96. https://doi.org/10.1007/S11125-020-09464-3

Garrison, D.R., & Kanuka, H. (2004). Blended learning: Uncovering its transformative potential in higher education. *Internet and Higher Education*, 7(2), 95–105. https://doi.org/10.1016/j.iheduc.2004.02.001

Kocoglu, Z., Ozek, Y., & Kesli, Y. (2011). Blended learning: Investigating its potential in an English language teacher training program. *Australasian Journal of Educational Technology*, 27(7), 1124–1134. https://doi.org/10.14742/AJET.908

Li, W., Zhang, Y., Wang, J., Ozaki, A., Wang, Q., Chen, Y., & Jiang, Q. (2021). Association of home quarantine and mental health among Teenagers in Wuhan, China, during the COVID-19 pandemic. *JAMA Pediatrics*, 175(3), 313–316. https://doi.org/10.1001/jamapediatrics.2020.5499

Means, B., Toyama, Y., Murphy, R., Bakia, M., & Jones, K. (2009). *Evaluation of evidence-based practices in online learning: A meta-analysis and review of online learning studies*. www.ed.gov/about/offices/list/opepd/ppss/reports.html.

Méndez Santos, M. del C. (2023). Análisis de los factores desmotivadores durante la enseñanza a distancia de emergencia causada por el COVID-19: El caso del español como lengua extranjera en el Instituto Cervantes de El Cairo. *Itinerarios*, 37, 295–322. https://doi.org/10.7311/ITINERARIOS.37.2023.14

Nunnally, J.C. (1967). *Psychometric Theory*. McGraw-Hill.

Risku, H. (2002). Situatedness in translation studies. *Cognitive Systems Research*, 3(3), 523–533. https://doi.org/10.1016/S1389-0417(02)00055-4

Salas-Pilco, S.Z., Yang, Y., & Zhang, Z. (2022). Student engagement in online learning in Latin American higher education during the COVID-19 pandemic: A systematic review. *British Journal of Educational Technology*, 53(3), 593–619. https://doi.org/10.1111/BJET.13190

Segre, G., Campi, R., Scarpellini, F., Clavenna, A., Zanetti, M., Cartabia, M., & Bonati, M. (2021). Interviewing children: The impact of the COVID-19 quarantine on children's perceived psychological distress and changes in routine. *BMC Pediatrics*, 21(1), 1–11. https://doi.org/10.1186/s12887-021-02704-1

Sun, P.C., Tsai, R.J., Finger, G., Chen, Y.Y., & Yeh, D. (2008). What drives a successful e-Learning? An empirical investigation of the critical factors influencing learner satisfaction. *Computers & Education*, 50(4), 1183–1202. https://doi.org/10.1016/J.COMPEDU.2006.11.007

Taquet, M., Geddes, J.R., Luciano, S., & Harrison, P.J. (2022). Incidence and outcomes of eating disorders during the COVID-19 pandemic. *British Journal of Psychiatry*, 220(5), 262–264. https://doi.org/10.1192/bjp.2021.105

Teräs, M., Suoranta, J., Teräs, H., & Curcher, M. (2020). Post-COVID-19 education and education technology 'solutionism': A seller's market. *Postdigital Science and Education*, 2(3), 863–878. https://doi.org/10.1007/s42438-020-00164-x

Tsang, J.T.Y., So, M.K.P., Chong, A.C.Y., Lam, B.S.Y., & Chu, A.M.Y. (2021). Higher education during the pandemic: The predictive factors of learning effectiveness in covid-19 online learning. *Education Sciences*, 11(8), 446. https://doi.org/10.3390/educsci11080446

Unger, S., & Meiran, W. R. (2020). Student attitudes towards online education during the COVID-19 viral outbreak of 2020: Distance learning in a time of social distance. *International Journal of Technology in Education and Science*, 4(4), 256–266. https://doi.org/10.46328/IJTES.V4I4.107

Vygosky, L.S. (1978). *Mind in Society: Development of Higher Psychological Processes*. Harvard University Press. www.jstor.org/stable/j.ctvjf9vz4

Yang, C. (2021). A study on blended learning of high-quality translation courses in the post-epidemic Era. *E3S Web of Conferences*, *253*. https://doi.org/10.1051/e3sconf/202125301073

Zheng, M., Bender, D., & Lyon, C. (2021). Online learning during COVID-19 produced equivalent or better student course performance as compared with pre-pandemic: Empirical evidence from a school-wide comparative study. *BMC Medical Education*, 21(1), 1–11. https://doi.org/10.1186/s12909-021-02909-z

12

STUDYING TRANSLATION ABROAD

A case study of Chinese international students' motivations during the COVID-19 pandemic

Yu Hao

Keywords: translator training; international higher education; mobility; motivations

1. Introduction

Individuals are thought to opt for international education to access valuable academic resources, world-class teaching staff and facilities, as well as qualifications that are recognised both internationally and at home. Engagement in overseas education is also reported to be driven by vocation-specific interests – some students expect increased employment opportunities in the local or global market with a degree from foreign universities (e.g., Cantwell et al., 2009; Rodríguez González et al., 2011). That said, not everyone cites educational or financial rationales; some individuals are drawn to the opportunity to spend leisure and vacation time overseas (Teichler, 2004; Stronkhorst, 2005). As students move away from family and existing social networks, self-discovery and personal growth may also occur.

In the context of translator training, little research has examined how different motivational factors influence translation students' choices between international and domestic education. Exceptions can be found, though, in a handful of studies that highlight the benefits of exchange programs, notably in enhancing second language (L2) proficiency (Pym, 1994) and intercultural competence (Rosiers, 2018). With respect to language acquisition, it is well-acknowledged that language mastery can often come from immersion in a naturalistic setting – ideally living in the country where the language is spoken, which provides exposure that is difficult to replicate elsewhere (e.g., Freed, 1998; Kinginger, 2009). Previous research has also explored

DOI: 10.4324/9781003440970-15

key questions, such as the level of language proficiency achievable through exchange and study abroad programs (e.g., Pellegrino, 1998) and the types of programs that best facilitate second language acquisition (e.g., Kinginger, 2008). In parallel, previous studies also suggest that studying abroad can foster a worldview and preparedness for global citizenship, thanks to direct engagement with the host culture and interaction with people from diverse backgrounds (Shaftel et al., 2007; Deardorff and Jones, 2012; Leung et al., 2014). These immersive opportunities can potentially enhance students' openness, emotional resilience, and adaptability to unfamiliar cultures and perspectives. Yet, other motivational factors that influence students' decision to pursue education abroad have not yet received much attention in the field of translation pedagogy.

This chapter presents findings from a case study that examines the motivational dispositions of a postgraduate Chinese international student cohort who studied translation and interpreting at an Australian university during the COVID-19 pandemic. In what follows, section 2.1 reviews the push-pull framework used to understand the phenomenon of international student flows and underlying factors that motivate students to study abroad. Section 2.2, with a focus on translation pedagogy, then reviews prior discussions about the motivations of translation students at various stages of their education (entry- and exit-points and the periods in-between) within different demographic and institutional contexts. Section 3 outlines the research scope, participants and methods of this case study. In section 4, we report on the motivational factors that shape students' choice of the study destination and mobility decisions, as well as their reflections on screen-based learning experiences during the pandemic. The chapter concludes with potential implications and suggested directions for future research.

2. Literature review

2.1 Motivations for studying abroad: a "push-pull" framework

For decades, educational researchers have studied the complex and evolving motivational factors that drive students to pursue studies abroad. Limited access to local educational resources can be one of the key motives for seeking opportunities abroad. International education is often viewed as a conduit to gaining overseas work experience (e.g., Oliveira and Soares, 2016) and facilitating pathways to immigration (Mazzarol et al., 2003). Many students also value the immersive cultural and social experiences that may come with studying abroad, including the opportunities to master a new language (or improve one's L2) (e.g., Goldstein and Kim, 2006), gain a metropolitan viewpoint, travel, and achieve personal growth (e.g., Anderson et al., 2015).

Many studies have applied a "push-pull" framework, originating in population migration studies, to analyse the factors affecting the flows of international students and their decision-making process (e.g., McMahon, 1992; Mazzarol and Soutar, 2002; Soutar and Turner, 2002). In this view, motivations for international education can involve a set of "push" and "pull" forces between the host and home countries. The push forces that operate within the home country relate to unfavourable conditions pushing people to leave. These include limited academic resources, a competitive job market, or social insecurity (Chirkov et al., 2007; Eder et al., 2010). In contrast, the pull factors operating in the host country then refer to those that make a study destination more attractive to international students than its competitors. More specifically, Mazzarol and Soutar (2002) contend that the decision process students are going through can involve three distinct but progressive stages: they must first decide "whether to go abroad", and "which country" then "which institution to go to" in two subsequent stages. In this decision-making process, push factors create a demand for international education in stage one, which, in tandem with pull factors that then come into play, decide the destination of study flows. In stage two, pull factors influence the selection of a host country (Mazzarol, 1998), such as financial costs (living expenses, travel expenses) and social costs (crime rates, racial discrimination, existing migrant community). Policies in the host country with respect to student work rights and post-study immigration pathways also contribute to this factor. In the last stage, pull factors relating to education then distinguish a particular institution from its "rivals", including university prestige, quality of education, staff expertise, alumni networks, facilities, among others.

More recently, many studies have set out to explore the motivations of international students during the outbreak of a global pandemic. COVID-19 has disrupted student participation rates and exerted a long-lasting and persistent effect on international education worldwide. For instance, in response to national border closures and lockdowns, many universities developed initiatives such as online or dual-delivery courses or the use of VR technology (e.g., Liu and Shirley, 2021) to engage students in the experience of learning abroad *virtually*. In this context, studies have examined the emerging factors (e.g., health-related issues, limited cross-border mobility) and the shifts in the balance of existing factors (e.g., several pull factors that may no longer have an impact) that influence students' decisions to study internationally (Santiso and Sanz, 2022; 2023). Although the world has gradually emerged from the shadow of the pandemic, it remains crucial to understand the decision-making process students went through in times of the pandemic and their perceptions of the alternatives to traditional study abroad experiences. This should be pertinent, in particular, to institutions that wish to develop an online program and/or program with significant international enrolments.

2.2 Motivations for studying translation

In the field of translation studies, previous research on motivation has predominantly focused on non-profit and collaborative translation efforts, i.e., motivations for volunteer translation mobilised by platforms like Wikipedia (Dolmaya, 2012), TED (Olohan, 2014; Fuente, 2015), or ¡Hjckrrh! (Marin-Lacarta and Vargas-Urpí, 2021) – a digital publication initiative for literary translation, among others. Amateur translators are reported to be motivated by a desire to share knowledge and ideas, effect social changes, and participate in global dialogue, which reflects a strong sense of altruism. Beyond their desire to impact others through their work, they are also motivated by some personal benefits they gain from these experiences, including enjoyment, growth, and intellectual stimulation.

In recent years, several studies have researched motivation within the context of translation pedagogy. For instance, Timarová and Ungoed-Thomas (2008) analyse the admission requirements of 30 conference interpreting programs in Europe, Asia, and North America. Alongside the evaluation of hard-core skills (such as language proficiency), motivation is often identified as a key predictor for a candidate's potential in aptitude and personality tests. Self-report motivations were viewed as indicators not only of the reasons students chose to engage in conference interpreting studies, but also of their commitment to mastering interpreting skills and the length of time they prepared to dedicate to this endeavour.

A handful of studies have solicited insights directly from translation students themselves. Li (2002) and Lung (2005) both focus on the "entry point", investigating what motivates incoming undergraduate students to study translation in Hong Kong. One of the strongest motives is "personal upgrading", i.e., through the accumulation of knowledge (language proficiency, translation) and education prestige (a university degree), students aim for promising careers and upward social mobility. According to Li (2002), over 80% of students did not initially intend to pursue a career in translation; rather, as L1 Cantonese speakers, they came to enhance their English and Mandarin Chinese, in the hope that this acquired language capital would give them an advantage in Hong Kong's job market. The majority (51.4%) wished to become executives in government departments or private enterprises. This aligns with the findings of Yan et al. (2010), who surveyed 45 interpreter trainees in the same region to find out their study motivations. Similarly, the students prioritised learning English and Chinese over the professional goal of being interpreters.

Wu (2016) surveyed 160 undergraduate and postgraduate interpreter trainees in China, aiming to understand their motivational behaviour and perceptions of (de)motivating factors *during* their degree program. It was found that, for the sampled student cohort, intrinsic motivations such as "ideal self" (i.e., the attributes of a qualified interpreter one wishes to possess) have a stronger impact than two other internalised extrinsic motivations: "instrumentality" (e.g., social recognition, economic rewards of the qualification) and "avoidance" (i.e., negative consequences of failure). Reflective essays collected from the students further show that the most frequently cited demotivational factors tend to be teacher-attributed (lack of feedback and explanation).

With a focus on the "exit point", Horváth and Kálmán (2020) surveyed a cohort of 50 postgraduate students who were about to graduate from Eötvös Loránd University, Hungary. All students express a desire to start their careers either as professional translators (56%) or interpreters (44%). It was not clear whether the survey question was kept open-ended to allow for other career options. Among the motivational constructs examined in this study, intrinsic motivation (i.e., interest in translation and interpreting), ideal self, and significant others (i.e., support from family, friends, peers, and teachers) have stronger effects than altruism, the dominant factor that motivates volunteer translators.

At the same time, our analysis of several surveys on the actual employment outcomes of graduates (Schmitt et al., 2016; Toudic, 2017a, 2017b; Hao and Pym, 2021, 2023) shows that, on average, only about a third of postgraduate translation students embarked on careers as professional translators or interpreters for any significant length of time. Another third went into language teaching, and the remaining third leveraged their languages in a wide range of occupations. Inquiries were made into the reasons why most graduates pursued careers outside of translation (see Hao and Pym, 2023 for more details). It is reported that factors pertinent to both industry hurdles (e.g., lack of extensive work experience, no suitable jobs) and demotivation (e.g., personal interest in other occupations) contribute to the relatively low number of graduates that become translators and interpreters. It is also frequently cited that translation and interpreting jobs are perceived as inherently unstable, temporary, and casual. This perceived negative image of the profession might explain the reason why many incoming students' primary motivation were already directed elsewhere (see Li, 2002; Lung, 2005).

The motivational disposition of translation and interpreting students remains relatively unexplored, with little research looking at motivations for studying translation abroad. To address this gap, the present study aims to explore the factors that shape the motivations of an international translation student cohort. A case study was conducted with 62 Chinese international students who chose to study translation and interpreting at an Australian university during and shortly after the COVID-19 pandemic, to understand their primary motivations, learning experiences, and career prospects before graduation.

3. The present study

Our purpose in this case study was twofold: 1) understand the motivations of translation and interpreting students for studying with an overseas university; and 2) investigate their satisfaction with learning experiences across two modalities of international higher education (on-campus and online) during the pandemic. Using students' reflective data, we explored these questions in a real-life context to gain a situated understanding of their concerns and aspirations. This study was exploratory in nature, as many variables involved at different levels were not controlled.

A postgraduate-level translation program based in Melbourne, Australia, was selected as a case study, in which more than 90% of its enrolled students were international and with a Chinese background. The program lasts from 1.5 to 2 years and has two intakes per academic year. The participants of this study were 62 current students and recent graduates from the chosen program;[1] the graduates in the sample had completed their studies within six months at the time of the survey (July 2022). This study primarily focused on the conditions that motivated translation students to pursue their education internationally. Our study was conducted following the first semester in which Australian universities returned partially to campus after the pandemic, adopting a hybrid approach that blends in-person and online instruction. Despite all participants being enrolled in the same overseas translation program, some students (n = 39, 63%) continued with distance learning and remained in their home country, while others (n = 23, 37%) returned to campus as soon as travel restrictions were eased. This variation in study modes provided us with a unique opportunity to examine the experiences of international students who engaged in both remote and on-campus studies. Our participants were from five different cohorts, all facing disruptions to their study abroad plans due to the pandemic: these include the first group of students that enrolled just before the COVID-19 outbreak in Australia in March 2020, three subsequent cohorts who began their studies when online learning was the sole option, and the final cohort that commenced in March 2022, when Australian universities went for hybrid learning. Around 90% of the students were female, and most of the participants were in their mid-twenties (ranging from 21 to 36 years, mean = 24.58, SD = 2.24). Mandarin Chinese was the first language (L1) for the majority of the participants (91.9%, n = 57); two were L1 Cantonese speakers, and three identified both as their primary languages.

The data-collection instrument was a bilingual questionnaire survey developed on the *Qualtrics* website (see Appendix). It asked the participants what motivated them to pursue the Master of Translation and Interpreting in an Australia university. In our working model, we considered three types of motivational factors (n = 20): "pull factors" (n = 8) and "push factors" (n = 4), influencing studying abroad decisions, as well as motivational factors specific to the study of translation and interpreting (n = 8). These items were derived partially from informal interviews with our students and from previous surveys that examined motivations to seek education in a foreign country (e.g., Mazzarol and Soutar, 2002; Bodycott, 2009; Wilkins and Balakrishnan, 2012). Each motivational factor was presented as a statement in the questionnaire survey; the participants were invited to rate the extent to which they agree with these statements, on a 5-point Likert scale ranging from 1 = strongly disagree to 5 = strongly agree. This should tell us the perceived impact of each factor on student decision-making.

Similarly, the participants were invited to evaluate their in-person and screen-based learning experiences, with a focus on the acquisition of translation skills, i.e., language and culture, translation, technology, personal and interpersonal, and service provision (EMT, 2017). Two open-ended questions were also included to elicit qualitative data. The student responses were made in English and Chinese, with the Chinese ones being translated by the researcher who is a NAATI accredited translator after data analysis.

4. Results

4.1 Motivations for studying translation abroad

We first examined the motivations of Chinese international students' for studying in a postgraduate translation and interpreting program in Australia during the COVID-19 pandemic (semester 1, 2020 to semester 1, 2022). When asked "Why did you choose to study translation at the University of Melbourne?", participants were invited to rate 20 statements that address motivational factors in our working model, on a scale from 1 = strongly disagree to 5 = strongly agree. The mean ratings of the three categories of motivational factors are shown in Figure 12.1: push factors (grey, n = 4), pull factors (white, n = 8), and translation-specific factors (black, n = 8).

In general, the participants' dispositions were shaped by all three types of motivational factors, with pull factors exerting a stronger effect than both push factors and translation-specific factors. That is, their decision to study abroad has more to do with the opportunities presented by the host country and/or institution and not so much with the avoidance of unfavourable conditions at home. Discipline-specific factors appeared to have the least impact.

Pull factors were placed higher in Figure 12.1, with the most prominent among them relating to what the institution could offer, i.e., top-quality education (1st, M = 4.45) and educational prestige (3rd, M = 4.16). Other pull factors that had a strong impact on the students' motivations included the desire to travel the world (2nd, M = 4.19), to socialise with people

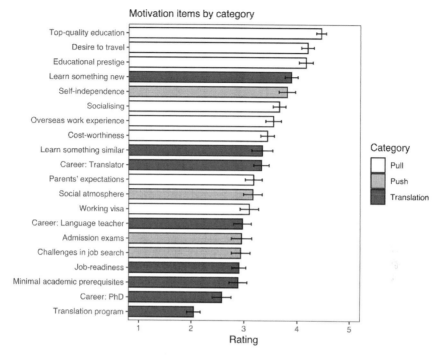

Motivation items by category

FIGURE 12.1 "Why did you choose to study translation abroad at the University of Melbourne?" Mean scores for 20 motivational factors by all 62 participants

from diverse backgrounds (6th, M = 3.66), and to gain overseas career opportunities (7th, M = 3.55). To provide context, during the COVID-19 pandemic, many attributes of the host country that are attractive to international students, e.g., the opportunity for travel and part-time work, became inaccessible to both those stranded overseas and those stuck in Australia's on-and-off lockdowns for two years. Against this backdrop, why did most of our participants prioritise the three pull factors, despite them being inaccessible at the time of their decision-making? This could be elucidated through the "forbidden" fruit theory (also known as the scarcity principle), which posits that people place a high value on objects or goals because they are unattainable or off-limits. Reflective notes from participants mirror this sentiment:

> things with the pandemic are beyond our control, but life does continue. The reason I chose Australia over elsewhere is that its Master program lasts longer, offering a better chance to literally go abroad and travel before I graduate.

Other factors were considered less important: parents' expectations (11th, M = 3.18) and post-study working visas (13th, M = 3.10).

In contrast with the above, except for over-reliance on parents (5th, M = 3.81), were placed relatively low on the list. It seemed that most students in their mid-20s sought to break away from their existing social networks and pursue self-discovery. At the lower end of the list were push factors such as job search challenges in China (16th, M = 2.94), admission exams for local programs (15th, M = 2.95), and concerns about the home country's social atmosphere (12th, M = 3.16).

At the same time, most discipline-specific factors did not leave a strong mark on the translation students' motivations for studying abroad. Here we measured students' intrinsic interest in this discipline at the entry-point and whether they envisioned themselves finding employment that would match their education at the other end. For instance, the students on average rated the statement "I wouldn't have chosen to study abroad if it weren't for learning translation and interpreting." 2.1 out of 5 (ranked 20th). Less than 10% of the participants strongly agreed or agreed, with over one-third of the participants strongly disagreeing with the statement (36.5%, n = 23). On the other hand, when asked about their ideal-professional self after graduation, the students showed a fair amount of enthusiasm for being "translator and/or interpreter" (M = 3.5), compared with the other two career paths – "language teaching" (M = 2.9) and "PhD" (M = 2.58). Around 40% of participants (n = 25) strongly agreed or agreed that after graduation, they wanted to work as translators and interpreters, with around one-third expressing the same degree of interest in language teaching (33%, n = 20) or a PhD (27%, n = 17).

4.2 Motivational dispositions of "online" and "in-person" groups

Further, we were interested in how students' motivations related to their geographical mobility decisions. The outbreak of the COVID-19 pandemic introduced significant challenges to higher education in Australia, as it did in many other countries worldwide. In-person teaching was discontinued in March 2020, and following the closure of national borders, almost 120,000 international student visa holders found themselves stranded overseas. In late 2021, after two years of online education during the pandemic lockdown restrictions, many Australian universities adopted a hybrid learning model that combined online and offline education. In this context, some students chose to return to campus (hereafter referred to as "in-person" students), while others continued to take online courses (referred to as "online" students).

The mean ratings for push, pull, and translation-specific factors by the two student cohorts are shown in Figure 12.2. In general, pull-factor items emerged as significant factors in all students' study abroad decisions, whereas push factors and discipline-specific factors played a more peripheral role.

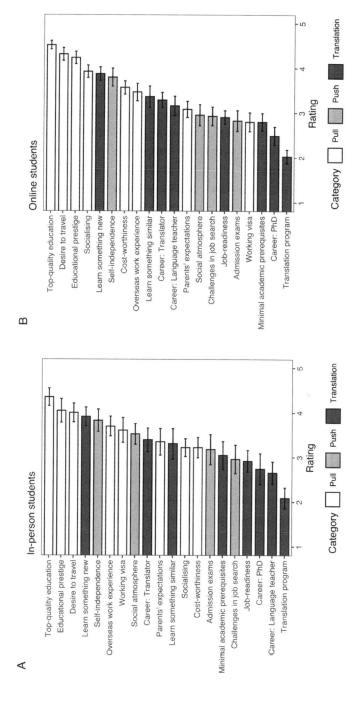

FIGURE 12.2   Average rating scores for the 20 motivational factors by in-person and online students

Motivational factors associated with education (e.g., high-quality education, educational prestige) and the advantages of studying abroad (e.g., the desire to travel, opportunities for socializing) were ranked higher, while several push factors (e.g., challenges in job searching) and translation-specific factors (e.g., an exclusive interest in translation) received lower ratings.

Despite the general trends, the two groups also demonstrated some divergent motivational dispositions in several aspects. Overseas work experience and post-study work visas were perceived as a pathway to immigration opportunities, significantly motivating in-person students' mobility and destination choices. However, these factors seemed to have a less pronounced impact on the motivations of those who chose to continue their studies online (post-study work visa per se, in-person: M = 3.61; online: M = 2.79). Not surprisingly, in-person students who prioritise immigration-related motivations also were more concerned with the social atmosphere of their home country than the other group (in-person: 8th, M = 3.52; online: 13th, M = 2.95).

With respect to their career prospects, both groups exhibited an interest in translation-related careers (in-person: 9th, M = 3.39; online: 10th, M = 3.29) but less enthusiasm for pursuing a PhD (in-person: 18th, M = 2.74; online: 19th, M = 2.49). Compared with their in-person counterparts, those remained online were more open to the idea of embarking on a language education career (in-person: 19th, M = 2.65; online: 11th, M = 3.15).

Similarly, several students who were hesitant to return articulated in their reflective notes that their primary motivation was neither to become translators nor to serve the Australian market. Instead, they wanted to enter the field of language teaching in their home country, where teaching English remained a stable and thriving profession (at the time). For instance, one student expressed concerns about how returning to campus could potentially interfere with their long-term career goals:

> My biggest motivation to study the Master of Translation and Interpreting at Melbourne was to better prepare myself for the National Exam for Teacher Certification back home. Becoming a language teacher has always been my dream, and passing this exam opens the door to stable and well-paid positions in state-owned public schools. One requirement for prospective candidates of this exam is to hold a Master degree: the more prestigious the university, the better. I like the flexibility that comes with online learning, because it allows me to balance my studies in Melbourne and my part-time English tutor jobs in China.'

With regard to flexible scheduling, our findings indicated that a significant proportion of online students were concurrently engaged in a variety of part-time roles across multiple occupations, leveraging their language skills.

Taken together, the different weightings given to these factors seemed to suggest that while in-person and online students were both motivated by high-quality education at a prestigious university, in-person students hoped this experience would increase their chances of employment outside of their home country while online students hoped for better opportunities within their home country as language professionals.

In order to examine the quantitative patterns at the motivation category level, the mean scores of motivation items rated by each student group were respectively combined based on their categories (see Figure 12.3). The intra-group and inter-group differences were analysed using a Linear Mixed Effect Model. As informed by Wald F tests (Kenward-Roger), the results show a significant effect of the motivation category, F (2, 1174) = 43.79, $p < 0.001$. In other words, the in-person and online groups were influenced by a combination of "push and pull" as well as discipline-specific factors that encouraged them to study translation overseas, although each motivational category impacted them to significantly varying degrees. Meanwhile, the analysis did not reveal a significant effect of inter-group difference, F (1, 60) = 0.11, p = 0.741, or a significant effect of the learning mode – motivation category interaction, F (2, 1174) = 1.13, p = 0.323. The results showed that there is some similarity between the motivational profiles of the two groups in choosing an overseas university for their postgraduate translation studies.

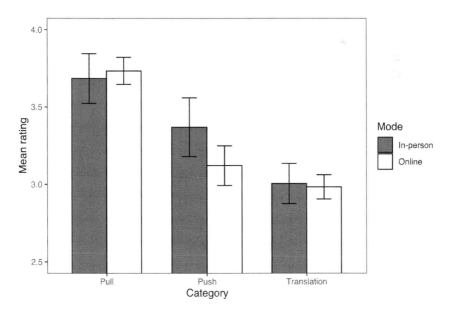

FIGURE 12.3   Combined mean rating scores of three motivation categories for studying translation abroad

Furthermore, *post hoc* tests reveal three meaningful significances: within the online group, pull factors were rated significantly higher than push factors, $M_{diff} = 0.612$, $p < 0.001$, and significantly higher than discipline-specific motivational factors, $M_{diff} = 0.750$, $p < 0.001$, while within the in-person group, pull factors were rated significantly higher than discipline-specific motivational factors, $M_{diff} = 0.679$, $p < 0.001$. Other comparisons were found to be not significant.

4.3 Translation competence acquisition in online learning

Now we turn to students' reflections on their screen-based learning experiences to understand how the pandemic has impacted the development of translation competence. Five categories of competence identified by the EMT group (2017, 2021) are considered here: language and culture, translation, technology, personal and interpersonal, and service provision competence. A statement for each competence was developed (see Appendix) to elicit self-report data from students, with responses on a scale from 1 = strongly disagree to 5 = strongly agree. Table 12.1 shows the mean ratings from all 62 respondents.

The quantitative data showed that "in-person" and "online" groups assigned similar ratings across competencies. A possible reason for this could be that, despite their different mobility decisions when Australia's border reopened in late 2021, both groups of students experienced online learning to similar extents. Not to mention that the "in-person" group had, at most, one semester of in-person learning at that time. For all students, while technology and translation skills seemed resistant to COVID-19 disruptions (translation per se, M = 3.05; technology, M = 2.82), the acquisition of the remaining skill sets faced challenges due to the lack of access to authentic language environments, in-person peer interaction, offline job placements (language and culture per se, M = 3.87; personal and interpersonal, M = 4.00; service provision, M = 4.00).

TABLE 12.1 Mean ratings for the disruption of skill acquisition by all 62 students

Skill	In-person		Online		All students	
	M	SD	M	SD	M	SD
Language and culture	4.04	1.02	3.77	1.20	3.87	1.14
Translation	3.13	1.22	3.00	0.97	3.05	1.06
Technology	2.83	1.37	2.83	1.21	2.82	1.26
Personal and interpersonal	4.00	0.95	4.00	1.30	4.00	1.17
Service provision	3.91	1.12	4.00	1.00	3.97	1.04

More specifically, students often found it difficult to interact with their peers in virtual learning spaces, which might also lead to a diminished sense of community. Several students, in their reflective notes on the overall experience, mentioned that studying abroad is perceived not only as an academic endeavour but as an invaluable chance to foster a cosmopolitan outlook. However, this might be compromised in the virtual study abroad experience, as the homogeneity of students' cultural and academic backgrounds could further limit this chance.

The situation aligned with the challenges in language acquisition faced by this international student cohort. As reported, many chose to study in Australia to immerse themselves in an English-speaking context, perceived as ideal for L2 language acquisition. Yet for many (n = 17, 27%), this expectation went unfulfilled due to the online learning mode.

Similarly, students' ability to develop service provision competence is reported to have also been hampered, as the numbers of job placements decreased during the pandemic and were rarely available to those who remained overseas. Some students nearing graduation voiced their concern about missing internship opportunities because they could not manage to return to the country, in a view that this could affect their employability and job readiness. For example:

I have never breathed the Melbourne air, but now it's coming to the end. I missed quite a few internships because I wasn't there. I find myself couldn't build up my networks let alone professional reputation.

5. Discussion and concluding remarks

This case study has investigated the motivations of a group of international students for studying translation at a foreign university against the backdrop of the COVID-19 pandemic. The results showed that their dispositions were influenced by all three types of motivational factors outlined in our working model, with pull factors exerting a stronger effect than push factors and discipline-specific factors. More specifically, attributes such as the host country's top-quality education, educational prestige, opportunities for overseas work experience and travel are appealing to the Chinese international students in our sample. It suggests that students made a proactive decision based on the positive attributes of the study destination rather than being compelled to leave due to unfavourable conditions at home. For university administrative teams and policymakers, it is crucial to understand the motivations and demands of international student cohorts from various ethnic backgrounds, which can help to refine educational offerings and further develop more focused student recruitment strategies.

The fact that this study was conducted during a transitional period, when Australia offered students the choice between online, on-campus, and dual-delivery hybrid learning modes, introduced an additional variable into our analysis: student geographical mobility decisions. We exploratorily divided the Chinese international student cohort into two groups: those who returned to campus once Australia reopened its borders for student visa holders, and those who remained overseas, continuing their studies online. Although the motivations of these two groups demonstrated similar patterns (as suggested by the quantitative analysis), we observed different dispositions in some respects. Compared to their counterparts who stayed online, students who returned to campus exhibited a greater interest in career development and residency opportunities in the host country (e.g., the "working visa" item in Figure 12.2) and were more susceptible to push factors operating in their home country (e.g., the "social atmosphere" item in Figure 12.2).

Further, the two cohorts showed divergent intended career trajectories. Despite a shared enthusiasm for becoming professional translators, the online group that remained at home showed a stronger preference for career paths leaning towards language teaching. This preference aligns with the findings of previous graduate employment surveys (e.g., Hao and Pym, 2023), where just over one-third of the translation graduates secured employment in this field for any length of time. In Hao and Pym (2023), the Chinese translation graduates who return to their home country are more likely to work as language teachers, with little trouble capitalising on their English skills. Taken together, the reason most students did not become professional translators might not be sorely due to their failure to meet industry hurdles, but possibly because their true passion has already lied elsewhere, such as in teaching. One possible implication for us is the need to avoid assuming homogeneity in students' career prospects (in tune with Li, 2002; Lung, 2005). Instead, programs should include specialised elective courses alongside training in core translation competencies to encourage customized learning plans.

The pandemic has a long-standing and persistent effect on international higher education worldwide. During the lockdowns, many universities were forced to either suspend their study abroad programs or pivot from traditional on-site instruction to online delivery. In this case study, we gathered student self-report data about the perceived impacts of such online transition on their acquisition of translation competencies. It seems that while translation technology has shown resilience to the disruptions of online learning, aspects such as language acquisition, intercultural communication, and service provision have been affected by restricted cross-border mobility and human interaction. More specifically, the students reported having limited opportunities to practice English outside of classroom settings; interactions with peers of similar ethnic and linguistic backgrounds did not meet expectations for cultural immersion (as indicated in their qualitative notes). Additionally, students experienced a diminished sense of community both amongst their peers (due to reduced human interaction), and within the translation profession (due to limited internship opportunities).

Given the current landscape, many higher education institutions have opted to retain online education as either an integral part of, or as an alternative to, the traditional on-campus curriculum after the pandemic. Therefore, if studying abroad *from abroad* becomes the new normal at least in some institutions, which could also be a relatively affordable option for students from less advanced social and economic status (SES) backgrounds, proactive measures should be taken to enhance experiential learning and cohort building. This could include developing tandem language learning partnerships with Modern Language programs and using new technology such as virtual reality (VR) artefacts to facilitate intercultural communication (for details, see Li et al., 2022; Liu and Shirley, 2021).

This case study was focused on a cohort of Chinese international students at an Australian university. These results should be relevant not only to the translation program in concern but also to other translator-training institutions that find themselves in similar situations, i.e., those with significant international student populations and/or those looking to develop their curriculum in an online format. Future research should examine the impact of academic discipline on students' decisions to join study-abroad programs in this field. Data gathered from student cohorts of diverse backgrounds across different geographical locations will further help us gain a more nuanced understanding of the motivations behind the mobility and studying abroad decisions of our translation students.

Appendix: questionnaire

Part one: personal details

1. Your name 姓名
2. Gender 性别
3. How old are you? 年龄
4. What is your first language? 母语

   Mandarin Chinese 普通话
   Cantonese 广东话

5. When was your first semester in the Master of Translation (and Interpreting)? 入学学期

   SEM-1 March 2020
   SEM-2 July 2020

SEM-1 March 2021
SEM-2 July 2021
SEM-1 March 2022

6. Have you taken any face-to-face classes in SEM-1, 2022?

在2022年第一学期，你是否参与过线下授课？

7. Which Master are you studying? 入学项目

200-point program
150-point program

Part two: motivations for studying abroad

8. Why did you choose to study translation at the University of Melbourne? You might be driven by multiple motivations, some of which are more prominent than others.

你为什么选择来到墨尔本大学就读翻译专业呢？也许你的动机有很多，一些动机和想法对你而言也许更加重要。

To what extent do you agree with the following statements? (1 = strongly disagree; 5 = strongly agree). 请问你从何种程度同意以下内容

I made the decision to study translation abroad because:
我选择出国学习翻译专业，因为

- I didn't want to sit for any entrance examination for local Master programs. ("Admission exams" in Figures 12.1 and 12.2)

  我不想参加国内硕士项目的入学考试。

- Finding/securing a job on the local market in China is difficult. ("Challenges in job search")

  目前在国内找不到好工作。

- I am concerned about the social atmosphere in my country. ("Social atmosphere")

  我对国内的社会氛围感到担忧。

- I wanted to learn how to live independently. ("Self-independence")

  我想过更独立的生活。

- A degree from a prestigious foreign university is highly recognised. ("Educational prestige")

  海外名校的文凭受到广泛的认可。

- I wanted to receive a top-quality education overseas. ("Top-quality education")

  我想在海外大学接受更高质量的教育。

- I was interested in gaining some overseas work experience via internships and part-time jobs. ("Overseas work experience")

  我想通过实习和兼职获得海外工作经验。

- I wanted to get a post-study working visa to live and work in the host country after graduation. ("Working visa")

  我希望获得学生工作签证，毕业后在国外工作和生活。

- I wanted to explore the world and visit different places. ("Desire for travel")

  我希望游历世界，造访不同的地方。

- My parents wanted me to study at a foreign university. ("Parents' expectations")

  我的父母希望我去国外大学学习。

- I wanted to make friends overseas. ("Socialising")

  我希望在国外结交朋友。

- I thought that what I could gain from this experience would be worth more than the amount of money my family has spent on me. ("Cost worthiness")

  我认为留学经历的收获远超过我的家庭所付出的经济成本。

- I wouldn't have chosen to study abroad if it wasn't to study translation and interpreting. ("Study translation")

  如果不是为了学习口/笔译，我不会选择出国留学。

- A translation degree is practical and can be applied to a range of career paths. ("Job-readiness")

  翻译专业很实用，毕业后就业面广。

- I wanted to learn something different from my background. ("Learn something new")

  我想学习一些和之前所学内容不同的新知识。

- A translation degree does not require much prerequisite knowledge. ("Minimal academic prerequisites")

  翻译专业对先前的专业背景要求不高。

- My bachelor's degree was highly relevant to translation and/or interpreting. ("Learn something similar")

  翻译和我在本科所学的内容高度相关。

- I wanted to become a translator and/or interpreter after graduation. ("Career: translators")

  毕业后我希望成为一名口译/笔译员。

- I wanted to become a language teacher after graduation. ("Career: language teacher")

  毕业后我希望成为一名语言教师。

- I wanted to do a PhD after graduation. ("Career: PhD")

  毕业后我希望继续攻读博士。

Part three: the impacts of COVID

9. Based on your experience, to what extent do you agree with the following statements? (1 = strongly disagree; 5 = strongly agree).

   基于自身经历，请问您从多大程度同意以下内容：

   - The lack of access to an authentic language environment makes learning more difficult. ("Language and culture" in Table 12.1)

     在线网课使学习变得更加困难，因为我无法获取纯正的外语环境。

   - Learning translation techniques online is more difficult than learning them face-to-face. ("Translation")

     与线下相比，在线课堂使得学习英汉翻译技巧更加困难。

   - Learning translation technologies (e.g., TM and MT suites) online is more difficult than learning them face-to-face. ("Technology")

     在线学习翻译技术（翻译记忆软件，机器翻译）相关内容比在线下学习更困难。

- Having limited in-person peer interaction makes it difficult to develop interpersonal skills (such as teamwork). ("Personal and interpersonal")

  在线学习不利于我的人际交往能力发展，因为面对面同伴互动的机会有所减少。

- The lack of job placements offline makes it difficult for me to gain industry experience, which may reduce my chances of landing a translation job after graduation. ("Service provision")

  线下实习机会的缺失会阻碍我获得相关行业经验，可能会大大减少毕业后找到翻译工作的机会。

10. What are your strongest motivations to study the Master of Translation and Interpreting at the University of Melbourne? Which aspects of your expectations have not been fulfilled? (Please write in English or Chinese, preferably in 100–140 words)

    你来到墨尔本大学学习口笔译专业最主要出于哪些动机？你觉得自己哪方面的预期没有实现？（请使用英文或中文简答，推荐字数100-140字）

10a. After the border restrictions were lifted, why did you choose to come to/ return to Australia? What benefits and drawbacks did you (and your family) consider when making this decision? (Please write in English or Chinese, preferably in 100–140 words)

    澳大利亚开放国境后，你为什么选择回到校园参加线下授课？当时你(和家人)在做决定时有哪些考虑，请和我们谈谈你的想法和心路历程 (请使用英文或中文简答, 推荐字数100-140字)

10b. After the border restrictions were lifted, why did you choose to remain abroad and take online courses? What benefits and drawbacks did you (and your family) consider when making this decision? (Please write in English or Chinese, preferably in 100–140 words)

    澳大利亚开放国境后，你为什么选择在线上完成学业？当时你(和家人)在做决定时有哪些考虑，请和我们谈谈你的想法和心路历程 (请使用英文或中文简答, 推荐字数100-140字)。

Note

1 Ethics approval of this research project was received from the Human Research Ethics Committees, Faculty of Arts, University of Melbourne (Ethics Authorization Number 1954388.1).

References

Anderson, P.H., Hubbard, A. and Lawton, L. 2015. Student Motivation to Study Abroad and Their Intercultural Development. *Frontiers: The Interdisciplinary Journal of Study Abroad* 26(1), pp. 39–52.

Bodycott, P. 2009. Choosing a Higher Education Study Abroad Destination: What Mainland Chinese Parents and Students Rate as Important. *Journal of Research in International Education* 8(3), pp. 349–373.

Cantwell, B., Luca, S.G. and Lee, J.J. 2009. Exploring the Orientations of International Students in Mexico: Differences by Region of Origin. *Higher Education* 57, pp. 335–354.

Chirkov, V., Vansteenkiste, M., Tao, R. and Lynch, M. 2007. The Role of Self-determined Motivation and Goals for Study Abroad in the Adaptation of International Students. *International Journal of Intercultural Relations* 31(2), pp. 199–222.

Deardorff, D. and Jones, E. 2012. Intercultural Competence: An Emerging Focus in International Higher Education. In Deardorff, D., de Wit, H., Heyl, J. and Adams, T. (eds.) *The SAGE Handbook of International Higher Education*. Thousand Oaks: SAGE Publications, pp. 283–303.

Dolmaya, J.M. 2012. Analyzing the Crowdsourcing Model and Its Impact on Public Perceptions of Translation. *The Translator* 18(2), pp. 167–191.

Eder, J., Smith, W.W. and Pitts, R.E. 2010. Exploring Factors Influencing Student Study Abroad Destination Choice. *Journal of Teaching in Travel & Tourism* 10(3), pp. 232–250.

EMT. 2017. *Competence Framework 2017*. www.ec.europa.eu/info/sites/info/files/emt_competence_fwk_2017_en_web.pdf.

EMT. 2022. *Competence Framework 2022*. www.commission.europa.eu/system/files/2022-11/emt_competence_fwk_2022_en.pdf

Freed, B.F. 1998. An Overview of Issues and Research in Language Learning in a Study Abroad Setting. *Frontiers: The Interdisciplinary Journal of Study Abroad* 4(1), pp. 31–60.

Fuente, L.C. 2015. Motivation to Collaboration in TED Open Translation Project. *International Journal of Web Based Communities* 11(2), pp. 210–229.

Goldstein, S.B. and Kim, R.I. 2006. Predictors of US College Students' Participation in Study Abroad Programs: A Longitudinal Study. *International Journal of Intercultural Relations* 30(4), pp. 507–521.

Hao, Y. and Pym, A. 2021. Translation Skills Required by Master's Graduates for Employment: Which are Needed, Which are Not? *Across Languages and Cultures* 22(2), pp. 158–175.

Hao, Y. and Pym, A. 2023. Where Do Translation Students Go? A Study of the Employment and Mobility of Master Graduates. *The Interpreter and Translator Trainer* 17(2), pp. 211–229.

Horváth, I. and Kálmán, C. 2021. Motivational Disposition of Translation and Interpreting Graduates. *The Interpreter and Translator Trainer* 15(3), pp. 287–305.

Kinginger, C. 2008. Language Learning in Study Abroad: Case Studies of Americans in France. *The Modern Language Journal* 92, pp. 1–131.

Kinginger, C. 2009. *Language Learning and Study Abroad: A Critical Reading of Research*. London: Springer.

Leung, K., Ang, S. and Tan, M. L. 2014. Intercultural competence. *Annual Review of Organizational Psychology and Organizational Behaviour* 1, pp. 489–519.

Li, D. 2002. Translator Training: What Translation Students Have to Say. *Meta* 47(4), pp. 513–531.

Li, C., Kon, A. and Ip, H.H.S. 2022. Use Virtual Reality to Enhance Intercultural Sensitivity: A Randomised Parallel Longitudinal Study. *IEEE Transactions on Visualization and Computer Graphics* 28(11), pp. 3673–3683.

Liu, Y. and Shirley, T. 2021. Without Crossing a Border: Exploring the Impact of Shifting Study Abroad Online on Students' Learning and Intercultural Competence Development during the COVID-19 Pandemic. *Online Learning Journal* 25(1), pp. 182–194.

Lung, R. 2005. Translation Training Needs for Adult Learners. *Babel* 51(3), pp. 224–237.

Marin-Lacarta, M. and Vargas-Urpí, M. 2020. Translators as Publishers: Exploring the Motivations for Non-profit Literary Translation in a Digital Initiative. *Meta* 65(2), pp. 459–478.

Mazzarol, T. 1998. Critical Success Factors for International Education Marketing. *International Journal of Educational Management* 12(4), pp. 163–175.

Mazzarol, T. and Soutar, G.N. 2002. "Push-Pull" Factors Influencing International Student Destination Choice. *International Journal of Educational Management* 16(2), pp. 82–90.

Mazzarol, T., Soutar, G. N. and Sim Yaw Seng, M. 2003. The Third Wave: Future Trends in International Education. *International Journal of Educational Management* 17(3), pp. 90–99.

McMahon, M.E. 1992. Higher Education in a World Market: An Historical Look at the Global Context of International Study. *Higher Education* 24, pp. 465–482.

Oliveira, D.B. and Soares, A.M. 2016. Studying Abroad: Developing a Model for the Decision Process of International Students. *Journal of Higher Education Policy and Management* 38(2), pp. 126–139.

Olohan, M. 2014. Why Do you Translate? Motivation to Volunteer and TED Translation. *Translation Studies* 7(1), pp. 17–33.

Pellegrino, V.A. 1998. Student Perspectives on Language Learning in a Study Abroad Context. *Frontiers: The Interdisciplinary Journal of Study Abroad* 4(1), pp. 91–120.

Pym, A. 1994. Student Exchange Programmes and Translator Training: Three Economic Principles. *Perspectives: Studies in Translatology* 2(1), pp. 41–50.

Rodríguez González, C., Mesanza, R.B. and Mariel, P. 2011. The Determinants of International Student Mobility Flows: An Empirical Study on the Erasmus Programme. *Higher Education* 62, pp. 413–430.

Rosiers, A. 2018. How Does a Study Abroad Experience Contribute to the Intercultural Competence of Student Translators? In: Deconinck, J., Humblé, P. and Sepp, A. (eds.) *Towards Transcultural Awareness in Translation Pedagogy.* Zürich: LIT Verlag, pp. 231–256.

Santiso, G.B. and Sanz, C. 2022. Study Abroad and Student Decision Making in Times of COVID: A Mixed Methods Study. *Frontiers: The Interdisciplinary Journal of Study Abroad* 34(1), pp. 45–60.

Santiso, G.B. and Sanz, C. 2023. Perspectives and Motives Involved in Study Abroad: COVID, Race and SES. *L2 Journal* 15(2), pp. 10–28.

Schmitt, P., Gernstmeyer, L. and Müller, S. 2016. *Übersetzer und Dolmetscher – Eine internationale Umfrage zur Berufspraxis*. DBÜ Fachverlag.

Shaftel, J., Shaftel, T. and Ahluwalia, R. 2007. International Educational Experience and Intercultural Competence. *International Journal of Business & Economics* 6(1), pp. 25–34.

Soutar, G.N. and Turner, J.P. 2002. Students' Preferences for University: A Conjoint Analysis. *International Journal of Educational Management* 16(1), pp. 40–45.

Stronkhorst, R. 2005. Learning Outcomes of International Mobility at Two Dutch Institutions of Higher Education. *Journal of Studies in International Education* 9(4), pp. 292–315.

Teichler, U. 2004. Temporary Study Abroad: The Life of ERASMUS Students. *European Journal of Education* 39(4), pp. 395–408.

Timarová, Š. and Ungoed-Thomas, H. 2008. Admission Testing for Interpreting Courses. *The Interpreter and Translator Trainer* 2(1), pp. 29–46.

Toudic, D. 2017a. *Graduate Employment Survey. Report to the EMT Network Meeting*.

Toudic, D. 2017b. *Maintaining standards in a changing market: the new EMT competence framework. PowerPoint presented*. PowerPoint presentation. Prague.

Wilkins, S., Balakrishnan, M.S., and Huisman, J. 2012. Student Choice in Higher Education: Motivations for Choosing to Study at An International Branch Campus. *Journal of Studies in International Education* 16(5), pp. 413–433.

Wu, Z. 2016. Towards Understanding Interpreter Trainees' (De)motivation: An Exploratory Study. *Translation & Interpreting* 8(2), pp. 13–25.

Yan, J., Pan, J. and Wang, H. 2010. Learner Factors, Self-perceived Language Ability and Interpreting Learning: An Investigation of Hong Kong Tertiary Interpreting Classes. *The Interpreter and Translator Trainer* 4(2), pp. 173–196.

INDEX

Note: Page locators in **bold** and *italics* represents tables and figures, respectively. Endnotes are indicated by the page number followed by "n" and the note number e.g., 111n5 refers to note 5 on page 111.

Printed and bound by CPI Group (UK) Ltd, Croydon, CR0 4YY

05/11/2024

01784181-0012